Sex *with* Shakespeare

Sex *with* Shakespeare

Here's Much to Do with Pain,
but More with *Love*

JILLIAN KEENAN

wm

WILLIAM MORROW
An Imprint of HarperCollins*Publishers*

HarperCollins books may be purchased for educational, business, or sales pro-
motional use. For information please e-mail the Special Markets Department at
SPsales@harpercollins.com.

FIRST EDITION

Designed by Sunil Manchikanti

Library of Congress Cataloging-in-Publication Data has been applied for.

ISBN 978-0-06-237871-2

16 17 18 19 20   OV/RRD   10 9 8 7 6 5 4 3 2 1

Some birds pair-bond for life.
This is for my Penguin.

Content Note

This book describes the sexual orientations and experiences of people who deserve discretion. To that end, I have gone to great lengths to shield their identities to such an extent that, in a few cases, even their own families would not be able to recognize them. Most names have been changed, as have, when necessary, some other identifying details, including nationality, occupation, educational background, or event location. When I did have to change identifying details, I made every effort to change them in a way that keeps feelings, motivations, cultural context, and emotional truth intact. Dialogue has been re-created to the best of my recollection and evokes the spirit of the conversations; when possible, I also pulled direct quotes from journal entries, emails, instant message conversations, and cell phone texts. I am grateful to Peng, Nikolai, and both Davids, who generously allowed me to use their real names.

In block quotes, I've usually followed the punctuation in *The Riverside Shakespeare*, Second Edition. However, from time to time, when I felt like it, I embraced literary anarchy and made my own punctuation choices.

I dislike trigger warnings. But some people feel they are

helpful, and I don't want to impose my personal preferences onto anyone else. So I will be clear: This book discusses themes and events that reflect the Shakespearean canon, including its darker elements. These include but are not limited to sexual and physical violence, rape, racism, homophobia, colonialism, drug and alcohol use, and disease.

Other sources of concern may include: tortured metaphors, magical realism, heavy-handed literary references, literal and figurative navel-gazing, my opinions, and the state of North Dakota. Each stands accused of traumatic potential of its own.

Should anyone here not know the loving art,
Read this, and learn by reading how to love.
By art the swift ships are propelled with sail and oar;
There is art to drive fleet chariots, and
Love should by art be guided.

I am ashamed to proceed,
But Venus whispers in my ear.
"What you blush to tell," says she,
"Is the most important part of the whole matter."

—*Ars Amatoria*, OVID
MENTIONED IN *The Taming of the Shrew*, 4.2

Contents

ACT ONE

Lovers and madmen have such seething brains,
Such shaping fantasies, that apprehend
More than cool reason ever comprehends.
The lunatic, the lover, and the poet
Are of imagination all compact.
One sees more devils than vast hell can hold;
That is the madman. The lover, all as frantic,
Sees Helen's beauty in a brow of Egypt.
The poet's eye, in a fine frenzy rolling,
Doth glance from heaven to Earth, from Earth to heaven;
And as imagination bodies forth
The forms of things unknown, the poet's pen
Turns them to shapes, and gives to airy nothing
A local habitation and a name.
Such tricks hath strong imagination,
That if it would but apprehend some joy,
It comprehends some bringer of that joy;
Or in the night, imagining some fear,
How easy is a bush supposed a bear!

—A Midsummer Night's Dream, 5.1

1.1 A Midsummer Night's Dream:
Stand and Unfold

It was on my mind again.

I tilted my head past the edge of the curtain and scanned the room. I was alone. Even the owner of the Internet café had run to the mosque across the street to pray. It was a holy moment in Oman. It was prayer time. All around the country, men and women paused their work to speak with Allah.

I needed to speak, too, but not with God. He was probably busy during prayer time. And I wouldn't want to make Him uncomfortable. I needed to talk about sex. I needed to be a little bit weird. And in His Majesty Sultan Qaboos bin Said al-Said's Sultanate of Oman, the few minutes of total privacy after the call to prayer were my best chance.

I slid a pair of black sunglasses under my pink hijab and retreated back to my computer. (The sunglasses were excessive in the dark café, of course. But they made me feel cool.) Safely ensconced behind a partition, I minimized a PDF of an article on postcolonial interpretations of *The Tempest* and opened a new browser window. After another quick glance over my shoulder to confirm that there was no one behind me, I typed the word *spanking* into the search bar and clicked enter.

I didn't want to communicate with God, but a higher authority wanted to communicate with me. This time, it was Oman's highest authority: the government. More specifically, it was the Omani Telecommunications Regulatory Authority. One of the TRA's stated missions was to protect social values.

In other words, they censor porn. And *they were onto me.*

I could only understand a few words of the Arabic warning that popped up on my computer screen to block me from my unsavory search request. But in my heart I knew what it said. My imagination filled in where language failed.

"Hi, Jillian," it read. "What the fuck is wrong with you?"

I scrunched my face into an old apple and ran my tongue across my teeth.

Oh, Omani Telecommunications Regulatory Authority, I thought, sighing. *I don't know.*

"You just tried to access sadomasochistic sexual material from a public Internet café," the Arabic script replied. "You've gone off the deep end. Now every moral authority in the Middle East is coming to arrest you."

Not likely, I thought. But I left a handful of rials on the front desk for the shopkeeper to find when he returned from prayers, and I fled anyway.

I walked home and sat on the edge of my bed. With a sigh, I reached up and pulled off my hijab. My ponytail spilled over my shoulder, and I absentmindedly pulled at the end of it. Minutes passed. Maybe hours, I don't know.

The porn blocker had a point. What the fuck was wrong with me?

A knock on the front door startled me out of my malaise. It was Sabihah, an elderly neighbor who had taken it upon herself to absorb me into her family when I arrived in her apartment building months earlier without male protection. I didn't have much choice in the matter. Sabihah insisted that I eat dinner with her each night and that I report my daily plans to her each morning. When she saw, to her horror, the collection of jeans in my bedroom, she even started to make clothes for me on her sewing machine.

"Were you with a man?" Sabihah demanded as soon as she saw me.

I smiled. It had been a while since someone had taken such a detailed interest in disciplining my choices. I didn't want Sabihah to worry about me. But it was a comfort that she did.

"No, Auntie," I replied, shaking my head. "There was no man. I went to use the Internet."

Sabihah narrowed her eyes.

"Okay," she said, with a curt nod. "Get in the car. Bring some clothes. Enough for two days. Don't dress like an American."

"Where are we going, Auntie?" I replied. "I have Arabic class on Saturday." (At that point, Oman's weekend, like neighboring Saudi Arabia's, fell on Thursdays and Fridays.)

"Don't argue with me," Sabihah scolded. "Hurry!"

That afternoon we climbed into a tattered gray sedan with Sabihah's adult daughter and drove to a tiny village deep in the desert to visit their relatives. The village was another world, a place where goats were more common than cars and sun-dried mud walls were typical. That night, after the men disappeared into another room, the other women and I chatted in a jumbled mix of Arabic, Swahili, and English and snacked on dates (but only in sets of odd numbers, such as three or five, Sabihah reminded me, with a sharp rap on my knuckles when I reached for one too many, because that was the practice of the Prophet Mohammed). Finally, sometime after midnight, the other women set mats on the floor and settled down to sleep.

I lay on my mat, stressed out. I was frustrated. I was awake. Soon, long, heavy breaths filled the room.

The others were asleep.

I stood up, grabbed a flashlight from my overnight bag, and pulled a long black abaya on over my pajamas. The door didn't have a lock. I slipped out into the village and walked down the dirt road as far as I could. Beyond the end of the road was the desert, and I kept walking. When I couldn't see any houses behind me, I stopped and passed my flashlight in a circle over the land. This seemed like a good place.

Out here, no one would hear me scream.

Years earlier, when I was in high school, I had developed a unique stress-relief ritual. I was sixteen at the time and reading *A Midsummer Night's Dream*. In it, a woman named Helena loves a man named Demetrius.

No—Helena doesn't love Demetrius, exactly. She craves him. Helena pursues Demetrius obsessively, while Demetrius, in turn, pursues Helena's childhood friend, Hermia. But unlike Helena, I didn't have a high school crush to pour my adolescent angst into.

So I borrowed hers.

One afternoon I walked to the edge of my empty high school football field, took a deep breath, and screamed Demetrius's name for as long as I could. Into his name, I poured all of my fear, desire, anxiety, and grief.

In the four years since, I'd developed the habit of yelling "Demetrius!" during moments of stress. An occasional scream releases pent-up energy, and as for the word *Demetrius*—well, why not? It seemed no less appropriate than *shit* or *fuck* or any other word I might want to yell in a moment of frustration. After I yelled "Demetrius!" at a college term paper and got an unexpected A, I even started to think of the ritual as a good-luck charm. Demetrius was my four-leaf clover.

I hadn't yelled his name once in the months since I had moved to Oman. This night seemed like a good time. If I were going to walk by myself, at night, into the middle of the desert, wearing cartoon duck pajamas and an abaya, just to scream the name of one of Shakespeare's least lovable male characters, it might as well be on the same day that I tried to find spanking porn in an Islamic public Internet café. Go big or go home, right?

I took a deep breath, filling my lungs with as much oxygen as I could stand to inhale. Then I coughed it all out in a start.

My flashlight had just passed over a pair of eyeballs.

I swung the light back in the direction of those eyes until I found their owner: a goat, sitting on the ground. He was alone. But I'd been in Oman long enough to know that wherever there was a goat, its owner would not be far away. I didn't want to wake anyone up.

So I couldn't scream. I spoke.

"Demetrius," I said, looking at the goat. "Hey, Demetrius."

The goat blinked. It was not impressed.

I sat on a rock and stared back at him. At that moment, my best friend in the world was an Omani goat.

I needed to get my shit together.

AT ITS MOST basic level, Shakespeare is physical and biological. It's even sexual. The metrical rhythm of iambic pentameter—the syllabic building block of Shakespeare's poetry—mimics the ba *bump* pattern of a heartbeat. His words circulate, speed up and slow down, skip beats, and flutter in perfect symmetry with the human heart. It's not an accident. I feel it in my bloodstream every time.

This story is about the Shakespeare Thing. And the Spanking Thing. But most of all, it's about the Love Thing.

I moved to Muscat, the capital city of Oman, roughly two months before my quiet midnight confrontation with the goat. I was twenty years old.

Oman is a thick slice of country in the Persian Gulf, wedged between Saudi Arabia, the United Arab Emirates, and Yemen. Oman's ruler, Sultan Qaboos bin Said al-Said, assumed control of the country after he overthrew his father in a palace coup in

1970, and today Oman remains one of the last absolute monarchies in the world. Although Sultan Qaboos is well respected and even beloved among Omanis, he also maintains strict control over the country. When I lived there, regulations governed even small minutiae of life in the sultanate. One law, for example, required that almost all buildings in Muscat be painted white, which gave the city a dreamlike quality. In its aesthetics, politics, and culture, Oman was a fierce mix of old and new. It was the kind of place where once, on my way to buy a frothy cappuccino and a flaky croissant, I got stuck in a traffic jam caused by a wayward camel. It was the kind of place where I could admire waves of perfect golden sand dunes—and then surf down them.

The Shakespeare Thing is what drove me to Oman in the first place. When I "stopped out" of college and moved to the Middle East, I told myself it was a responsible choice. I had just spent a term at Oxford, where I studied under a tutor who specialized in "Shakespearean cartography"—the study of how maps and mapmaking interact with Shakespeare's plays. (Yes, that's a real thing.) I followed that with a summer research fellowship, for which I read about Shakespeare, wrote about Shakespeare, watched Shakespeare, and did little else.

But as much as I loved Shakespeare, he wasn't an employable plan. As the imaginary career counselor inside my head reminded me, I needed to pick up a useful skill. Oman seemed unfamiliar and exciting, but, more to the point, people spoke Arabic there. I decided I would learn Arabic, renounce my less-than-practical Shakespeare habit, and equip myself for a reasonable job. In Oman, I thought, I could finally break up with William Shakespeare and start my grown-up life.

And I wanted to sexually neuter myself. There was that, too.

Which brings us to the Spanking Thing.

In *Notes from the Underground,* Dostoevsky wrote: "There are things which a man is afraid to tell even to himself, and every decent man has a number of such things stored away in his mind." That's true. Here's what I, for decades, was afraid to tell myself: I'm obsessed with spanking.

I don't use the word *obsessed* casually. Plenty of people enjoy an occasional erotic swat, but that is not me. It would not be accurate to say that spankings "turn me on," or that I "enjoy being spanked." Those phrases don't describe obsession.

What would be accurate is to say that all day, every day, for my entire life, I've thought about spankings. Spanking is not *part of* my sex life; spanking *is* my sex life. (To be honest, I could almost drop the word *sex* from that sentence.) My fetish is my sexual orientation, or maybe just my orientation. It isn't something I chose, or an experimental phase, or a "preference," or a trend that I opted into. It's the core of my sexuality, and an innate, unchosen, and lifelong center of my identity. My phone is saturated with pictures of wounded butts—not only of my own, but photos of my friends' bottoms, too. Every morning I wake up to dozens of text messages in our group chat, where my fetishist friends and I swap photos and stories about our adventures in gluteal perversion. If I had to give up sex—*all* kinds of sex—or spanking, I'd flush sex like a drug smuggler ditching his stash in an airport bathroom. My fetish isn't something I do. It's something I am.

That is what I mean when I say I'm obsessed with spankings.

It sounds weird, I know.

BDSM, the blanket term for sexual identities on a spectrum with my own, has a lot of definitions: bondage and discipline, dominance and submission, and sadism and masochism. But even within those categories, there are subcultures. As for corporal punishment enthusiasts, like me, the broader BDSM community calls us spankos. But I can't stand that word. I suppose it's short for *spankophile*, but the abbreviation makes my skin crawl. It sounds like a processed food product, and there is nothing more thoroughly unerotic than that.

The linguistics of BDSM are as complicated as its practice. No semantic approach can satisfy every perspective. *Paraphilia*, for example, is the most formal, clinical term for my obsession, but I'll use the word *fetish* instead, since it's more widely understood. I'll also use the word *kink* at times, since fetishes and kinks often overlap. But there is also a significant difference between the two. Put simply, it's possible to opt into kink. But fetishes are not chosen.

I identify as a masochist, a bottom, and, in rare cases, even a submissive, depending on the context, so all three words will appear at different times. But that should not imply that those terms are interchangeable, because they're not. Masochists aren't necessarily submissive, and submissives aren't necessarily masochists. And the term *vanilla*—the most common way to describe people who aren't kinky—does not imply that a person is boring or conservative. (Just as fetishists aren't necessarily interesting or adventurous.) Plenty of vanilla people explore kink as an accessory to sex. The difference is that fetishists explore sex as an accessory to kink. Our fetish is our baseline. It is our first, and most fundamental, need. This is about identities, not activities.

I can't promise to satisfy everyone with my word choices. I have to write from my own perspective, and in my own voice.

But I can promise to avoid the word *spanko*. I don't want to think about cans of spray cheese.

By the time I moved to Oman, I had come to recognize my fetish as the center of my sexuality. I had often wondered what caused this bizarre obsession, but eventually I gave up. It was exhausting to psychoanalyze my erotic life. Recognition and experience didn't translate into comfort. The psychological and social implications of my inner life were so disturbing to me that I could rarely force myself to confront them. Wasn't I a feminist? And a pacifist, too? How could I fantasize about scenarios and interactions that were, I feared, eroticized domestic violence, internalized patriarchy, proof that I was, at my core, messed up? My commitments to peace, women's rights, gender equality, and nonviolence seemed absurd alongside the dark and frightening underworld of my fetish. I hated myself for the hypocrisy.

I left home to "fix" myself. Instead, it took only a handful of weeks and one briefly unattended Internet café for my resolve to fade.

But my confusing sexual identity wasn't my biggest worry. My biggest worry, I had started to realize, was the Love Thing. It was a problem so vast I couldn't wrap my head around it.

I had no idea how to love someone. I mean this in a romantic sense, but, to be honest, also in a platonic one. Babies learn to talk from hearing adults speak to each other, right? (Otherwise, our vocabularies would be limited to "Who's the pretty baby?" and "Peekaboo!") I think it's the same with love. Kids learn to love from watching adults love each other. As long as a child sees a parent love someone—a spouse, a friend, a religious leader, a colleague, whomever—she can learn how healthy love begins, thrives, overcomes conflict, and lasts.

Even one example might be enough. Just *one* single healthy and loving relationship between adults could be all a kid needs to learn how to love.

My point is: If a kid has never seen someone scramble an egg, it's not easy for her to figure it out on her own. And, for now, let's just say my family doesn't cook.

IT ALL STARTED with Helena. For me, she is everything. As I sat alone that night, in the middle of the Omani desert, feeling gross and broken and alone, Helena had my back. I needed a friend, and she, as best friends do, showed up.

In the desert just beyond the goat, the faint outline of two figures appeared. It was Helena and Demetrius. They were in the middle of a fight.

No, not literally. To be clear, I don't hallucinate Shakespeare characters (although that would be awesome). What happened that night is that I understood, for the first time, just how books interact with our lives. The characters we love become more than friends. Through them, we can pass our anxieties, questions, fears, and insecurities to an external source of strength; confront what is internal in an external forum.

Literature is a *conversation*. Books are walkie-talkies, not radios. That night, as I sat next to a goat in the warm midnight Omani desert, I let these characters sink into my life.

I spoke to them. And they spoke back.

At first, though, Demetrius and Helena ignored me. They focused on their fight.

"I love thee not; therefore pursue me not," Demetrius yelled at Helena. He wanted her to stop following him. She, as always, refused.

"You draw me, you hard-hearted adamant!" she shouted back.

I sighed. I always hated this part. In this scene, Helena, who loves Demetrius, follows him into a forest while he yells at her to go away. But she stays with him. I had watched Helena and Demetrius have this fight onstage a dozen times, and imagined it a hundred more. But no matter how many times I revisited this conversation, I couldn't find a reason to like it. Why did Shakespeare include such a cold, cruel scene in this lighthearted play? It didn't fit.

A Midsummer Night's Dream is Shakespeare's most joyful exploration of sensuality and the infinite variety of sex. Its world is sex uncensored, joyful, and diverse. I could find a huge spectrum of sexualities reflected in its characters. I saw passionate monogamy in Hermia and Lysander, confident polyamory in Oberon and

Titania, playful anthropomorphism in Titania and Bottom, and loving bisexuality or homosexuality in Oberon and Puck.

But in Helena and Demetrius, I just saw assholes. The problem was that damn scene.

From its beginning, *A Midsummer Night's Dream* provokes questions about sexual consent. Does Hippolyta sincerely consent to marry Theseus, or was she kidnapped and coerced? To what extremes should Hermia go to avoid a forced marriage? When Oberon puts the fairy potion on Titania's eyes to trick her into falling for Bottom, is that comparable to putting a date-rape drug in her drink? We should ask ourselves these questions. *Midsummer* isn't just a play about sexual awakening and sexual exploration. It is, at its core, a play that grapples with questions about sexual freedom, self-determination, and consent.

Even more than that, this is a play about people who *do* consent. Which brings us back to my girl Helena.

Helena isn't an easy woman to love. She's whiny and self-pitying. It's hard to sympathize with her desperate fight for Demetrius, who seems so unworthy. We first hear about Helena before we see her, when Lysander reveals her romantic history with Demetrius. Lysander's description of Helena is friendly and sweet. But her first appearance onstage is far less flattering. In fact, she's pathetic. She whines about Demetrius, oblivious to her best friend Hermia's far more serious plight of being forced to marry against her will. And her love of Demetrius is even worse. What kind of monster leaves his fiancée for her best friend? What kind of woman keeps chasing him, even after that betrayal?

What kind of people talk to each other this way?

"Do I entice you? Do I speak you fair?" Demetrius shouted at Helena. He ran his fingers through his hair, frustrated, and kicked the toe of his boot against a sand dune. "Or rather do I not in plainest truth tell you I do not nor I cannot love"—his voice caught in his throat, and he turned his back to Helena—"you," he finished.

I stayed at my seat, next to the sleeping goat, and watched them fight.

"And even for that do I love you the more," Helena replied, wrapping her hands around her stomach. She stood there, looking at Demetrius's back. Then she made a decision.

"I am your spaniel, and Demetrius, the more you beat me, I will fawn on you," she said.

The starkness of those words, my least favorite line in the play, hung in the air. Demetrius looked down. I looked up.

And for the first time, perhaps, we both listened—*really* listened—to Helena.

"Use me but as your spaniel—spurn me, strike me, neglect me, lose me," she said. "Only give me leave, unworthy as I am, to follow you. What worser place can I beg in your love (and yet a place of high respect with me) than to be uséd as you use your dog?"

Demetrius stood there, frozen. Then he sat down on a sand dune, his body hunched over and his forehead in the palms of his hands. He swallowed. His next words had none of the rancor of his earlier threats. Suddenly, he sounded tired and sad.

"Tempt not too much the hatred of my spirit, for I am sick when I do look on thee," Demetrius said, unable to make eye contact.

Helena walked over to the dune and settled down next to him, the tips of her fingers sinking into the sand. "And I am sick when I look not on you," she replied.

Demetrius looked at the ground for long seconds. Finally, he looked up and met Helena's eyes.

"You do impeach your modesty too much, to leave the city and commit yourself into the hands of one that loves you not," he muttered, furrowing his brow with amazement. "To trust the opportunity of night and the ill counsel of a desert place with the rich worth of your virginity."

Helena shrugged. "Your virtue is my privilege," she said, simply. She put her hand on Demetrius's ankle, and, for a second, he let it rest there. Then he stood up, abruptly, and shook his head. Their détente was over. He demanded again that she leave him alone, and ran off. His outline disappeared into the desert.

I expected Helena to jump up and follow him, as she always does. But this time she didn't. Instead, she looked over at me, acknowledging my presence for the first time, and smiled.

Then she shook her head. My breath caught in my throat.

No matter how many times I had watched Helena and Demetrius have this fight, the words had always been the same. It was always hard to watch Helena debase herself in the face of Demetrius's obvious scorn. On paper, that scene is sad, unfunny, and doesn't make sense within the context of the play. Taken at face value, their fight is exactly what it appears to be: Demetrius is selfish and cruel, and Helena is ridiculous and pathetic. This interpretation relies on the worst stereotypes of both genders, since it requires us to accept that men are unfeeling and inconstant in love, and that women are clingy, desperate, and lacking in self-respect. Which is why, for years, I hated that scene.

But I'd never seen it like I did that night—so soft, so honest, so compassionate. I had never before seen Demetrius's obvious pain. I'd never seen Helena's strength.

We tend to skim over Shakespeare's most challenging scenes, like this one, or play them for absurd laughs, because otherwise they're too hard to digest. We can't confront lines like "The more you beat me, I will fawn on you" because *Midsummer* is a comedy, and if people were to engage with the literal or even figurative meanings of those words, it wouldn't be funny anymore. Even worse, we gloss over lines like:

> *You do impeach your modesty too much,*
> *To leave the city and commit yourself*
> *Into the hands of one that loves you not;*
> *To trust the opportunity of night,*
> *And the ill counsel of a desert place,*
> *With the rich worth of your virginity.*

At face value, that's a rape threat. How can we stomach a rape threat in a romantic comedy? If we reduce Helena to a pathetic cliché and Demetrius to a cruel player, how can we smile and be satisfied at the end when they end up together?

We can't.

That interpretation is unfair to these characters. They deserve better. Demetrius is not a monster, and Helena is not a pathetic damsel in a tower, waiting for a man to climb up her hair. Her actions throughout the play prove otherwise. She's relentless and unstoppable. She knows what she wants, and latches onto it like a lioness on the hunt. She's not stupid, either. So why would she invite the object of her affection to "beat" and "strike" her? Why, if Helena isn't silly, self-effacing, and desperate (an interpretation I've seen in too many performances), does she ask for this treatment?

Maybe it's what she wants.

How might the possibility that Helena and Demetrius are kinky change their relationship? How might that possibility change this frustrating and challenging scene?

Look again at the first words of their exchange. Demetrius says, "Do I entice you? Do I speak you fair? Or rather do I not in plainest truth tell you I do not, nor I cannot, love you?" Already, something is wrong. We can't take this scene at face value. From at perspective, Demetrius is just angry with Helena for follow-him into the forest. But there's more at stake here. Demetrius nuine pain—and I can prove it.

espeare wrote the majority of his verse in iambic

pentameter—a poetic form in which each line has ten syllables. Those syllables break into five so-called "feet," with two syllables per foot: an unstressed syllable, followed by a stressed syllable (ba *bump* / ba *bump* / ba *bump* / ba *bump* / ba *bump*). Demetrius's first two lines—"Do I entice you? Do I speak you fair? / Or rather do I not in plainest truth"—are perfect iambic pentameter. But the third line—"Tell you I do not, nor I cannot, love you?"—isn't. It has one extra syllable.

That might seem minor, but it's not. Breaks in the verse form are significant in Shakespeare. They're the clues that Shakespeare left us to understand his characters. Irregular iambic pentameter can indicate a lot of things: extreme anger, mental illness, or inebriation. But in this scene, I don't think those possibilities fit. Demetrius isn't drunk or mentally ill. And if Shakespeare wanted to suggest anger, I suspect he'd put the irregularity in the line "Do I entice you? Do I speak you fair?" which seems like a more appropriate place to emphasize rage. Demetrius isn't as angry as his words suggest. In this context, I think the irregular pentameter indicates emotional turmoil or pain.

In other words, Shakespeare says that it crushes Demetrius to tell Helena that he does not—or *cannot*—love her.

If it's so painful for Demetrius to treat Helena this way, he's not just a jerk who doesn't love her. There must be some more nuanced explanation. Something happened.

Coming to terms with the details of our sexual identities is hard for everyone. That's especially true for people who have non-normative sexual identities. It was hard for me to accept that I'm a fetishist. I was in denial for a long time. This process is often even more difficult for sadists. I can't imagine how scary and confusing it must feel to realize, in the early stages of sexual development, that you long to "hurt" the people you desire. Many sadists have told me that, at first, their fantasies terrified them. And in the early stages of awareness, it doesn't necessarily help when sadists and masochists first meet. It's overwhelming. We feed into each other, and the realization that our fantasies could become realities is the scariest thing of all.

What if this conflict explains the mystery of why Demetrius got engaged to Helena and then abruptly left her to pursue Hermia instead? What if he couldn't confront the terrifying implications of a relationship in which both he and Helena started to become aware of some scary sexual impulses? Helena and Demetrius aren't very old. They're teenagers. There's no way they've had enough experience to understand their sexual selves yet.

I've been there. Once, when I was fifteen, years before my first kiss or even my first date, I got into a playful pillow fight with my friend Dan. (Pillow fights are a common way to test the waters of rougher play.) The fight had escalated into teasing and playful threats when, abruptly, Dan grabbed a remote control and slapped it across my butt, hard, two times. We both froze.

"I'm sorry," he said.

"It's fine," I replied, a bit too soon.

The rest of the afternoon was awkward, and I left not long after. The next morning, Dan emailed me.

"I'm so sorry about yesterday," he wrote. "I don't know what's wrong with me. I'm such an asshole."

Remembering that letter, my heart aches for him. Dan and I have long since lost touch, and I can't make assumptions about his sexuality. But I can let my experience and impressions of how humans interact influence my assumptions about Demetrius. Here's what I know: teenagers are awkward, easily embarrassed, and scared of their sexual impulses. And I believe that when humans—especially young adults—treat each other badly, it's often motivated by fear rather than by cruelty.

I don't think Demetrius is cruel. I think he's scared.

I was, too.

What if his voice cracks with pain, not anger, when he tells

Helena that he cannot love her? What if Helena's response is not just shameful degradation?

> *And even for that do I love you the more:*
> *I am your spaniel; and, Demetrius,*
> *The more you beat me, I will fawn on you.*
> *Use me but as your spaniel; spurn me, strike me . . .*

What if that line—"The more you beat me, I will fawn on you"—is not a silly moment of hyperbolic desperation, but rather the most honest moment in the scene? Helena's first line in that section—"And even for that do I love you the more"—is not perfect iambic pentameter. It has one extra, unstressed, syllable. We call that a "weak ending." (Those are also, unfortunately, known as "feminine endings.") There's another weak ending in the final line.

Consider this: to make his verse perfect, Shakespeare only had to remove the word *the* from the first line. Then it would be "and even for that do I love you more"—perfect iambic pentameter. By including that unnecessary three-letter word, Shakespeare forced a weak ending.

It's not a coincidence. In Shakespeare, little is.

And as her speech progresses, Helena's verse becomes more regular. She's gaining power and rhythm as she speaks:

> *Neglect me, lose me; only give me leave,*
> *Unworthy as I am, to follow you.*
> *What worser place can I beg in your love*
> *(And yet a place of high respect with me)*
> *Than to be uséd as you use your dog?*

What if this portion of Helena's dialogue isn't silly self-debasement? What if it is instead the most explicit and brave declaration of sexual consent in the Shakespearean canon? Better still, what if Demetrius's next remark isn't a rape threat anymore?

You do impeach your modesty too much

. . .

To trust the opportunity of night,
And the ill counsel of a desert place,
With the rich worth of your virginity.

There was nothing ominous about the way I'd just heard Demetrius speak those lines. He said them sincerely, amazed and confused at Helena's willingness to take such a risk to follow him. That night, displaced from Shakespeare's magical forest to Oman's vast desert, Demetrius's implication transformed even as the words remained the same. He underlined the fundamental question at the core of every sadomasochistic relationship: Demetrius asked Helena how she could trust him enough to submit herself to physical risk at his hands—and Helena assured him that she can, and does.

Isn't this a more powerful, and more empathetic, way to explain their relationship than merely "Demetrius is mean" and "Helena is pathetic"?

Let's listen to these characters. Try to hear them as they speak. The way Helena describes her love for Demetrius is unpalatable to a lot of people—it's not my exact cup of tea, either, by the way— but she says it's "a place of high respect" to her. (And after all, this is the same play in which another character declares: "I woo'd thee with my sword, and won thy love doing thee injuries.") Let's take Helena at her word.

Maybe Helena does want Demetrius to treat her that way. Maybe that's what he wants, too.

Or maybe not. Maybe in Helena, and in all Shakespeare—hell, in all literature—I only see what I want to see.

But, if so, who cares? The people who crowded into the standing-room section of Shakespeare's Globe Theatre for the first performance of *Midsummer* weren't academics and noblemen. There are no gatekeepers here. Shakespeare's plays were, and are, soap operas: designed for mass appeal. We all have our own versions, and those interpretations are as valid as anyone's. In "Hamlet: My Greatest Creation," one of my all-time favorite essays, Norman Holland argues that the reader has as much responsibility for the creation of great literature as the author, since literature is nothing without reader response. Characters are like clouds: we all see different animals hidden in them.

Shakespeare created Helena, but I can too. My Helena is kinky. In *Midsummer*, she chooses the love she wants. It doesn't matter what we think of Demetrius or whether we approve of their dynamic. Helena loves him unflinchingly, and for that she deserves our respect. *A Midsummer Night's Dream* is a play about consent, and its message is clear: not only can we consent to sex, we can consent to love. It only demands our honesty.

In the desert, I looked up to see if Helena was still with me, and she was. I walked over to her and sat down. The goat stayed behind me.

In *Hamlet*, Shakespeare wrote that the purpose of theater is to "hold a mirror up to nature." But it wasn't until I sat next to Helena that night and looked into her eyes that I felt, with a sudden jolt of recognition, that Shakespeare might be holding a mirror up to me, too.

If I could find myself reflected in Shakespeare's world, maybe that meant I wasn't as unnatural as I feared.

"I thought I was the only one," I told Helena. "I've been lonely for a while."

Helena winked. "The story shall be changed," she told me.

Then she jumped up, dusted the sand off her abaya, and ran into the desert, still following Demetrius—determined to change her story, and mine.

I realized that I could figure out the Shakespeare Thing. That with time, I could even work through the Spanking Thing. But the Love Thing wouldn't be so easy. Love is a tricky bastard.

I would need some help.

IN PLATO'S *Symposium,* a group of philosophers comes together to discuss the thorny problem of how to understand *eros,* the Greek word for passionate love and desire. After dinner and wine, these intellectual giants present their theories. First, Phaedrus argues that love inspires bravery. Pausanias, meanwhile, draws a line between love that is "attracted to the bodies rather than the minds" and love that is "inherently stronger and more intelligent." Eryximachus says that "the body of every creature on earth is pervaded by Love," which is "the source of all our happiness." Socrates concludes that love is the longing for a missing good.

But I return to Aristophanes's speech most often. He describes an ancient world of three human genders, each of which had two faces and four limbs. These ancient humans also had two sets of genitals: one gender had two sets of female genitals, the second gender had two sets of male genitals, and the third gender had one of each. These original humans always had the support of their other halves, which gave them power. The gods grew envious of that power, so they ripped these humans in half, splitting their essence into different bodies. Today, we lonely half-humans, now with only two eyes and two legs each, wander the world trying to find the other halves of our original selves. We push ourselves together like locks and keyholes, hoping to find the combination that comes closest to what we lost.

That, Aristophanes says, is sex.

"We human beings will never attain happiness until we find perfect love, unless we each come across the love of our lives and thereby recover our original nature," he warns. "'Love' is just the name we give to the desire for and pursuit of wholeness."

I want to be whole. And who am I to argue with Aristophanes about how to make that happen?

Now, I don't have a symposium of legendary Greek philosophers in my living room. But I can look to what I do have, and have always had: a symposium of Shakespeare's characters inside my head. And I can bring them together whenever I want. Could this Shakespearean symposium teach me how to love? Could they make sense of the whole impossible issue?

"To say the truth, reason and love keep little company together now-a-days," another one of Shakespeare's characters from *A Midsummer Night's Dream* warned me. His name is Bottom.

Of course that's his name.

Bottom had a point. But, on the other hand, I'd been sitting on a rock, in my ridiculous duck pajamas, staring at a goat for the better part of an hour. I was in no position to nitpick what was or was not reasonable. (Or, for that matter, sane.) I pushed Shakespeare's words of caution aside.

Instead, I looked to his dare from *Hamlet:* "Stand and unfold yourself."

Challenge accepted.

ACT TWO

One fire burns out another's burning,
One pain is less'ned by another's anguish;
Turn giddy, and be [helped] by backward turning;
One desperate grief cures with another's languish:
Take thou some new infection to thy eye,
And the rank poison of the old will die.

—*Romeo and Juliet*, 1.2

2.1   The Tempest:
Were I Human

It's an odd thing for a teenage girl to fall in love with a fish, but I did.

My mom took me to my very first Shakespeare play, at the Utah Shakespeare Festival in Cedar City, when I was fifteen. It was *The Tempest*. An actor named David Ivers played Caliban—the half-human, half-fish "monster" who inhabits a magical island. Caliban crept onstage, his body covered with seaweed and boils, and opened his mouth to speak.

"As wicked dew as e'er my m-m-mother brush'd with raven's feather from unwholesome fen drop on you both!" he hissed at Prospero. "A south-west blow on ye, and blister you all o'er!"

My chest swelled with his words, and, for the first time in years, I really breathed.

From Caliban's first moments onstage, I was transfixed. I had been an unhappy kid, and I was an unhappy teenager, but Caliban was a revelation. As Ivers played him, Caliban was angry and abused, flinched easily and often, and stuttered every time he said a word that began with the letter *m*. He slid down my throat, like a living fish, and into my stomach to writhe and thrash against the acid inside.

It was his stutter that really stuck in my head. Why *m*? I imagined there must be a reason.

At the theater's bookshop, my mom bought me a small paperback copy of *The Tempest*. It was my first Shakespeare play. I couldn't wait until we got home to read it, so instead I sat on the floor of the shop and hungrily pawed through each page. As I circled all the *m* words, a picture came into focus. All of the most important and painful things in Caliban's life begin with the letter *m*: Master. Miranda. Man-i'-th'-moon. Murder. Mother.

RUDYARD KIPLING SUPPOSEDLY said that since God could not be everywhere at once, he created mothers in his stead. If that's true, God fashioned my mom in his Old Testament image: angry, vengeful, at once capable of breathtaking generosity and fearsome rage. She could match Prospero at his magical best and furious worst. As a child, I regarded her with equal parts awe and terror. My mother was a woman who, before my birth, had walked with gorillas in Rwanda and traveled to China only shortly after Nixon did. She kept a slide projector filled with images that astonished me—animals I'd only seen in picture books, and people who looked unlike anyone I had met on the sidewalks and in the strip malls of Phoenix, where we lived. She wasn't the kind of mom who baked cookies. Instead, she taught me to make umeboshi rice balls: Japanese pickled plums nestled inside fluffy rice and crisp sesame seeds. We made the rice balls only that one time, when I was six, and the salty plums had made my face pucker and wince at their tang. But for the next three years, "umeboshi rice balls" was always my improbable answer when people asked about my favorite food. I imagined my mother in green mountains, crouched only steps away from the baby gorilla who had reached out to touch the tiny white stars on her black gloves, like Adam reaching for God on the ceiling of the Sistine Chapel. I was so proud to be her daughter.

I felt certain that my mother was the most brave and magnificent woman who had ever lived.

As I got older, she began to include me in her adventures. My mom loved books, and her travels were usually inspired by things she had read. She inserted herself into the physical worlds of her stories, even when those stories took her to the literal ends of the earth. When I was fifteen years old, she read about Ernest Shackleton, the British polar explorer who was stranded with his crew on Antarctic ice floes for almost two years, and arranged for us to sail on a Russian polar icebreaker to Antarctica. A penguin tried to feed me by vomiting on my foot. I watched the nutritious brown gel roll off the toe of my green boot and onto the snow beneath, and knew that my childhood wasn't typical. My mom made it clear that, in her mind, dreams came true through force of will. She taught me to question conventional values and find my own priorities. Travel was her priority. I have no memories of my mom buying expensive clothes for herself or visiting a salon: throughout my childhood, she cut and dyed her own hair in the bathroom. Her house was infested with cockroaches that terrified me: I found them in my shoes and, once, even under the sheets in my bed. But when I begged her to hire an exterminator, she refused. My mom saved her money for adventures. Like God creating the world, she built for herself the worlds and dreams she had learned in books. "Follow your bliss," she often told me.

My mother's passion was matched only by her frenetic inconsistency. Her rage was chronic. She was incapable of playing low status, even when it would have been in her best interest to do so. When the police pulled her over for speeding, which happened a lot, she refused to apologize and beg her way out of a ticket. Instead, she yelled, threatened, and antagonized the police, telling them that their radar guns were defective or that they'd been incompetently trained.

This tactic did not work. She got a ticket every time.

"Can you believe this?" she'd exclaim, brandishing her ticket in the air with the indignant outrage of a red-haired Norma Rae.

"Yes, I can believe it," I'd say. "Stop arguing with the police. You're never going to win!"

She'd laugh.

"I know, I know," she'd say. *"But can you believe this?"*

She saw herself as endemically two steps shy of a greatness that had been snatched away.

"I had the idea to open a coffee shop long before Starbucks," she insisted often.

Although my mother and I lived alone, I felt like there were two other people with me in her house. I could never predict which version of my mother would wake up each morning. She reacted to the exact same provocations in terrifyingly different ways. The first time I saw snow, for example, I made a snowball and threw it at her. She laughed and playfully told me to stop. When I threw a second snowball at her, only seconds later, she slapped me in the face.

"You're not crying because it hurts," she said, more than once. "You're crying because you're embarrassed."

Although we stayed in the same house and school district throughout my childhood, my mom made me enroll in a different school almost every year. By the time I entered sixth grade, I'd attended seven different schools. I never understood it, but I came to expect and even embrace her pattern: every June, my mother found a reason to hate the school I was in, and would move me to another. The following September I'd start at a new school, in a new room of strangers.

My mom went through distinct but short-lived phases of her own: she had a macrobiotic phase, a mountaineering phase, a Unitarian phase, and more. Her relationships were similarly short-lived: friends drifted in and then, after the inevitable dramatic blow-up, disappeared. I knew my father, who split up with my mother when I was two, but I suspect there might have been a medical explanation for his emotional unavailability: he was incredibly intelligent, but found it impossible to empathize, pick up on basic social cues, or even maintain eye contact during conversations. There were no other relatives. Uncles existed, but I didn't know them. An aunt existed, too, and cousins. But I didn't meet them, either. My grandparents died and disappeared without funerals. Family was not a plural concept. My family was my mom.

It must have been so hard for her. My mom didn't have any help. She was a single parent with a full-time job, and she hadn't learned nonviolent parenting techniques during her own childhood. When she was mad at me, which was often, she expressed it with the same uncontrolled impulsivity with which she lived the rest of her life. She flew into screaming rages, saying and doing cruel and unfair things I knew she didn't mean.

The first person I loved was also the first person I feared. The implications of that are not lost on me.

THE TEMPEST IS all about power—having it, losing it, and seizing control of it.

The play starts with a shipwreck: sailors caught in a life-threatening bout of powerlessness against the elements. As the storm rages, Prospero, a sorcerer and the deposed former Duke of Milan, and his daughter, Miranda, watch the chaos at sea from the safety of their magical island. (Caliban and Ariel, two non-human native inhabitants of the island who Prospero has forced into captive servitude, also live there.)

Like the shipwrecked sailors, Miranda begins this play about power confronted with her own powerlessness. She is dismayed by the suffering she imagines aboard the sinking vessel, and fears that her father caused the storm. She begs him to calm it, saying: "If by your art, my dearest father, you have / Put the wild waters in this roar, allay them." Then she sadly remarks that if she had been "any God of power," she would have intervened to save the ship.

Unlike her father, Miranda is at the mercy of things she can't control.

The rest of the play explores the same issues of power and powerlessness. Prospero schemes to confront his brother, Antonio, for throwing him out of power as Duke of Milan. Caliban schemes to murder Prospero and take back the island, which had previously belonged to his mother. In their own subtle ways, every character tries to re-negotiate his or her place in the power structure of the play.

But I was stuck on Caliban. Like Ariel, he was an original inhabitant of the island. Prospero befriended, educated, and then enslaved him. To explain this dramatic change of treatment, Prospero says that Caliban tried to rape his daughter, Miranda: "Thou most lying slave, whom stripes may move, not kindness! I have used thee, filth as thou art, with human care, and lodged thee in mine own cell, till thou didst seek to violate the honor of my child."

Caliban doesn't deny the accusation. "Oh ho, oh ho!" he replies. "Would't had been done! Thou didst prevent me. I had peopled else the isle with Calibans." In other words, Caliban admits that he had hoped to reclaim power over his stolen island by using Miranda as a sex object to create a race of his children.

My sympathy and affection for Caliban clashed with my growing commitment to gender equality. I worried at the realization that I cared so much for a character who treated Miranda that way. Miranda was the one who deserved my love and sympathy; instead, I gave those things to her attacker. The literary characters we love can challenge our affections just as much as the people we love—and from the worst perspective, Caliban is an alcoholic, homicidal rapist.

But there is a more charitable way to understand his character, and I clung to it. Caliban's native home was invaded by colonizing foreign powers. After initial displays of kindness and even love, they tricked Caliban, took control of his island, and forced him into slavery. Prospero calls Caliban "filth," and that's how he treats him. When Caliban insults Prospero early in the play, Prospero threatens to punish him with torturous cramps.

Miranda, too, is controlled and dominated by Prospero, although the control that Prospero exerts over his daughter is less overt. But Miranda and Caliban react to their respective powerlessness in different ways. While Caliban is angry and vengeful, Miranda is careful and calm. It's no accident that she ends the play in the middle of a chess game—an apt metaphor for the calculated ways she deals with the characters who overpower her throughout the play.

I am no chess player. The physicality of Caliban's rage felt closer to home.

There is something so vulnerable and childlike in Caliban. When Prospero first arrived on the island with his baby daughter in tow, we are told, Caliban didn't know how to speak—so Prospero, presumably, taught Caliban to speak alongside Miranda. Caliban tells Prospero:

> *When thou cams't first,*
> *Thou strok'st me and made much of me, wouldst give me*
> *Water with berries in't, and teach me how*
> *To name the bigger light, and how the less,*
> *That burn by day and night; and then I loved thee.*

That line always hit me where it hurt. Caliban has memories of a Prospero who loved him and educated him, but he also has memories of a Prospero who says Caliban can only be influenced through "stripes," "not kindness." I could have said the exact same thing about my mom.

My feelings for her confused me. The intense love and loyalty I felt for one version of her clashed with the fear and contempt with which I regarded her other self. The first version of my mother was warm and encouraging; when I was seven or eight, she often sat next to me in the bathroom while I took baths so she could write down the poems I dictated aloud from the tub. She was support-ive, and assured me with confidence that my childish poems were wonderful, and that maybe I could even publish one. But the other version of my mother, her second self, once beat me with a dustpan in that same bathroom. Even from an early age, I felt a deep sense of guilt that whenever I thought of that bathroom, it wasn't the poetry I remembered first. Alongside so many good memories and such extraordinary privilege, it felt unfair and ungrateful that the bad memories stuck.

I knew that, for the most part, nothing bad had ever happened to me. I had almost everything a person could want, and so much more.

But maybe love and family are like eyebrows: you notice when they're not there.

OF COURSE, THERE was one more reason that Shakespeare's manifesto on power and powerlessness was so attractive to me: my nascent sexuality also revolved around power exchange.

I've always been kinky. My fetish appeared early, long before I knew anything about kink or the diversity of sexual lifestyles. As a child, I pored over any book that mentioned spanking, paddling, or thrashing. *Tom Sawyer* and *The Whipping Boy* went through many early reads, as did, believe it or not, key entries of the Oxford English Dictionary. ("Spank: To strike, especially on the buttocks with the open hand.") In one mortifying childhood memory, I told a friend that I wanted to rewatch the paddling scene in *Dead Poets Society* three or four times because I was "curious about the sound editing" of that moment.

I did lots of "book reports" and elementary school projects on corporal punishment.

Many, *many* "book reports" on corporal punishment.

Even as a toddler, my sexuality existed. By the time I was five, I was already prototyping my sexual identity (and no doubt ruining the otherwise pristine childhood memories of a few friends) with twisted games of House. From the outside, it looked like the standard childhood game: we climbed into a playhouse and pretended to be a family.

On the inside, things got weird. With the fevered specificity of a tiny Orson Welles, I manipulated our scenarios so that whoever was pretending to be the mom or dad that day ended up chasing us around the playhouse with a belt, yelling that we needed to be "punished." This style of play thrilled and, on a deeper level, profoundly satisfied me. I was a glutton for these play punishments.

But even at that age, we all sensed that there was something shameful about our game. We never played House with adults nearby.

Most fetishists have funny stories about the strange ways our sexuality leaked out in childhood. When my friend Tom was eight or nine, his parents took him to Home Depot. While they looked at merchandise, Tom wandered over to a computer terminal—the kind that employees could use to search for inventory—and, for reasons he still can't quite explain, and despite the fact that he had never been spanked himself, impulsively typed "I want to spank 528,984,777,000 girls!!!!!" onto the screen. (He doesn't remember the exact number he wrote; he just mashed his hands against the keyboard until the number reached a height that was sufficiently impressive to an eight-year-old.) Tom stood at the terminal for a minute, transfixed, just as I have always been, by the mere sight of that word. But when the euphoric fog of self-disclosure cleared, Tom realized he wasn't alone—a middle-aged man was standing right behind him, wearing an expression that confirmed he'd read Tom's confession.

Tom didn't even bother to delete his words. He just fled the scene of his crime.

As I got older, I stayed weird. My copy of Roald Dahl's *Boy* (which details his childhood canings in the British school system) went through so many rereads that its cover fell off. The dictionary was my first erotica: I looked up the definitions for *spank, paddle, thrash,* and *whip* so often that, after a few years, my dictionary automatically fell open to those pages. I could say that I was haunted by sexual fantasies about domination, submission, and pain, but that would be a euphemism. I wasn't haunted by fantasies about "domination" or "submission." At that point, I wasn't even familiar with those terms. I was haunted by specific fantasies about being bent over for a severe punishment, as I cried and begged for forgiveness. Alone in my room, I sometimes rolled up a pillow, put it under my hips to force my bottom into the air, as if I were draped over someone's knee, and lay on my stomach to drink the confusing cocktail of satisfaction and self-loathing that came of that position.

I realize that all this raises the obvious question of whether I was spanked as a kid—that is, hit repeatedly on my butt in the specified and deliberate way I fetishize—and how that played into my emerging sexuality. But that question is a pinch more stinging than bees, and it will take me this whole book to answer it. For now, feel free to make assumptions. But be forewarned: those assumptions will probably be wrong.

WHEN I WAS ten years old, I changed schools (and, for the first time, stayed put for a few years) and met a misanthropic ballerina named Peng (rhymes with "lung"). Before long, she was my best friend. I admired Peng's languid, graceful body and her enviable straight hair, which looked so perfect compared to my frizzy blond mess. But Peng's outward elegance was tempered with enough inner deviance to make our friendship possible. It was Peng's idea the first time we covered a rival's house with toilet paper; the secret language we invented to insult classmates was her idea, too.

But Peng's best idea, by far, was the Green Notebook.

It was 1999. That year, Peng and I (like everyone else in our generation) played a video game called *The Legend of Zelda: Ocarina of Time*. The green notebook was our way to keep the story going during class.

Link is the hero of the game. He begins his quest to save the world of Hyrule as a child, but when the battles become too challenging for his age, he goes into hibernation at the Temple of Time under the care of Rauru, the game's so-called "Sage of Light." Seven years later, Link wakes up as an adult and continues his quest.

Link's hibernation period was our window of opportunity. What if Link wasn't asleep during those seven years? What if, instead, he was training for the battles to come? Wouldn't that be a good story? Peng and I relished the chance to flesh out this part of Link's narrative without contradicting the game we loved.

We filled a green three-ring binder with paper and a bag of multicolored pens, assigned colors to each character, and passed the notebook back and forth during classes. Peng wrote as Rauru. He spoke in gray ink. I wrote as Link, who spoke in green ink.

In our story, Rauru was a strict—*very* strict—teacher and mentor figure to Link. (Both Rauru and Link are male, and have no biological relationship; to this day, most of my favorite erotica emphasizes that dynamic: male, platonic, educational.) I didn't control both characters, but just as I had done years earlier when my friends and I played House, I manipulated our scenarios so that Rauru ended up giving Link severe, detailed beatings, with all kinds of implements: straps, sticks, and more. At night, I taught myself to masturbate to the thought of those stories.

More than a decade later, when the green notebook came up in conversation, I asked Peng if she remembered the experimentally masochistic scenes that, in hindsight, seemed so obvious and embarrassing to me. She didn't. It was my first experience of the kind of love that Shakespeare described as "painted blind"—every time I had let my freak flag fly and done something twisted, Peng didn't even notice. I loved her for that.

"LET'S RENT A MOVIE," Peng suggested at a sleepover one night in 2001, when we were fifteen. At Blockbuster, I stumbled onto a French film called *The Piano Teacher*. The back of the tape said that it was about a piano student who gets involved with his masochistic music teacher. Intrigued and titillated, I grabbed Peng and insisted that we rent this movie. She shrugged and, as usual, tolerated me.

The Piano Teacher is about a middle-aged piano teacher named Erika, who has a domineering mother and a father who is institutionalized in a psychiatric asylum. Erika and one of her piano students, Walter, become attracted to each other, and he tries to kiss her. Erika tells Walter that she'll have a relationship with him only if he is willing to satisfy her masochistic fantasies, which she describes in a letter. Walter is repulsed. Their relationship climaxes when Walter attacks Erika in her apartment, in exactly the way she requested, and beats and rapes her. Erika seems shaken and unsatisfied by this encounter. The next day, when she sees Walter at a concert, he ignores her.

At the end of the film, Erika removes a knife from her purse and casually inserts it into her own chest.

Peng was bored. I sat frozen on the couch, wearing a mask of stricken, sunken-eyed horror. (When beginning to explore a divergent sexual identity, *do not* turn to French cinema.) Did Erika's character speak for me? Was she my sexual destiny? Were my only choices to follow my superego into the light of normative (if frustrating and unsatisfying) vanilla sex, or to follow my id into the suicidal hellscape of a French psychosexual drama?

American pop culture wasn't any better. In *Six Feet Under,* an otherwise sexually open-minded and nonjudgmental character who cheats on her submissive boyfriend complains, "If only he enjoyed nice, normal, perfectly average sex." *Friends* and *Frasier* are speckled with occasional jokes about the perversity of kink, only some of which felt lighthearted and benign. Even *Sex and the City,* which I hoped might be a refuge of sexual positivity, devoted an episode to Miranda's shock and disgust when she finds spanking pornography in a date's apartment. None of those references are problems by themselves—most people don't share my fetish, so it makes sense for pop culture to portray it as something unusual. And kink often is funny! But the problem was how relentless those messages were. I *never* got to see my burgeoning sexuality in a healthy or happy light. According to my culture, I was one of two things: a punch line for a prerecorded laugh track, or a freak.

In 2002, I went to a local movie theater with a few high school friends. We didn't have a specific movie in mind; instead, we had planned to show up at the theater, check out our options, and pick something. We asked the ticket taker what was playing that hour. He listed a few options—including a new movie, starring Maggie Gyllenhaal and James Spader, called *Secretary.*

"What's *Secretary* about?" my friend Karen asked the ticket taker.

"It's about a woman who gets into a sadomasochistic relationship with her boss," said the guy behind the glass, with a chuckle.

I launched myself at the ticket booth, elbowing strangers out of my way. People leapt to the sides as I plowed through the group like a linebacker. A baby flew out of his mother's arms and landed in a tree.

"We'll see that one!" I yelled, pounding on the counter. "Four tickets, please!"

No, that's not what happened. But that's how it felt. Here's what really happened.

"That one sounds okay," I said, shrugging casually. "What do you guys think? Want to see that?"

"Okay," my friends agreed.

Oh, the ticket taker had undersold this movie. It's not just about a woman who has a sadomasochistic relationship with her boss; the two characters seem to have a specific interest in spanking. Other kinks do show up, such as pony play—at one point, the main character wears a saddle—but *Secretary* was close to right up my alley. Every time the secretary makes a typo on an office document, her boss calls her into the office, bends her over his desk, and spanks her. I was overwhelmed to see a version of my fantasies onscreen. It was the first time I realized I wasn't the only one who had them.

But even *Secretary* was hard to swallow. (Years later, I would learn that the film was based on a far more complex short story by Mary Gaitskill.) In the movie, the masochistic lead character, Lee, has a sad backstory, with a history of psychiatric institutionalization and self-mutilation. (At one point early in the film, she presses a boiling hot teakettle against her naked thigh, exhaling with relief as her skin burns.) In her bedroom, Lee keeps a hidden box, decorated with colorful rainbow stickers, full of razors, spikes, and other implements that she can use to hurt herself. *Secretary* seemed to suggest that sadomasochistic relationships are merely an alternative form of self-mutilation.

In the absence of James Spader, was I supposed to start cutting myself?

I longed for Caliban because I longed to uncage myself, and the ravenous sexual terrors in me, from the antiseptic place where I was starving us to death. I longed for Caliban's ugly honesty and the unselfconsciousness of his impulses. Pop culture, hygienic and un-nuanced as it was, gave me nothing to hold on to. Only Caliban could speak to me about what it is like to feel infested.

"Peace and happiness can only come from God," someone told me once. "Our Heavenly Father is an awesome force that brings us to our knees. His will controls everything. Can you imagine that?"

Could I imagine an awesome force that would bring me to my knees? Could I imagine submitting to a higher authority and giving up control under threat of severe punishment? Could I imagine obedience, bondage, pleasure, pain, sacrifice, and suffering blended together in a holy mélange?

Yes. I could imagine that.

AS A KID, I had imagined that if I learned my mother's triggers, I could navigate her land mines and she would settle into a consistent place as the generous, loving half of herself who I adored. Failing that, I reacted to my mom's unpredictable moods with a terrible fantasy: I longed for illness. When I was eight, I read a novel about a little girl with leukemia. I envied that girl so much. In the book, the little girl's parents brought her flowers and sat by her bed. They cried and brushed the hair away from her face. I wanted someone to brush the hair away from my face. I wanted my mother to be as gentle and maternal as the mother of the little girl in the book. And I assumed that if I got sick, she would be.

I could picture it.

"Go on without me," I would whisper in a hoarse voice, as my loved ones gathered around the bed in a frozen tableau of grief. "Live. Dance. Sing. Love. I will always be with—" And then my head would fall against the pillow, my hair scattered around my face like a halo. Outside, a gentle rain would begin to fall.

"She's gone," my mom would say, her voice cracking.

"A great light has gone out," the nurse would whisper, as a single tear ran down her face.

Yeah, that sounded good.

Karma obliged. When I was fifteen, only a few months after my mother introduced me to Caliban for the first time, my hand went numb. It didn't get better for weeks. My mom worried it was a brain tumor, but after almost a year of tests, a neurologist had another idea.

"It looks like this is multiple sclerosis," he said.

"Oh, that's a relief!" my mom said, brightly. "After all, nobody wants to hear 'brain tumor.'" She laughed. I pursed my lips.

"Nobody wants to hear MS, either," the neurologist replied. "But we'll do what we can. I'm swamped with appointments this afternoon, but here's a coloring book. It can answer some of your questions." He handed the coloring book to me. It was my sopho-more year of high school.

My mother took me back to school, and I went to math class. I hated math. I had dropped out of the honors track, which meant that Peng and I weren't in the same classes anymore.

I sat alone in the back row and pulled the coloring book out of my backpack. It flopped open onto my desk. It was designed for a younger child, most likely one who had a parent with MS. The pages of questions and answers were illustrated with black car-toon outlines of happy figures. I flipped through the thin book and learned that multiple sclerosis is one of the more baffling degener-ative neurological diseases. It has no known cure. It can cause pa-ralysis, blindness, and other problems with the potential to screw up my social life.

I understood why they put this information in a coloring book. I suddenly wanted something to do with my hands.

One page caught my eye. On it, the black-and-white outline of a little boy asked the question: "Do people who can't walk still have fun?"

"Yes!" cheered the empty outline of his mother, from her wheelchair.

I shoved the coloring book into my backpack and left the class-room.

When I got home that evening, I walked into the living room and put *Zoolander*, the Ben Stiller comedy about male models, into the VHS player. I sat on the couch and stayed there for four days, watching *Zoolander* over and over, dozens of times. Once again, my body had let me down. It was too fragile, too carnal, too vulnerable to pain. I wanted to be Ariel, who is light, airy, ethereal, and unburdened with physicality. (Even Ariel's name likely comes from its similarity to *aerial*.) Instead, I felt like Caliban, Ariel's antonym—dark, heavy, sad, scared, and tied to the earth. Every time *Zoolander* ended, I rewound to the beginning and started again. The lines of the movie became a meditative refrain. I felt myself drift away.

"I'm pretty sure there's a lot more to life than being really, really, ridiculously good-looking," said Derek Zoolander from inside the TV.

There was a soft tap on the living room window. I glanced over and gasped with surprise.

Caliban was there.

I ran up to the window and pressed my hands against the pane.

"What are you doing here?" I whispered, amazed. It was the first time a Shakespeare character had stepped off the page and into my life. I opened the door and gestured for Caliban to step inside. But he refused. He didn't want to come in.

Caliban is always on the outside.

Prospero never learns how to love. Indeed, his emotional detachment isn't specific to love—Prospero seems to misunderstand the language of all human emotions. Ariel, a nonhuman, has to explain it to him:

ARIEL
Your charm so strongly works 'em
That if you now beheld them, your affections
Would become tender.

PROSPERO
Dost thou think so, spirit?

ARIEL
Mine would, sir, were I human.

Prospero's books are not enough for love. The raw depths of human emotion can only be accessed through the wild, unclean underworld of our bodies. Love demands us to reject the cerebral and physically surrender to nature. In *The Tempest*, Shakespeare proves it.

Prospero couldn't guide me to my nature. Only Caliban could.

"Somewhere beyond right and wrong there is a garden," wrote the classical Persian poet Rumi. "I will meet you there."

I like to think Caliban lives in that garden. Somewhere beyond right and wrong seems like the only place where I can speak to him.

So I stepped outside. Sea air filled my nostrils.

"You smell like a fish, Cal," I told him. "A strange fish."

He smiled. I met his eyes.

"I don't want to have a body anymore," I said.

"Why not?" Caliban replied.

"My body is my enemy," I told him. "It hurts; it breaks. It wants things I can't want."

Caliban nodded.

"Yes," he said. "I understand you."

I shook my head.

"I don't think anyone understands," I muttered. "I—"

My voice broke. The acid inside my stomach felt rough, and violent, like a storm-tossed sea that sinks ships. I thought of the awful moment, at the end of *The Tempest*, when Caliban resubmits himself to Prospero's slavery. "How fine my master is!" he says. "I am afraid he will chastise me." And: "I shall be pinched to death."

Caliban's story always ends this way.

I looked down.

"I have the most disgusting things inside my head," I admitted.

Caliban looked at me for long seconds. Then he put his hands on my shoulders and leaned down to speak in my ear. "Be not afeard," he whispered.

> *. . . the aisle is full of noises,*
> *Sounds and sweet airs, that give delight and hurt not.*
> *Sometime a thousand twangling instruments*
> *Will hum about m–m–mine ears, and sometime voices*
> *That, if I then had waked after long sleep,*
> *Will m–m–make m–m–me sleep again: and then, in dreaming,*
> *The clouds m–m–methought would open and show riches*
> *Ready to drop upon m–m–me that, when I waked,*
> *I cried to dream again.*

Tears welled in my eyes, threatening to escape. I pressed the heels of my hands into the sockets. I needed to believe, more than anything else, that even we monsters could surrender to nature without becoming monstrous.

"Stay with me, Cal," I begged him. "Teach me to hear the same instruments that you do."

Caliban held my hand, wrapping my fingers in his own webbed fins.

"Not everything that looks scary is something to fear, sweetheart," he said. "Give in to your own gravity."

Then he reached up and, with a gentle touch that left a streak of seawater on my temple, pushed a lock of hair behind my ear.

I leaned my head against the fish scales on his shoulder and sobbed.

A FEW MONTHS later, my mom was mad again. I don't remember why.

"I hope you *die* of MS," she shrieked, standing on the step outside our front door. I was on the sidewalk. We were nothing if not dramatic.

I was torn. On the one hand, I'd just won. Every vulnerable place in me had already calcified into armor. She couldn't hurt me. Her comment was merely a claim check I could save for later, to make her feel guilty in one of her good moods. And she didn't literally mean what she had said, of course: no one had spent more time researching homeopathic treatments for my disease than my mom. I knew that she often said and did things in anger that she would later regret. (Once, a year earlier, I had cut the back of my wrist with a kitchen knife, in a performative attempt to demonstrate how painful her mood swings were for me. "If you're trying to kill yourself," she had replied, "you cut the wrong side." Then she got in her car, drove away, and left me alone in the house, still holding the bloodstained knife.)

But on the other hand, I was pissed off. I thought she was being a bitch, and I told her so.

"Get out," she said. "You don't live here anymore. I wash my hands of you."

"I wash my hands of you" was my mom's favorite phrase. She yelled it all the time, to declare her cyclical disinterest in motherhood. She had shrieked it the first time she threw me out of the house, when I was nine years old, and had remained an Olympic champion at figurative handwashing ever since.

I tossed a few things in my school backpack and left, rolling my eyes. Getting thrown out of the house loses its dramatic weight the third or fourth time around, it turns out.

"I have lost my daughter," Prospero admits at the end of *The Tempest*.

A few weeks later, I walked into my high school registrar's office and announced that I would not return for the following semester. Nothing inspires action like disease. If I was destined to waste away, I sure as hell wasn't going to waste away in Arizona.

There are brave new worlds to find.

2.2 The Winter's Tale:

An Aspect More Favorable

The first time I met John, my hair was wrapped up in a blue bandanna.

I was seventeen. By that point, my MS diagnosis had convinced me that what they say is true: I should seize-or-whatever the day. So I dropped out of high school, signed up for a correspondence course that would let me finish my diploma through the mail, and flew to Seville, Spain. (My mom, to her credit and my gratitude, had paid for my flight and some other expenses, like a Spanish class. She was always in favor of adventure, and I'd been right to assume that her remark about my death could be deposited for cash.)

I stumbled into my new apartment in Seville, struggling under the weight of my heavy backpack, and John, one of my three new roommates, was the first person I saw. He was sitting on the couch in our living room, watching a Spanish-dubbed episode of *Felicity*. John had the tall, broad-shouldered build (and, I'll be honest, the slightly receding hairline) of a television marine. He was handsome.

"Hi," I said. "Is Seville in the same time zone as London?"

"I'm not sure," he said. "What time is it in London?"

I slid the bandanna off my hair.

John was twenty-four and a recent law school graduate from Oklahoma. He had come to Spain to drag his feet against the undertow of time that was pulling him toward the corporate legal world. John was an avid surfer, and he supported that passion with construction jobs. But since John, like me, didn't have a Spanish work visa, the jobs he could find were infrequent, short-lived, and under the table. So he supplemented his lifestyle with another illegal line of work: selling drugs. Wherever there were loud British or American college travelers, butchering the simple Spanish they had learned in high school, John was there to put them at ease with his slight Oklahoma drawl—then offer them cheap bags of cocaine.

John didn't use his own product, but that didn't stop him from offering it to me a few nights after I moved into the apartment. Our two other roommates, Kylie and Ana, both college exchange students at the University of Seville, had invited some friends over for a party.

"How do I know it's not cut with anything weird?" I had asked, eyeing the line. We were alone in a bedroom.

"Don't you trust me?" John said.

I narrowed my eyes.

"I met you like four days ago, and already you've offered me drugs," I said. "So, no, I don't 'trust' you, Mr. Stock Character from an After-School Special."

John laughed. "Come here," he said.

I walked over to him. He wrapped a hand around my jaw.

His hand was big. I *noticed* that his hand was big.

"Open your mouth," he said. There was something about John's voice. I wanted to do what he told me to do.

I opened my mouth.

"If this is cocaine," John explained, wetting the tip of a finger on his other hand and tapping it in the powder, "this will make you feel numb, okay?" He slid his finger between my lips and dabbed the powder against my tongue.

I closed my lips and rubbed my tongue against the roof of my mouth.

It did feel numb.

Look—this was not my finest moment, or John's. Don't judge us yet. (God knows there will be plenty of opportunities for that.) As much as I wanted to, I couldn't just skip ahead to the fun parts. In *The Winter's Tale*, Shakespeare wrote:

> *There's some ill planet reigns;*
> *I must be patient, till the heavens look*
> *With an aspect more favorable.*

And I, too, had to be patient. My ill planet was coming to the end of its short-lived reign. I just had to get through my bourgeois cliché of a coke phase first.

"Can I do it alone?" I asked. "I don't want you to watch me."

John shrugged.

"Sure," he said, leaving. "I'll come back to check on you in a minute."

I looked at a mirror above the dresser, staring into my own eyes. (Movies had taught me that moments of self-destruction are supposed to follow a dramatic moment with a mirror, so I followed the script.) I gazed for a few seconds—that seemed sufficiently emotive—and then bent over the table, stuck a rolled-up euro in my nose, and inhaled regret in a fine white snow.

Outside the room, I could hear the music and happy chatter of the party. There was a knock on the door.

Euphoria rushed through my veins. This was great.

"Come in," I called. John walked in. He eyed the rolled-up bill in my hand.

"How do you feel?" he asked.

"It's awesome, I think," I said, hopping up and down. "But I don't feel much yet. Should I do another line?"

John chuckled. "Let's start with just one," he said, leaning against the wall. "If you want more later, I'm always here."

At the beginning of *The Winter's Tale*, one of the characters declares that "a sad tale's best for winter," and this winter play does, indeed, begin as a sad tale. At the beginning, Leontes, the King of Sicilia, indulges in jealous fantasies, convincing himself that his pregnant wife, Hermione, has been unfaithful and that the child she carries is a bastard. Mad with jealousy and rage, Leontes throws Hermione into prison and orders that her baby be left to die in some desolate place. But the servant he orders to abandon the baby instead names her Perdita (which means "little lost one") and leaves her to be raised by a shepherd.

The first half of the play is brutal and tragic. I imagine it lit in shadowy grays and blues.

But *The Winter's Tale* is Shakespeare's meditation on resurrection and rebirth. If its first half is dark, the second half is bright and full of joy—impossibly so, in fact. As soon as the action shifts from the Sicilia of the first three acts to the Bohemia of the final two, the story brightens. There are improbable coincidences, and happy resolutions to unresolvable conflicts. (There is even a joke about "dildoes." Why don't our high school teachers ever tell us about *that*?) Leontes's wife, Hermione, whom everyone had believed was dead, even returns in a final scene in which she appears to be miraculously resurrected from a frozen statue.

That's the great mystery of *The Winter's Tale*: how does a frozen woman start to thaw?

Sicilia was sad. But don't worry: Bohemia promises more.

"Wait," I said to John, still bouncing with energy on the balls of my feet. "Why did you give me that line for free?"

John smiled.

"Consider it an investment," he said.

KYLIE AND ANA already had friends through their university, so John and I gravitated to each other. We hung out all the time. The sexual tension between us was obvious and immediate—he had literally put his finger in my mouth after less than a week, after all.

One morning, I walked into the living room, rubbing the sleep out of my eyes. John was there, ironing a pair of his jeans. He handled the fabric with tender, almost loving care.

I giggled.

"What are you doing, John?"

He blinked at me.

"What does it look like I'm doing?" he said.

"Who irons jeans?" I asked, squinting. "That's weird."

John frowned.

"It's not weird," he said.

"Yeah," I insisted. "It's super weird."

John shrugged.

"I like things a certain way," he said.

Before I dropped out of high school and enrolled in the diploma-by-mail course, I had been a B student, with the occasional A or C. I did not think of myself as fancy college material. But Stanford had expressed interest in me after I won an Arizona State Shakespeare high school competition a year earlier, so I had sent in an application. By coincidence, John had graduated from Stanford. I didn't yet know if I'd been accepted, but asking John questions about college was a good excuse to talk to him.

"Why aren't you in high school?" he asked me.

"Why aren't you in a law firm?" I replied.

The next morning, I called the airline and canceled my flight back to Arizona.

At seventeen, I was well above Spain's age of consent, which at that point was only thirteen. (In 2013 Spain raised it to sixteen.) But John was from the United States, where the number eighteen carries a special magic. I didn't care about the seven-year age difference between us, but it seemed like John did. Although we hung out every day—I imagined that it was like dating—everything was chaste: we never kissed; we never even held hands. But we ate most of our meals together, watched movies, and lost hours in flirtatious conversation. One night, we saw a movie (it was *The Passion of the Christ*—John chose it) and then stood outside the theater, talking, until dawn, despite the frigid air. I told John about *The Tempest* and loaned him the shredded paperback copy I had dragged with me to Spain. We ate paella. We ate gazpacho. We had a screaming fight with our landlord, Carlos, about whether the Grand Canyon is in Arizona.

"What is the name of the river at the bottom?" Carlos shrieked in Spanish, as we stood on his roof, drinking wine.

"It's the Colorado River, but that doesn't mean the Grand Canyon is in Colorado," John yelled.

"I am literally from Arizona!" I roared, gesticulating with my wineglass for emphasis. "I know where the canyon is!" Wine sloshed over the rim onto the roof.

"Americans are so stupid!" Carlos screamed.

"You are such an asshole!" I yelled back. (We had crushed quite a few cups of wine.)

The next day, Carlos came to the apartment while we were watching TV.

"I looked it up," he said, with a shrug. "You're right." Carlos plopped down on the couch next to us and pierced a corkscrew into a new bottle of wine. John and I exchanged a triumphant glance. This was international diplomacy at its drunken best.

Life in Seville was exciting and fun. I found a part-time job at a nearby café that was willing to pay under the table for a foreign waitress to serve its English-speaking customers and began to collect the knowledge that builds a life: a place to buy books, a place to see movies, a place to get groceries. I learned how to cook lentils. I made a few friends.

Although he had never touched me, it seemed as if John's interest was not platonic. All the signs were there. As Leontes puts it, "Is whispering nothing? / Is leaning cheek to cheek? is meeting noses?"

"What's that ring?" John said one afternoon, gesturing to a silver band on my left hand.

I fiddled with it.

"A guy named Mohammed gave it to me in Cairo a few months ago," I said. "It's dyeing my finger blue."

"So you're spoken for?" John said.

I was startled.

"No," I said. "Mohammed was just a friend."

In Seville, John and I fell into a routine. He took Spanish classes in the mornings. Most evenings, when neither of us had work, we walked to a nearby park, bought a bag of pistachios from a street vendor, and sat on a bench to talk and snack.

"What is life, on a scale of one to ten?" he asked me one afternoon, as we sat in the park.

I thought for a moment.

"Life is a nine point seven," I finally said.

Months later, John told me that question was his personal "test." (An admission that annoyed me, by the way. Who has a girlfriend test?) He asked every girl he was interested in to rate life. "Nine point seven," he said, was the moment his interest in me graduated from sexual attraction to something more. It was the highest rating he'd ever heard.

"You're close," he told me, at the time. "Life is a ten."

"We're only point three degrees apart," I argued. "That's nothing. You'll condemn me over point three degrees?"

John grinned.

"I might have to," he said.

Back in Arizona, my mother collected my college admission and rejection letters as they trickled into her mailbox. One afternoon, I went to an Internet café to check my email and found an email from her. The subject line said: "Congratulations!!!!!" It was a list of all the universities that had accepted me.

I ran across town and into the school where John took Spanish classes. His class had just ended, and students were filing out of the classroom. I yelled John's name from the lobby below. He leaned over the edge of the balcony to look at me.

"You were right," I shouted in English, causing heads to turn. "Life is a ten!"

John smiled—with only a touch of embarrassment—and jogged down the stairs to meet me.

"What's going on?" he said, putting his hands on my upper arms.

"I got into Stanford!" I told him. John dropped his book and swept me up in a big hug, lifting me so the tips of my toes left the floor.

"That's my girl," he said.

"Will I like it there?" I asked him.

"You'll love it," he replied.

Stanford had organized a special weekend for admitted students to visit the campus, sit in on a few classes, and chat with current students. I obviously couldn't go, but I felt detached from the pre-college experience my friends were having back home. So I satisfied my curiosity by reading comments on an online message board for college applicants from an Internet café in Seville. I never wrote a comment. I just read other people's conversations.

One afternoon, as I browsed this website, I noticed a comment that would stay in my mind for years to come. In response to a long discussion thread about financial aid and how to pay for college, one guy wrote:

I'm eighteen, and I'm a senior. A few years ago, my mom died of MS. After she died, my dad started drinking more and doing meth. One night, he struck me. So they put me in foster care. I live with my high school principal now. He helped me with my college applications, but he can't help me with tuition. I inherited a few thousand dollars after my mom died, but not much. And I don't talk to my father anymore, so I can't get any help from him. Do you guys know anything about scholarships or work-study options? I live in North Dakota, and it's hell. There's no way I'll stay here. I'm definitely going to college. I'm not sure how I'll pay for it, but I'll find a way, come hell or high water.

In the days that followed, I thought a lot about the kid who had written that post. I was humbled by his sad story, which put my own "problems" into stark perspective. And the remark about his mother's death was memorable, for obvious reasons. In the year since my MS diagnosis, I had studiously avoided learning about the scarier details of my disease. As far as I knew, it wasn't fatal. But this kid's story threw that supposition into doubt.

He seemed great, though: resilient, hardworking, and honest. I hoped that some college would give him a generous scholarship. I wondered what he looked like. I couldn't picture his face.

I imagined him with a baseball cap.

As much as I longed to talk to someone about what I'd read, I couldn't talk to John. He was my closest friend in Seville by far, but I hadn't told him about my disease. And I didn't plan to. Instead, I went online. I did a search for "died of MS," and discovered that, for the most part, I'd been right. Usually, MS isn't fatal.

But sometimes it is.

"Do not weep, good fool, there is no cause," Hermione, Leontes's wife, scolded from inside my computer. "Life is fatal, too." She was wearing a prison uniform.

"Can't you let me mourn?" I asked her. "Can't I feel sad for a minute?"

"No," she replied. "I refuse to let you pout."

Hermione doesn't cry. "I am not prone to weeping, as our sex commonly are," she says, when she fears her lack of tears will turn the lords against her at her trial. "I have that honorable grief lodg'd here which burns worse than tears drown." To reassign Katherine's words from *Henry VIII*, Hermione lets tears "turn to sparks of fire."

Shakespeare's strongest women do not weep: they burn.

So I focused on happier thoughts. I read blogs by current Stanford students, browsed an online version of the student newspaper, and looked at photos of the campus. The university even sent out a "game" to admitted prospective students, which just required the player to click on the word *Stanford* as it bounced around the screen.

Stanford. Stanford. Stanford. Stanford. Stanford.

But whenever I tried to ask John other questions about Stanford—what the dorms were like, which of the required freshman-year humanities courses I should choose—he refused to answer.

"You have to figure it out on your own," he told me.

"You won't even help me choose a humanities course?" I said.

"No," he replied.

JOHN WAS SO hard to understand. For weeks, I had wondered how a guy like him had ended up selling drugs. His side job seemed so dark. And John was an optimist: How did someone who proselytized life's highest "rating" get into cocaine? I needed answers.

One night, I convinced John to let me come with him to pick up some "product" in a neighborhood called Las Tres Mil Viviendas, which is so dangerous that postal workers, ambulances, and firefighters reportedly won't go there without a police escort. (I was stupid.) John's "colleague," Javi, seemed tense and nervous, but

John, an obvious foreigner in perfectly pressed jeans, seemed un-afraid. It fascinated me.

"Stay in the car, Jillian," John told me as we pulled up to the house.

"I want to come in with you," I said.

"No," John said. "This isn't a field trip. Stay put."

John and Javier disappeared inside the house. I slouched in my seat.

Wasn't the car also a stupid place to be?

After minutes passed, I opened the door and got out of the car. I wandered up the street. It seemed like any other urban neigh-borhood. Firefighters really couldn't come here without a police escort?

The door of the house opened and John and Javi walked out. From my place on the far side of the road, it looked like they were arguing. I jogged back to the car to meet them.

When John saw me, his face changed.

"What the fuck did you do, Jillian?" he said.

I slid into the backseat.

"I didn't do anything," I said. "I felt conspicuous here in the car."

"And you don't think it was conspicuous to wander around this neighborhood?" John said. He seemed mad. I was gratified to dis-cover that I could shake his unnerving calm.

"In dangerous places, I think sometimes it's safest to act like I belong." I shrugged. "Like I have nothing to worry about."

From the driver's seat, Javi started laughing.

"Do something about that one, John," he said, in Spanish.

"I plan to," John muttered in response. Then he switched to English and twisted around in the passenger seat to face me.

"I am never bringing you here again," he said. "So don't even ask."

"I have some news for you, John," I snapped. "Sitting in a car isn't fun. I don't even want to come back here."

After that, John would sometimes disappear for a night. I knew he was in Las Tres Mil.

I had some questions.

"What's the story with the coke, John?" I asked him over lunch at an outdoor café.

"Why?" he replied, raising an eyebrow. "Do you like it?"

"Yes," I said. "I like it a lot. I need to be careful with that stuff." (Since that first party, I hadn't developed a regular habit, but I did do a line from time to time, and could imagine its addictive potential.)

John laughed.

"Yeah," he agreed. "It can have that effect."

I pushed a few apple cubes around my glass of sangria with a straw.

"But you know that's not what I'm asking," I continued. "I want to know how a nerd who irons his jeans ends up selling drugs in Spain."

"I'm the nerd, huh?" he said. "You're the one who showed up at the apartment with a backpack full of books."

"They are *plays*, John," I replied.

"I think you just proved my point," he said.

"And you just changed the subject," I replied. "I asked you to explain the drugs."

John leaned back in his seat.

"Why don't *you* explain the drugs, Jillian?" he said. "Why do you keep using? Even I stopped using last year. Cocaine is not a good choice."

To my own surprise, I replied:

"I guess I'm not a good girl."

John raised an eyebrow.

I have a talent for ruining a moment. Right then, I poked an apple cube with my straw too hard and knocked over my sangria. Ice cubes scattered across the table. John and I both jumped up, away from the mess. Red liquid dripped onto the pavement below.

The Winter's Tale's tonal change, from downbeat to upbeat, seems abrupt. But it's not an accident. Different places bring out different versions of ourselves. When *The Winter's Tale*'s action shifts from Sicilia to Bohemia, the tone shifts, too. Shakespeare was aware of this shift: he even foreshadows it in the very first lines of the play, when Archidamus, a Bohemian lord, tells his Sicilian friend: "If you shall chance, Camillo, to visit Bohemia . . . you shall see, as I have said, great difference betwixt our Bohemia and your Sicilia."

Even the title of the play hints at a seasonal transition: after winter, there is always a spring.

Shakespeare's Bohemia is a kind of never-never land, a perfect place that cannot exist in real life. This is literally true. Several scenes, for example, reference a Bohemian seacoast—which, as the literary scholar Andrew Gurr and others have pointed out, was a geographical improbability, since Bohemia, the present-day Czech Republic, does not have a coastline. Some people think that Shakespeare just made a mistake. Others (those Shakespearean cartographers!) have suggested that Bohemia did, in fact, command a small strip of coastline along the Adriatic Sea between 1575 and 1609.

But I'd rather think of Bohemia as Shakespeare's intentionally impossible utopia. In Bohemia, the inhibitions of Sicilian social norms disappear and the characters are free. This kind of contrast runs throughout the Shakespearean canon: one place is cold and restrained while another place is hot and feral. (There are similar tonal contrasts between the court and the Forest of Arden in *As You Like It,* and between Venice and Cyprus in *Othello.*) In Sicilia, Perdita is the "little lost one," who is born in a prison and almost left to die. But in Bohemia, she grows into a confident, self-assured young woman, and falls in love.

Spain was my Bohemia. I was becoming a more confident, uninhibited version of myself.

PERHAPS CONFIDENCE IS contagious.

The next night, John and I went to a friend's apartment for the evening. Everyone had a few glasses of wine, and the platonic veneer of our friendship began to fade into teasing jokes and taunts. Things escalated into a pillow fight when, apropos of nothing, John spoke.

"Jillian," he asked, in the same casual tone of voice. "Have you ever received a severe spanking?"

My heart stopped. His question—and the fetishistic specificity of its phrasing—hit me like a truck. I felt transparent, as if even my skin could not hide my self. I couldn't breathe, let alone respond, so I giggled and said nothing. The conversation moved on, and John didn't revisit the issue. But that question, so bizarre in its pointed rhetoric, lingered. I couldn't ignore it.

The next day, as we sat in a room in the apartment we shared, I swallowed my embarrassment and fear.

"Last night—why did you ask me that question?" I asked. My chest was tight.

"What question?" John said. He seemed genuinely confused.

"I can't say it," I replied, covering my face with my hands. "You have to figure it out yourself." My heart thrashed against the bones of my rib cage. Although my face, still hidden in my hands, was pointed at my feet, I knew he was looking at me.

I didn't want to be looked at.

"I have no idea what you're talking about," John said. "Honestly."

I dropped my hands from my face and met his eyes.

"Come on, John," I said. "That question. Why did you ask me *that question*?" I filled my eyes with speechless messages.

Recognition washed over him.

"Jillian!" John breathed. There was an expression on his face that I had never seen before or since; an odd mix of delight and surprise, understanding and lust. Speech is the only antidote to isolation in this lonely world, and the most powerful of all words—I understand you—hovered beneath his breath, unsaid.

John said my name again. He wrapped his arms around my shoulders in a hug.

"No," I moaned. I pulled away from him and put my face back into my hands. "Don't look at me. Please stop looking at me."

"I want to look at you," he said.

"Well, *I* don't want to look at me," I replied.

In *The Winter's Tale*, Autolycus says: "Though I am not naturally honest, I am so sometimes by chance." But, then again, in the same play he also warns: "What a fool Honesty is." So this could go either way.

After that, every conversation was tinted with danger. (In hindsight, I recognize this period as a negotiation in disguise.) What flirting is to vanilla relationships, implied "threats" are to my kink.

"Do you like Eminem?" I asked John one night over a pitcher of sangria. (It was 2004, and I was a white teenager with probable mental health problems. Of course I liked Eminem.) John shook his head and listed some other musicians as examples of what he did like. I hadn't heard of any of them.

"That's because you haven't been educated about music," he said.

"Or because you're super old," I replied.

"Careful," he warned.

Days passed this way.

The stakes of our relationship were already high, every

interaction charged with anticipation, when John and I both raised them.

One evening after dinner, he and I sat at the base of the Torre del Oro, a squat, cream-colored tower along the Guadalquivir River. I leaned against him, and he wrapped his arms around me. We sat like that for a while, watching as the sky darkened and the lights of Seville flickered on across the river. Given the romantic spot (and the intimate way we were sitting), I started to wonder if John would ever make a move.

John, I would learn, was thinking about something, too.

He pushed me away and looked at my face. He took a breath.

"Okay," he said. "I want you to listen to me. You're not going to touch coke ever again. You're not going to buy it, from me or anyone, and you're sure as hell not going to use it. I'm serious. I'm going to watch you and make sure you obey me on this. Am I understood?"

There's a kind of kinesis that happens between submissives and dominants when a rule is introduced. It's good. (And how often do people drop the word *obey* in casual conversation? The word alone sent a spark down my spine.) It's a powerful, almost trancelike feeling.

I argued with him anyway.

"You're the one who gave me the coke in the first place, John," I pointed out.

"I don't care," he said. "You're better than that. No excuses."

"Yeah." I sighed, picking at the grass along the riverbank. "You're right." (Say what you will about sadomasochism: I never used cocaine again.)

John hugged me.

"Good girl," he said.

Kink is a trust fall. I wanted to trust him.

"I need to tell you something, John," I said. Then I paused for a long time, working up my courage. He waited.

"I have this, like, disease thing," I finally said. I continued to rip blades of grass with my fingers. "It's okay. It's not contagious. But there's no cure. And it could mess me up, maybe."

As I described my MS to him, something welled in my chest. Tears pricked the backs of my eyes. I was nervous. I didn't want to ruin the game we'd been playing for the past few weeks. When *The Winter's Tale* finally becomes happy and comedic, nobody wants to revisit the dark parts from the first acts. Nobody wants to shatter the perfect illusion of flirtation. Nobody wants to go back to Sicilia.

"Oh, shut up," said Hermione, stepping out from inside the Torre del Oro. "My husband threw me in prison and tried to kill our daughter. What do you have to complain about?"

The crotch of her thin prison smock was stained dark red with dried blood.

Hermione had a point. I blinked back the tears.

John and I stayed there, on the riverbank, talking for hours. He told me about his mother's cancer, and about how much he admired the way his father had supported her through chemotherapy. I shared my fears that it would be cruel, and selfish, to ever ask someone to tie his or her happiness to mine. By the time we walked home, John could see me more clearly than ever before, and didn't flinch away from the sight.

"You're stronger than you look, you know," he said.

"Does that mean you think I look weak?" I teased.

"Jillian, I think you look just about perfect," he said. "That should be obvious by now." I blushed. He had never been so direct before. A hummingbird thrashed against the bones of my rib cage.

Too hot, too hot!
To mingle friendship far is mingling bloods.
I have tremor cordis on me; my heart dances,
But not for joy—not joy.

AT THE END of *The Winter's Tale,* the statue of Hermione unfreezes and comes to life.

From a scientific perspective, this moment is only possible if Hermione merely pretended to be dead, and conspired with her best friend Paulina to stage this miraculous revival. (After all, King Leontes, Hermione's husband, never actually saw Hermione die—he took Paulina's word for it.) This literal interpretation gets some support from the text: when Leontes first sees the "statue," he remarks that it has aged, saying: "Hermione was not so much wrinkled, nothing / So aged as this seems."

But mythology suggests another possibility. After Hermione's death—or "death"—Leontes fell into grief and regret. He commissioned a statue of Hermione: a clear literary homage to Ovid's *Pygmalion* myth, in which a man carves a statue of his ideal woman that magically comes to life. A mythological interpretation of this scene would suggest that Hermione really did die, and Leontes's regret miraculously revived her. This angle also has basis in the text: when Hermione sees Perdita, her daughter, she floods her with questions as to how Perdita survived the past sixteen years—which presumably Hermione would already know the answers to if she had faked her death and lived in hiding with Paulina during that time. Paulina herself acknowledges the unreality of this miracle: "That she is living, / Were it but told you, should be hooted at / Like an old tale." And yet, preposterous as it seems, Hermione does, against all odds, come to life.

"If this be magic," Leontes marvels, "let it be an art / Lawful as eating."

Neither the natural and scientific nor the artistic and mythological possibility is conclusive. But, as Scott Crider argues, Shakespeare may have purposefully designed this ambiguity to "interrogate the essence of the relationship between art and nature, between the mimetic and the real."

So what revives Hermione: nature or art?

We don't have to choose. As Polixenes, the king of Bohemia, tells Perdita earlier in the play, art and nature function in symbiosis with each other more often than we realize: "This is an art / Which does mend nature—change it rather—but / The art itself is nature." What if love itself necessarily blurs the lines between art and nature? Early in the play, even Leontes himself recognizes love's impossible possibilities:

> *Affection! thy intention stabs the centre.*
> *Thou dost make possible things not so held,*
> *Communicat'st with dreams—how can this be?*

Like Hermione, it was time for me to unfreeze.

Being honest with John about my disease was the responsible choice, but for days I worried that I had derailed whatever relationship we'd started to build. We still hadn't even kissed, although, for weeks, we'd been flirting and going on chaste "dates." As days passed, I began to suspect that I had knocked myself into the friend zone. Maybe he would never make a move.

Then one night, as I sat in my bedroom reading, there was a knock on the door.

"Come in," I called. It was John. He was wearing jeans and a white T-shirt. My hand immediately went to my hair and smoothed it into place.

"Kylie and Ana left a note," he said. "They took the bus to Cádiz. They're gone."

"Oh," I replied. "We're alone tonight?"

"We're alone all weekend," John said.

"So this is our chance to burn the place down," I joked.

I expected John to leave, but he didn't. He paused. Then he took another step into the room and picked up my stuffed monkey from a shelf on the bookcase. He fiddled with the monkey's red bow tie.

"Do you know how frustrating you are?" he finally said, rubbing the back of his neck with his hand. I stayed on my bed and looked at him. An uncharacteristic calm washed over me.

"I am not frustra-*ting*," I replied, in a soft voice. "You are frustra-*ted*."

John leaned against the wall opposite my bed. I leaned against the wall behind me. We faced off, looking at each other, for seconds. He looked more nervous than I felt.

"Do you want water?" John asked, abruptly. "I want some water."

"Sure," I said. "I want some water."

He pushed himself off the wall and left the room. A second later, I heard a sink turn on.

I pulled my feet up onto the bed and rested my chin on my knees. The position made me nervously aware that I was wearing a skirt. I almost never wore skirts. My legs felt exposed and vulnerable. I fiddled with the hem, pulling it toward my knees.

In the kitchen, I heard the sink turn off for a minute, and then turn on again.

My eyes fell on a pile of folded clothes stacked on my desk. I had left my flat, wooden hairbrush on top of them. It felt like Chekhov's gun: a weapon that, once introduced into a scene, must fire. I jumped off the bed, picked it up, and shoved it into my sock drawer, out of sight. As I slid the drawer closed, John walked back into my room. I turned around.

"Here," he said, handing me a glass.

I took a sip.

John closed my door.

I turned away and put the water glass on top of my cupboard. I stood there, looking at the clear liquid inside. My senses felt heightened. I heard the soft hum of the air conditioner. I heard my skirt brush against my legs. I heard my breath.

Behind me, I heard the door lock.

"You're sure no one is here?" I asked. My chest felt tight.

John's hand appeared on top of my own. He detached my fingers from the water glass. I turned around to face him.

"I'm sure," he said.

I swallowed.

"Are you okay?" he asked.

I nodded.

"Are you nervous?" he asked.

I nodded again. He put his right hand on my waist.

"Is this what you want?" he asked.

I didn't move. I didn't breathe.

He stepped closer to me, and put his right hand on my chin. Then he tilted it up, toward his face, and kissed me. His mouth was warm and wet.

It was my first kiss. My fingers trembled.

John stepped away from me and sat on the edge of my bed. He reached out for my hand and pulled me, gently, toward his knees.

"Come here, Jillian," he said.

His voice was thick and rough with emotion.

That night, for the first time in my life, I left my head and fell into my body.

2.3 Romeo and Juliet:

These Violent Delights

Shakespeare is physical. He has to be. His words can't survive imprisoned on the page. They belong inside our bodies. To savor Shakespeare, read him aloud. Otherwise, how could we appreciate the pulsing *s* sounds, rising momentum, and climactic release of Sonnet 129? It's not a poem, it's an orgasm:

> *Th' expense of spirit in a waste of shame*
> *Is lust in action, and till action, lust*
> *Is perjur'd, murd'rous, bloody, full of blame,*
> *Savage, extreme, rude, cruel, not to trust,*
> *Enjoy'd no sooner but despiséd straight,*
> *Past reason hunted, and no sooner had,*
> *Past reason hated as a swallowed bait*
> *On purpose laid to make the taker mad:*
> *Mad in pursuit and in possession so,*
> *Had, having, and in quest to have, extreme,*
> *A bliss in proof, and prov'd, a very woe;*
> *Before, a joy propos'd, behind, a dream.*

All this the world well knows, yet none knows well
To shun the heaven that leads men to this hell.

—SONNET 129

Cerebral doesn't work for sex, and it sure as hell doesn't work for Shakespeare. The Bard too often seems distant and unapproachable, but that's all wrong. He doesn't live inside an ivory tower. He lives behind your rib cage, and in my pelvis, and all the parts of our bodies where the blood flows. Shakespeare is raw. Shakespeare is bloody. Shakespeare is physical.

Romeo and Juliet is physical, too.

JOHN AND I did not have sex that night in my bedroom, by the way. Sex didn't even cross my mind. We both gave into impulses that run deeper than that.

Over John's knee, my hair spilled past my shoulders and into my face.

"Are you comfortable there?" John asked, in a low voice. He reached down with his left hand to gather my hair on one side of my neck.

It was hard to answer questions with my stomach in my throat.

"Am I supposed to be comfortable?" I murmured.

John chuckled.

"I guess not," he replied. He reached back to grab the edge of my skirt, and pulled it up to my waist.

I winced. I was not wearing sexy underwear. Come to think of it, I didn't even own sexy lingerie. My underwear that night had polka dots.

John pulled those down, too. I heard him inhale.

"Your ass is amazing," he said.

I blushed with pleasure. I wasn't going to argue. I'll always be grateful that my fetish fixates on a body part I happen to love.

"It was convenient of you to wear a skirt on the same night that we have the apartment to ourselves," John teased, stroking my butt. I wriggled to adjust my position, but only managed to disrupt my balance. I grabbed John's ankle to steady myself.

"That's just a coincidence," I insisted.

"Is it?" John asked. "We've been dancing around this for a while now."

I swallowed. The truth was, I had known that Kylie and Ana would be out of town before John told me. So why had I worn that skirt?

I turned my head to the left, to look up, over my shoulder, at him.

"Are you still frustrated, John?" I murmured.

Around me, John's body changed. His leg muscles tightened, the pressure of his left hand on my lower back increased, and his torso shifted forward. The gentle things he had been doing to my butt with his right hand stopped. The next time he spoke, it was in a rough voice I had not heard before.

"Jillian," he said. "You have no idea."

If I'm honest, that first spanking, as cathartic as it was, was also a mild disappointment. It just didn't quite match my fantasies. (Fetishes are nothing if not detailed to the point of absurdity.) It didn't hurt as much as I wanted it to, for one. John, to his credit, had proceeded with caution—it was our first time, and it's far better to hurt someone too little than to hurt her too much. I was also disappointed that I didn't cry that night. Years later, I would learn that many spanking fetishists regard tears as comparable to orgasms—desirable, but elusive. Like anyone else, I shouldn't have been surprised to not "climax" my first time.

The biggest disappointment, though, was that I didn't bruise. Bruises are to kinky people—or, at least, bruises are to me—what I imagine hickeys are to vanilla teenagers. I wanted to bruise because I wanted physical proof that it had happened; I wanted confirmation that my deepest fantasy had come true. I wanted my body to display a record of touch.

"Now you have something to think about the next time you're tempted to use drugs," John said afterward, with a wink, as we sat on my bed in a tangled web of limbs and emotions.

I rolled my eyes.

"You're the most hypocritical dealer ever," I said. "I want a refund." I stuck out my hand.

John frowned.

"But I gave you those lines for free," he replied. "I didn't make you pay."

I giggled.

"Actually, I think you just did."

THE NEXT MORNING, I discovered that what I lacked in bruises I made up for in embarrassment. I woke up alone in my bed, thirsty and needing to pee, and couldn't bring myself to leave the room. I had never been so mortified. John's room was just down the hall.

I couldn't bear to see him.

I peeled myself out of bed and cracked open the door. I tilted my head toward the hallway, straining to hear a sound. The apartment was quiet. Where was John? He never worked on Sunday, when the entire city of Seville shut down, but it also didn't sound like he was in the apartment. Maybe he had woken up early and fled. I *hoped* he had.

This was the kind of situation in which I would've liked to scream "Demetrius!"

I stepped into the hallway, as quietly as possible, and tiptoed into the kitchen. I filled a teakettle with water and put it on the stove.

I watched the pot, waiting for it to boil. John walked into the kitchen.

"Shit," I said, when I saw him.

"Good morning to you, too," he replied, sticking his hands in his pockets. "How are you feeling?" His lips twitched as he fought to suppress a laugh.

"Go away," I said. "I'm making tea."

He sat at the cheap plastic table we'd put in the middle of the kitchen.

"I like tea," he ventured.

"Go away," I said again.

"Where do you want me to go?" he asked. "I live here."

"I want you to go *away*," I repeated. "I'm processing. And making tea."

"What are you processing?"

"I'm processing you, I guess," I replied, with a shrug.

For a moment, John paused.

"You're something," he finally said.

I looked over my shoulder.

"I'm some*one*," I corrected. Then I turned off the burner on the stovetop, poured boiling water into my mug, and sat down at the table next to him. John didn't say anything. I took a sip. We sat there for a few minutes, quietly.

I finally broke the silence.

"So," I said. "You're pretty fucked up, huh?"

John burst out laughing. I laughed, too. We both laughed so long and hard that it was unreasonable; we laughed until the tension dissipated; we laughed until I had tears in my eyes. Eventually, we caught our breath.

"I want to be your boyfriend, Jillian," John said.

Something inside me fluttered.

"Um, yeah," I replied, rolling my eyes to hide my nerves. "After that mess last night, you had better want to be my boyfriend." He laughed again.

I liked him so much. John made me nervous in the best ways; at the same time, he made me unselfconscious in the best ways. Our relationship felt as natural and necessary as water.

He called me "little bird."

We didn't talk about our kink even as we explored it. John had first raised the topic, not me, so for months I reassured myself that I was merely satisfying his interest, not my own. I wasn't one of those weird masochists, I insisted. I was just a girl who loved a sadist. I couldn't acknowledge my complicity in my own fantasies even as they came true. We had to navigate BDSM ourselves, and it was tricky. There were no guidebooks—or, if there were, they weren't available in the tiny English-language section of our neighborhood bookstore. Neither of us had a laptop, and I wasn't yet desperate enough to conduct that particular research from a public Internet café. We were so young: I was still seventeen, and John was twenty-four. As worldly and experienced as I thought he was, we were both kids, playing with a potent drug.

Romeo and Juliet also play with dangerous sexual drugs. Shakespeare's story about two star-crossed lovers from feuding families is one of my favorite plays, and Juliet is one of my favorite characters. But, despite what we've been told a million times, *Romeo and Juliet* is not a love story—it's a lust story. Even Juliet, magnificent and perceptive as she is, almost recognizes this; early on, she describes her relationship with Romeo as "too rash, too unadvis'd, too sudden." *Romeo and Juliet* isn't a story about young people in love. It's a story about two young people who desperately hope for love, with tragic results.

Their lust never becomes something better.

It's all about physical and sexual attraction. Romeo makes that clear the first time he sees Juliet, when he says that Juliet has "beauty too rich for use, for earth too dear." A few lines later, he says, "Did my heart love till now? Forswear it, sight! For I ne'er saw true beauty till this night." If Romeo sees Juliet's beauty as "too dear" to exist on earth, how can we expect them to handle the day-to-day realities of love, like aging and paying the cable bill? Who is going to clean the litter box?

Other than John's first question, when he asked me if I had "ever received a severe spanking," and our subsequent chat, when I couldn't bring myself to even say the word, John and I talked about our kink only a few times.

One conversation, if I can even call it that, happened a few weeks after John told me he wanted to be my boyfriend. He had moved out of the group apartment we shared and into a studio in Triana, on the other side of the river. (I was glad when John moved out. I wanted to look nice around him, so it was a relief to be able to wander the apartment in sweatpants again after he left. More to the point, John and I were also glad to have a place to "play" without having to worry about Kylie, Ana, or, God forbid, Carlos hearing something untoward.)

One afternoon, we made scrambled eggs in his new apartment. We cooked eggs all the time. Eggs were cheap.

"Did you do this stuff with your other girlfriends?" I asked, stirring.

"Make scrambled eggs? Sometimes," John joked.

I shot him a glare.

"That's not what I meant," I said.

He sighed.

"With Luce, yes," he said. He had mentioned Luce to me before. She had been one of his college girlfriends. "But I think it—well, I think it got a little out of hand with her."

"What does that mean?" I asked.

John winked.

"Would you like to find out, m'dear?" he joked. He could drop in and out of his drawl at will. It was cute. He used it against me.

"No, I'd rather not," I replied. And then, after a pause: "You didn't, like, actually hurt her, did you?"

John leaned against the doorframe and squinted.

"I don't actually hurt *you*, do I?" he asked.

"Fair enough," I said.

The eggs were done, as was the discussion. That was our big conversation about consent, boundaries, and the role of kink in our past and current relationships. (To be clear: This is not a healthy model. This is an example of what not to do.)

But his last question was reasonable. Was he hurting me? Technically, he was. I was shocked by how much it could hurt. Every time, I thought the pain was more than I could take—and yet, somehow, I did take it, and always came back for more. By that point, we had graduated from using his hand to using wood and leather, and our play style had evolved from the tentative, improvisational tone of our first time to something much more intense and disciplinary. (Throughout that conversation, I had purple welts on my butt and thighs from the night before.) We played rough. We weren't having sex yet—for months into our relationship, I remained a virgin—but the kink was satisfying on its own. Intercourse was almost irrelevant.

That's one of the biggest misconceptions about kink. The notion that BDSM (or, in my case, spanking) is just a form of foreplay to sex couldn't be more wrong. Spanking is like a dance or a massage: it *can* be erotic, but it doesn't have to be. (Years later, my friend Abby put it this way: For us, spanking isn't exclusively sexual—it's *inclusively* sexual. We can sexualize it when, and if, we choose.) This paradox is perhaps best illustrated by the fact that our spanking "pornography," in my experience, often doesn't include sex. It really is *just* spanking. A person can be kinky and asexual at the same time, and many are. Even for those of us who are kinky and sexual, kink often stands alone. Spanking was dinner. Sex was dessert: I didn't need it, or even want it, after every meal.

"Is love a tender thing?" Romeo asks his best friend, Mercutio. "It is too rough, too rude, too boist'rous, and it pricks like thorn." Mercutio shrugs.

"If love be rough with you," he advises, "be rough with love."

I adored it. The pain and ritual were a drug. Besides Shakespeare, kink was the only thing that could free me from the confines of my neurotic, self-conscious, insecure mind and release me into my body. Other details from the BDSM spectrum made guest appearances, but spanking was the fetish. It was the focus. And it was fun.

Spanking has some themes. Submission and dominance are two of them, of course, but there are others. Obedience. Discipline. Authority. Accountability. Respect. Punishment.

Those are good words. Someone out there, I promise you, is masturbating to that list of words right now. Wordplay is sex play. This is a verbal fetish.

As John and I continued to play, I tried to justify our lifestyle with science. Pain releases endorphins, which can cause a euphoric high, similar to the high that long-distance runners describe. There is an artery in the pelvic region called the common iliac artery, which supplies blood to both the genitals and the butt; when blood rushes down that artery to one of the two regions, it also rushes to the other region and can cause a kind of blood engorgement. Fear and lust have a similar effect on the brain, and provoke a symmetrical list of symptoms: sweaty palms, racing heart, churning stomach. Maybe my fetish, I decided, was just a reasonable conclusion to that tangled web of nerve endings and blood vessels.

Of course, those physiological rationales didn't explain the side of the coin that John was on, but he didn't feel the need to justify anything. He didn't seem afraid of his sexuality, as I was. Science babble did not interest him. He focused on a different detail of the physical response.

"The harder I spank you, the wetter you get," John told me once, when I was inelegantly draped over his knee.

I pushed my torso up and twisted around to look at him.

"Gross!" I declared, indignant. "I don't want to hear that!"

"It's not gross, it's great," he replied. "But do you want to argue with me while I'm in this position and you're in that position?"

I had never felt so good.

"Wisely and slow," cautioned Friar Lawrence, who advises Romeo and Juliet throughout the play. "They stumble that run fast."

I longed to understand him. John, I discovered, was a kindergarten-through-high-school-product of the Catholic school system.

"Ah," I joked. "That explains it."

"What?" he replied.

"Nothing," I said, smiling. "Are you still Catholic?"

John frowned.

"I think everyone has a God-shaped hole inside his chest," he finally said. That didn't answer my question.

Another time, I asked him why he was named John. "It's such a clean name for a messy guy," I said.

"My mother chose it because she had never met a John she didn't like," he explained. "Until me, I guess." He smirked.

We found lines the wrong way: by crossing them. Once, after a spanking, John tossed his belt on the bed. Against the brown leather, I could see dark smudges of something wet. I reached out to touch it, and my finger came away red. It was blood. I showed him.

"Wow," John said.

"Really?" I asked. "We broke the skin? Are you sure?"

He ran his hand over my butt, surveying the damage.

"It's not bad," he said. "It just looks like pinpricks. Like red sweat."

That intrigued me. I wanted to find a mirror and see for myself.

Then I imagined us from the outside and was dismayed by the sight. My boyfriend had just spanked me bloody. And I was *thrilled*.

DUKE
So then it seems your most offenseful act
Was mutually committed?

JULIET
Mutually.

DUKE
Then was your sin of heavier kind than his.

—*Measure for Measure*, 2.3

"Does this stuff worry you, John?" I asked, still bent over the bed. "Are we—?" I broke off. I couldn't finish the thought.

"You worry too much," he replied.

From then on, those extremes were not rare. People don't realize how often (or how easily) spanking can cross into blood play, or strip away patches of skin.

But it was impossible to shake the fear that our "brawling love" was sick. After all, that was the official psychiatric consensus. At that point, the *Diagnostic and Statistical Manual of Mental Disorders* still listed sadism and masochism as serious mental illnesses. (The psychiatric establishment has a shameful history with sexuality. Homosexuality was once classified as a mental illness; so was masturbation. Even today, the most recent *DSM* still lists sadism and masochism as mental illnesses if they cause distress to the individual—just as it once did for "ego-dystonic homosexuality.")

I didn't have any old friends in Spain. I longed to call Peng and tell her everything. But how do you start that conversation?

As private as my personal life had become, the political borders of my worldview expanded like never before. Shortly after I moved to Seville, a series of simultaneous, coordinated bombings terrorized the Madrid commuter train system, killing 191 people and wounding thousands more. Three days later, the Spanish people went to the polls for their 2004 presidential elections. International politics seemed more urgent and relevant than ever. I couldn't read enough. The following month, *60 Minutes* broadcast a story about American soldiers torturing prisoners at Abu Ghraib prison in Iraq.

"See, that is sick," John told me, pointing to a news photo on a computer screen. "*That's* what is deranged. Can't you see the difference between that and what we do?"

"Don't joke, John," I said.

"I'm not joking," he replied.

When I wasn't reading about international politics, terrorism, and the wars in the Middle East, I read books. I was thrilled to have been admitted to Stanford, but I was also terrified. My admission felt like a fluke. I wouldn't fit in at a fancy college. My only hope, I decided, was to get a head start: I'd read the classics. So I raided the English-language section of the nearby bookstore and filled my room with giants: Orwell, Joyce, Faulkner, Plath, Fitzgerald, Nabokov, Austen, Dickens, the Brontës, Salinger, Plato, Hawthorne, Dickinson, Bradbury. And Freud, who made me mad. And Cervantes, who made me laugh.

Oh, and Dostoevsky.

"Promise me you'll start with *The Brothers Karamazov*," John told me. "You'll love it."

And I did love it. Masochists love Russian novelists.

"If we ever do something that you can't take, you can say 'red' and I'll stop," John told me one night over dinner, as I squirmed on a hard chair. "You know that, right?"

I did not know that, actually.

"Like red light, yellow light, green light?" I asked.

John nodded.

"Exactly," he said.

"In that case," I replied, "red light."

He raised his eyebrows.

"I have to take that seriously, Jillian," he said. "Was that a joke?"

I pushed my food around my plate with my fork.

"It was a joke," I admitted.

"Okay," John replied. "If you say that again, make sure you mean it."

We still weren't having sex, but every moment was sexual. To his credit, John almost never pressured or rushed me, despite the fact that our atypical relationship dynamic and the age difference between us empowered him to do so. He controlled when and how we played with pain; I controlled, for the most part, when and how we experimented with pleasure. And along the way, sex did happen: first, I gave him my anal virginity at a Hotel California during a weekend trip to Málaga. We didn't have lube, so John made do with spit and sunscreen, and that was my first time.

"You do realize that didn't count as my *virginity*-virginity, right?" I announced after. But then John took my "*virginity*-virginity" on a red tile apartment floor in Barcelona a few months later, so those semantic calisthenics were ultimately pointless.

"Oh, my God," John said once, a few weeks after we'd started having sex, as we lay on the bed in his apartment in Seville. "Yesterday, we had anal sex in the morning, and you gave me a blow job that night. And I didn't take a shower in between."

I sat up straight. He was right.

"Oh, my God," I repeated.

I leapt off the bed and sprinted to the bathroom.

"I'm going to die!" I yelled, scrambling to put paste on my toothbrush. "Go get me some antibiotics!"

John was laughing.

"You'll be fine," he said. "Did it taste . . . weird?"

I poked my head out of the bathroom. My cheeks were puffed

out like a chipmunk's to contain the unreasonable amount of frothy toothpaste I had just inhaled.

"Are you asking me," I said around the toothbrush, as foam threatened to spill past the edges of my mouth, "if your penis tasted like *my poop*?"

John shrugged.

"I guess," he said.

I disappeared back into the bathroom and spat the toothpaste into the sink. If it is possible to spit emphatically, that is how I expelled the paste from my mouth.

"No!" I screeched. "Why the hell would you ask me that?"

"Don't cuss at me, bird," John replied coolly. "You know better than that."

I stuck my head back into the bedroom and pointed a bottle of Listerine at him.

"Don't start," I threatened. "Don't you dare."

John's eyebrow flickered.

"Well, if there was ever a moment to wash your mouth out with soap . . ." he said with a grin.

I locked the bathroom door.

If accidental ass-to-mouth play seems like an inappropriate topic to mention in a chapter about Shakespeare's most "romantic" play, by the way, don't blame me. Blame Mercutio, Romeo's best friend. He's the one who first raises the subject of anal sex, when he teases Romeo about what kind of woman he should find:

> *If love be blind, love cannot hit the mark.*
> *Now will he sit under a medlar tree,*
> *And wish his mistress were that kind of fruit*
> *As maids call medlars, when they laugh alone.*
> *O, Romeo, that she were, O that she were*
> *An open-arse, and thou a pop'rin pear!*

Mercutio's joke is a double entendre, of course. (And not a very subtle one, at that.) *Open arse* is self-explanatory. But during Shakespeare's life, it was also bawdy slang for a medlar fruit. That joke appeared as early as the fourteenth century, when Chaucer used *open arse* to describe the fruit in "The Reeve's Tale." And when we consider that Shakespeare's words were meant to be heard, not seen, the term *pop'rin pear* quickly becomes a phallic play on *pop 'er in.*

In other words, Mercutio encourages Romeo to look for a girl who will, let's say, slide into "literature" through unexpected doors.

The heady euphorias of every spanking were followed by intense, inexplicable lows. Without fail, twelve to sixteen hours after intense play, I'd crash into tears, self-doubt, and depression. I wanted to cry, fight, or curl up and hide—and, more often than I'm proud to admit, that's exactly what I did. Years later, I'd learn that this phenomenon is called "sub drop." The physical pain of BDSM play causes endorphins and adrenaline to spike, and when those hormones subside, the return to normalcy often feels sad and confusing. ("Dom drop" can happen to tops, too.) But since John and I didn't yet speak the language of our world, we didn't understand my depressive moments. Sometimes John dealt with my moods by spanking me, and suddenly, almost like magic, endorphins flooded back into my bloodstream and I felt better. More often, though, I looked for reasons to pick fights and John shut down.

"i wonder if you even care about me, john [sic]," I emailed him once, in the throes of sub drop, for no apparent reason.

"Sooner or later, every girlfriend writes me an email in all lowercase letters," John said, sighing, later that night. (I winced at the realization that I had become a cliché and redoubled my commitment to grammar.)

And there was still the risk that my disease might, at any second, ruin everything.

I was spending the night at John's apartment and had just finished brushing my teeth. I put my toothbrush in the coffee mug John used as a holder and looked up at the mirror above the sink. Juliet's face, instead of my own, gazed back at me from the glass. But something was wrong. She looked gray, stiff, and cold, as one dead in the bottom of a tomb.

I could feel it coming before it happened. At first, it was just an energy in my fingers and hands that ran down the map of my skeleton. Then a wave of paralysis hit, and my body folded up into itself, out of my control, like an old, crumpled grocery list. A second later, I was on the floor of the bathroom. My body curled over my arms. I couldn't stand; I couldn't move. I couldn't even cry. It hurt. Nothing had ever hurt so much.

The bathroom door opened.

"Jillian, what the hell?" I heard John say.

I couldn't speak, so I kept my eyes closed.

I felt John's arms wrap around me, and he lifted me up off the cold blue tile of the floor. In the same moment, the transient paralysis began to fade away, like the moment a wave pulls back from the beach. I began to cry.

"Hey, now," John said gently. "If you wanted me to carry you, you could've just asked."

I tried to laugh, but the sound mixed with my tears and came out in a strangled choke.

John carried me into his bedroom and set me down on his bed. I could finally move my hands again, and I used them to cover my eyes while I cried. John sat next to me.

"I don't know what that was," I said. "But I don't want you to see me like this."

"You're my gal," John said. "I'm here."

I pressed my face into his chest.

The next day, we decided to move to Barcelona. I was ready for a change of scenery. And John, to my surprise, had found a low-level job at a Spanish law firm there. He'd just turned twenty-five. It seemed as good a time as any to grow up.

"I can't tell you to stay away from drugs when I'm selling them," John explained with a wink.

Right away, Barcelona was wonderful. I rented a room near Hospital de Sant Pau; John, meanwhile, moved into his own apartment nearby. (My waitressing job didn't follow me to Barcelona, so at this point I was mooching off John and occasional checks from my mother, who had no idea what was happening on our far side of the world.)

I HAD ENTERED Spain on a tourist visa, so I still had to leave the European Union every three months. John and I had satisfied this detail by taking the ferry to Morocco while we lived in Seville, so from Barcelona we decided to shake up the routine and buy cheap flights to Switzerland for the weekend instead. We landed in Geneva and immediately hopped on a train to the Alps. I'd heard good things about a small town in the Bernese Oberland called Gimmelwald, which I wanted to see.

We arrived in the Alps and spent the night at a cheap motel at the base of the mountains. It was May, only a month before my eighteenth birthday. There was a computer in the hotel lobby, so that morning I used it to check my email. I had some spam, which I deleted. My mother had forwarded me a chain email about toxins in lip balm, and I also deleted that. And there was an email from my high school class president. Apparently someone had forgotten to take me off the list when I dropped out. The subject line was: "BEST PROM EVERRRRRR!"

Was it prom already?

I deleted that email, too. I didn't care about prom.

John and I walked from our hostel to a tram station and took the tram up into the Alps to Gimmelwald. It was a tiny town of less than two hundred people, perched on the side of the mountain at an elevation of more than four thousand feet. We wandered through Gimmelwald until we found a picturesque farm with a perfect view of the mountains.

We sat on the grass and gazed at the landscape around us. It was incredible. Huge mountains filled the sky—360 degrees of massive brown crags, like hunks of perfect Swiss chocolate topped with powdered sugar. Small villages were scattered among the bright green fields at the bases of the peaks.

"It's amazing," I said.

"I miss the ocean," John replied. I turned to look at him. It wasn't like John to be morose.

"Why do you love surfing?" I finally asked.

John moved to sit behind me and wrapped his arms around my shoulders so I could fall back into him, like a chair.

"It's peaceful," he said. "I only have to think about my breath, my board, and the water. Sometimes the wave curls around me and makes a crisp blue tube. It's perfect in there. It's the most perfect the world can be."

"It sounds nice," I said.

"I can teach you," John replied, getting animated with excitement. "There's a wave I dream about called Cloudbreak. It's in Fiji. It's an almost perfect left. If I could surf any wave on earth, that's the one I'd pick. I want to take you there."

I ran my hand up his pants to the long scar on his calf. It was from a surfing accident years before. John had been surfing the Banzai Pipeline, a wave in Hawaii that is notorious for its shallow water and sharp reefs, when he fell. The leash that tethered him to his surfboard wrapped around some coral, trapping him underwater. As he struggled to free himself, John's leg ripped open against the reef. The resulting scar was thick and ugly, and the long seconds he'd spent underwater, out of control, had left him with a profound fear of being unable to breathe. I was never, ever allowed to touch John's neck. That was a real rule, not like one of our fun rules I could break at will. Whenever anyone touched his neck, it reminded him of choking.

"I don't have good balance," I confessed.

John laughed.

"I'll take you somewhere safe, bird," he said, hugging me. "There are some good spots for beginners in Portugal. You can ride some little waves. We'll hop across the border and I'll show you the ropes. You'll see: surfing is the best way to feel real."

I relaxed into his hug. This felt like love. But I couldn't say it.

Instead, I said, "I love it when you talk about surfing."

"I belong in the water," John replied with a nod.

Since we were outside, and therefore I was "safe," I decided to mess with him. I opened my bottle and splashed some water in his face.

John recoiled from the spray, blinking with surprise as water dripped from his hair into his eyes.

I giggled.

"You shouldn't have done that," he finally said, in a familiar tone of voice.

Startled at his reaction, I jumped to my feet and ran. John took off after me, and we raced across the field. He caught up with me—it didn't take long, I'm slow—and tackled me to the ground. He wrestled me onto my back, sat on top of me, and put his hands on my shoulders.

"That was a mistake," John said, pointing at my face.

"You said you like water," I squealed, laughing as I struggled to get away. "I was just helping!"

His hands went to his waist, and he unbuckled his belt.

"Oh, my God," I exclaimed. "John, we're outside! We're in a field!"

"You should have thought of that before," he said, as he pulled his belt off through the loops on his pants. I tried to squirm away, but John wrestled me over onto my stomach, folded his belt in half, and whipped it across my butt. He was kneeling on the backs of my legs, straddling them, so I couldn't escape. I folded my arms and hid my face in them. On the far side of the field, a spotted black-and-white cow was looking at us.

Shakespeare hides Romeo and Juliet's sex scene inside the break between scene 3.4 and scene 3.5, by the way.

I ROLLED OVER onto my back, basking in the Alpine mountain scenery and the afterglow that comes with a really satisfying spanking.

"Get up, bird," John said. "Someone is going to see us." He was already standing up.

I pointed at his waist, where his belt had been restored to its more traditional place.

"That is a dangerous object," I said dramatically. "I need a minute to recover. You don't know how it feels."

John snorted.

"I grew up in Oklahoma," he said. "Of course I know how it feels."

The dark implication was a bucket of ice water. Nothing puts a frost on sex quite like psychology.

I hopped to my feet.

"Fine, I'm up," I said. "Happy?"

"As a matter of fact, I am happy, darlin'," he drawled, grinning.

We collected my water bottle from the far side of the field, rode the tram back down the mountain, and then took a series of trains back to Geneva.

At a stationery shop in one of the Swiss train stations, I bought a pad of paper and a blue pen. On the next train, when John leaned against the window and fell asleep, I pulled out the notebook and began to draw. I drew rolling waves, crested with froth and bits of spray. I'm not an artist, but I rocked that wave drawing. It looked great. I was proud.

John was still asleep. I crawled over to his seat and poked him in the ribs. He grumbled and turned away.

"Wake up," I whispered, poking him again. My excellent wave drawing demanded admiration. "The train is on fire."

That did the trick.

"What?" he muttered, waking up.

"Nothing," I said. "I made you a drawing." I pressed it into his hand.

John looked at it for a long time. Then he touched a wave with the tip of his finger.

"This is beautiful," he finally said. "Thank you."

"You like it?" I asked.

"I love it," he replied.

"I'm glad to hear that," I told him. "Because it would mean a lot to me if you got this tattooed on your back."

"What?" he asked.

"I'm kidding," I said, laughing.

It can be hard to accept that *Romeo and Juliet* isn't a love story. There is so much beauty there—beautiful language, beautiful moments—which can feel undercut by the realization that the play is about childishness and lust rather than real love. But love and communication are the same thing. And the characters in *Romeo and Juliet*, including the title characters, don't communicate. More than a romance, *Romeo and Juliet* is a bloodbath. ("Here's much to do with hate, but more with love," Romeo claims at the beginning of the play, but I've wondered if perhaps the opposite is true.) Six people die. And the reason they die, more often than not, is that they didn't talk to each other. In *Romeo and Juliet*, Shakespeare couldn't be more clear about the importance of communication: at the end of the play, if a single letter were delivered on time, Juliet and Romeo would likely survive. When the lines of communication fail, love fails.

Romeo and Juliet is a play about children, and John and I were children, too. We didn't ask each other the right questions, or have the necessary conversations. I shouldn't have ignored the ominous implications of John's remark that his childhood taught him what it feels like to be hit with a belt; at the same time, he should have shared himself with me through more than hints. And I should have shared myself with him. But, instead, I tucked my legs under me, leaned against his shoulder, and we watched Switzerland pass us through the window of our high-speed train.

We arrived back in Geneva and headed straight to the airport. Hotels were expensive, and we had an early flight home to Barcelona, so John and I had decided to sleep in the departures terminal. Airports are free.

We walked inside and looked for a comfortable place to sleep. Under my pants, I could feel the telltale deep, prickling itch that told me something was healing.

"I'll be right back," I said. "I need to run to the bathroom."

"Going to survey the damage?" John joked.

"No," I glared. "I just need to pee."

"Sure, sure," he said, sarcastically. "You *hate* all of this."

"Watch my backpack," I ordered.

I left John alone and wandered through the deserted terminal until I found a bathroom. Friar Lawrence was already inside, washing his hands over a sink. I rolled my eyes.

"This is the girls' bathroom," I said. "But I suppose you're here to tell me that 'these violent delights have violent ends,' right?"

"That's right," he said gravely. "Don't forget."

He shook the water off his hands and grabbed a paper towel. Then he walked out, letting the door swing closed behind him.

I checked under the stalls for feet. When I felt confident I was alone, I locked the door, stood in front of the mirror, and pulled down my jeans and underwear. I twisted around to look at my butt in the mirror. It looked okay. No, it looked great. In the months since that first spanking, John and I had discovered, to our mutual delight, that I could bruise beautifully. And there it was: a purple-and-pink aurora borealis on my ass.

I wondered what kind of dress I would have worn to prom.

I pulled up my underwear and, with my pants still wrapped around my knees, hopped into a stall. I peed, and then stepped back out. The line of sinks was in front of me. A sudden, infuriating thought sprang to mind.

I dashed to the bathroom door, unlocked it, and ran out into the airport. Friar Lawrence was nowhere in sight. I sprinted across the terminal to the automatic exit doors, which whisked open before me. To the right, in the darkness, I could just make out the distant, brown-robed figure of the friar. I ran down the pavement after him.

"Hey, asshole," I shouted. He turned around and waited until I reached him. I skidded to a stop.

"What the fuck was that?" I yelled, pointing toward the airport. "Was that some kind of shitty metaphor? Are you also washing your hands of me now?" I reached out and shoved him in the chest. He fell back a step.

"Stop worrying, child," he replied, taking one of my hands in his own. "Not everything in your life is about your childhood. Sometimes a soap bar is just a soap bar."

He squeezed my palm, then turned away to resume his walk toward Geneva.

I stood there, huffing and watching him go.

Back in the airport, I found John upstairs. He had set our backpacks against a wall and was using his own as a pillow. I settled on the floor next to him and put my head on my own backpack. It felt hard. I shifted on the floor, trying to find a comfortable position, but it was useless. I wouldn't be able to sleep that night.

We lay there, listening to the soft murmur of the airport.

I turned my head to look at John. His eyes were open, too.

"I missed my prom," I told him.

John looked at me for a few seconds, then stood. He walked over to a nearby display case of glass figurines and held out his hand to me.

"Dance with me here, little bird," he said.

I peeled myself off the floor and walked over to take his hand. He pulled me into his arms. I put my hand on his shoulder; he put his hand on the small of my back. And right there, on the second floor of the Geneva airport, surrounded by sleeping travelers and one night janitor, I rested my cheek on his chest and we danced. Tiny sparks of light bounced off the glass figurines in the case and scattered across the floor of the terminal.

"Hey, look how the floor of heaven is thick inlaid with patines of bright gold," Lorenzo, from *The Merchant of Venice,* called over to me from the arrivals lobby, where he was dancing with his wife, Jessica.

Then it was silent, save for a few occasional snores. We danced to the music I imagined in my head.

2.4   The Taming of the Shrew:
Rough with Love

John grabbed my upper arm.

"We're going home," he growled, as he dragged me down a busy Barcelona street called Passeig de Gràcia. "I'm going to spank you until you learn to be more considerate of my time."

He stepped off the curb and lifted a hand to hail a taxi.

I had just turned eighteen. Like many teenagers, I had a problem with tardiness. John didn't like that. Luckily, my punctuality (or lack thereof) was something I could control. If I felt restless—in other words, if I wanted to play—I could leave twenty minutes late for a date. Or if I unintentionally arrived on time, I could slip into a café and wait a few minutes to be tardy. It was a reliable and predictable way to get a spanking, when I wanted one.

But this time wasn't part of a plan. My subway train had gotten stuck inside a tunnel, which is why I was late to meet John at an after-work movie for which he had already bought tickets.

"It wasn't my fault," I told him. "The train stalled. If you need to spank someone, go find the subway conductor."

"It *was* your fault," John corrected. "You have to plan to arrive fifteen minutes early. You can't plan to arrive right on time. Things happen that you don't expect, as you're about to discover."

A taxi pulled up to the corner. John grabbed my shoulder and, with a firm nudge, pushed me into the backseat. He slid in after me, then leaned forward and recited his address. Our taxi pulled into the stream of traffic.

The driver was in earshot, and likely understood English, so I settled for a vague complaint: "This isn't fair."

"Nonsense," John replied. "You're too argumentative."

I had to concede the point. I was too argumentative. He was right, and it stressed me out. The scraps of information that I'd found on the Internet suggested that I was "submissive," but that word didn't seem right. I never acted or even felt submissive. I had spent the entire span of my sexual maturity fantasizing about this kind of relationship, but now that I had it, I was holding back. To steal from *Henry VI, Part 3:* if John was "stern, obdurate, flinty, rough, re-morseless," wasn't I supposed to be "soft, mild, pitiful, and flexible"? But I was none of those things. I argued, complained, bargained, negotiated, and did everything a submissive wasn't "supposed" to do. I couldn't help myself. Spankings hurt. I craved and fantasized about them, but I also feared them. This confused me.

Years later, I would learn that I'm a bit of what the kink community calls a "brat"—someone who is a bottom, but has a play style that is more sassy or combative. In mature, healthy kink, responsible "bratting" isn't shameful; it's just a different point on the kink spectrum. But I didn't know that yet. At the time, it felt like I'd failed at normalcy and failed at kink. I couldn't even succeed at being messed up.

The taxi arrived at John's apartment building. He dragged me into the elevator.

"Have you considered the possibility that you're an agent of patriarchy?" I growled, once the doors closed. "And if patriarchy is terrorism, that makes you a terrorist." (I'd recently stumbled onto the selected writings of Andrea Dworkin.)

John ignored my elementary discourse on gender politics.

"I think sometimes you're late on purpose," he mused. "Either way, we're going to break you of this unattractive habit."

"That's not true!" I exclaimed, bristling with indignant embarrassment. Maybe conviction would cancel out the fact that he was, technically, correct.

John stuck his hands in his pockets. "I think," he said, leaning against the wall of the elevator, "you just need *discipline*." Then he grinned.

Damn it. That boy could be sexy.

"I have never been late on purpose," I lied. "You're paranoid."

"Maybe I am," he replied. "But that doesn't change anything."

"I bet you like it when I'm late," I grumbled under my breath. If John heard that, he didn't respond.

The elevator arrived at the seventeenth floor. John grabbed my upper arm and pulled me toward his apartment. When he got inside, he pointed at the couch in his living room.

"Bend over the end of that sofa," he said. "And don't you dare test me on this one." Then he left the room and disappeared down the hallway. A second later, I heard the air conditioner in the other room click on.

While he was gone, I did what I'd been told. I bent over the arm of the sofa, rested my elbows and forearms on a cushion, and dropped into the arch of my back. I loved this position. It made me feel sexy.

John walked back into the room, rolling up his sleeves.

WHAT IS ABUSE? It's a question I've often asked myself. After all, the consensual interactions that feel so erotic and necessary to me would be considered abusive in other contexts. This is what interests me most about *The Taming of the Shrew*.

It's easy to forget that *The Taming of the Shrew* is a play within a play, but it is. In the first scene, a group of people play a trick on a drunk beggar, Christopher Sly, who has passed out in an alehouse. They put rings on his fingers and place him in a lavish bed. When he wakes up, they treat him like a nobleman. At first, Sly is bewildered when these strangers insist that he is a lord. But they assure him that a play will cure his amnesia and "melancholy," so he agrees to watch it. It is only in that form—as characters in this play within a play, performed for people who are themselves pretending to be something they are not—that Kate and Petruchio, the central characters of *The Taming of the Shrew*, appear.

Their story is controversial. At the beginning, a wealthy young man named Lucentio falls in love with a beautiful woman named Bianca. But there's a catch: Bianca's father, Baptista, has declared that she cannot get married until her older sister, Katherine, does. Finding a husband for Katherine, Lucentio learns, will be difficult. Katherine has a terrible reputation around town. People say that she is rude, hostile, mad, and ill-tempered: in other words, a "shrew." No one wants to marry her—which is fine with Kate, since she dislikes all of them, too.

Meanwhile, Petruchio arrives in Padua and decides that he wants to marry Katherine—or, rather, that he wants to marry the wealthy inheritance her father guarantees. But in their first meeting, Kate and Petruchio's relationship accelerates beyond the financial. After they spar in perfect symmetry—it's a jousting match, not a conversation—Petruchio announces to Baptista that he "must and will have Katherine to my wife." At this, Kate uncharacteristically has no sassy retort.

On the day of the wedding, Petruchio is late. The moment

when Kate fears that Petruchio has left her at the altar is a rare glimpse of sincerity. Her tearful disappointment is no game. Kate, this woman who refuses to do anything she doesn't want to do, *wants* to marry Petruchio. He eventually shows up and, after the wedding, he takes her back to his house.

Once they are alone, Petruchio begins the uncomfortable and alarming process of "taming" Kate. He inflicts on her the same tactics that Elizabethan falconers used to tame their birds, which emphasized deprivation of food and sleep. (Petruchio inflicts this deprivation in the guise of "love," insisting that Kate is too good to eat his inferior food or sleep in his inferior bed.) These scenes can be difficult to watch, especially for people who believe, as I do, that Kate and Petruchio share a real and meaningful love. But their "taming" process is mutually exhausting. When Katherine does not eat, neither does Petruchio.

In the final scenes, Kate and Petruchio return to Padua to visit her family. On the road, they share a climactic denouement when Petruchio asks Kate to pretend that the sun is a moon, and she does. "Be it moon, or sun, or what you please," says Katherine, " . . . henceforth I vow it shall be so for me." Soon after this, they kiss.

The play ends back in Padua. Kate, in front of the same people who dismissed her as "mad" and "curst," delivers a long speech about the "love, fair looks, and true obedience" that women owe their husbands. Her use of the word "true" is significant. In this moment, as in the rest of the play, Shakespeare screams in our ears not to forget that there is a difference between what is "true" and what is play.

Above all, *The Taming of the Shrew* is a play about *playing*. Innkeepers pretend that Christopher Sly is a lord. Servants pretend to be noblemen, and noblemen pretend to be teachers. Kate pretends to believe that the sun is a moon, and that an old man is a young virgin. Shakespeare saturated this play with so much pretense, in fact, that we cease to notice it—just as we forget that a play-within-a-play narrative frames everything. Lucentio even cautions us to not let "counterfeit supposes [blear] thine eyne." That is, we shouldn't let false impressions cloud our sight. Yet despite this warning, we still forget.

Shakespeare wrote many plays within plays, including the ones in *Hamlet* and *A Midsummer Night's Dream*. But *The Taming of the Shrew* is the only one where the play within a play destroys its narrative frame and becomes the play itself. That detail fascinates me: Kate and Petruchio's story appears so real, and so powerful, that it takes over.

But their relationship is a literal fantasy. It's play.

Should we hold play to the same standards as reality?

Masochism and sexual fetishism existed during Shakespeare's life, of course, and I have no doubt that he was aware of them. One of the most graphic literary descriptions of kink—frankly, it sounds like a spanking fetish to me—appeared in a 1599 collection of epigrams and elegies by John Davies and Christopher Marlowe, which Will Shakespeare, then thirty-five years old, likely would have read:

> *When Francus comes to sollace with his whoore*
> *He sends for rods and strips himselfe stark naked:*
> *For his lust sleepes and will not rise before,*
> *By whipping of the wench it be awaked.*
> *I envie' him not, but wish I had the powre,*
> *To make my selfe his wench but one halfe houre.*

Thomas Middleton and John Fletcher's seventeenth-century play *The Nice Valour* includes a character, Lapet, who delights in submitting to beatings and even writes a book about how to optimize the experience of being beaten. Sixty-seven years after

Shakespeare's death, Robert Dixon addressed masochism in *Canidia, or the Witches: A Rhapsody in Five Parts*, which describes a "bumpkin lout" who

> *. . . beg'd for Rods, would madly rail,*
> *If Lictors with Rods did not brush his Tail*
>
> *. . .*
>
> *And so furious was the Lown,*
> *That he must see the Blood run down.*
> *Thus he delighted above measure,*
> *To feel at once both Pain and Pleasure.*
> *The more tormented, the more he itcht,*
> *None can say, but he was bewitcht.*
> *He was conjur'd into Venus Arms,*
> *No otherwise than by Whipping Charms.*
> *We taught him upon Rue to feed,*
> *To stop the Urine of his Seed,*
> *For fear [there] should be more of his Breed.*

As John Yamamoto-Wilson has pointed out, these early references to masochism are not without judgment: Dixon's masochist is "bewitched" and must eat rue to prevent him from passing his affliction to a new generation, and in *The Nice Valour,* the masochist's name—Lapet—is French for "the fart." In a 1639 disquisition on sexual masochism, *Of the Use of Flogging in Venereal Affairs,* by Johann Heinrich Meibom (which was, according to David Savran, the authoritative text on the subject for two hundred years), the author "rejoice[s]" the fact that if such a "perverse" case were to occur in Germany, the masochist would be "severely punished by avenging flames"—that is, he or she would be burned alive.

When Shakespeare himself wrote about kink, it was in much more subtle (and compassionate) ways. Cleopatra describes a "stroke [that] is as a lover's pinch, which hurts, and is desired," and there are powerful sadomasochistic allusions in *Measure for Measure* and *King Lear,* too. In the scenes where Petruchio "tames" Kate by depriving her of food, sleep, and new clothing, it's worthwhile to consider that sensory deprivation (in other words, deprivation of sight, hearing, touch, smell, and taste, along with the associated loss of control) is a kink of its own. Who's to say how Kate and Petruchio get down?

Kate and Petruchio are performers. Before they meet each other, they play the roles of a shrew and a madman—and later, while he "tames" her, they are still playing. But it's a game for which they wrote the rules themselves. That's the only thing that matters.

Kate and Petruchio are in love. They fall in love almost from the first moment they set eyes on each other. In fact, their mutual attraction is so strong that they joke about cunnilingus during their very first conversation:

PETRUCHIO
Come, come, you wasp, i' faith you are too angry.

KATHERINE
If I be waspish, best beware my sting.

PETRUCHIO
My remedy is then to pluck it out.

KATHERINE
Ay, if the fool could find it where it lies.

PETRUCHIO
Who knows not where a wasp does wear his sting? In his tail.

KATHERINE
In his tongue.

PETRUCHIO
Whose tongue?

KATHERINE
Yours, if you talk of tales, and so farewell.

PETRUCHIO
What, with my tongue in your tail?

From a modern perspective, it sounds like Petruchio is joking about putting his tongue in Kate's butt. (And if we learned anything from Mercutio and *Romeo and Juliet,* it's that Shakespeare is not above anal bawdry.) But in Elizabethan England, *tail* was actually slang for vulva, not ass. With that in mind, read their conversation again. Imagine that *sting* is a sly reference to orgasm. This time, Kate teases Petruchio about whether he can "find" a rather critical (if sometimes elusive) target of female sexuality, and Petruchio proves that he does indeed know exactly how to find it.

Even today, female sexual satisfaction is often swept under the rug. But not so with Kate and Petruchio. From the very first time they meet, their relationship is built on a foundation that emphasizes *her* sexual satisfaction over even his own. To Petruchio, Kate comes first (in every sense of the phrase).

Many people assume that Shakespeare's stories are fundamentally male fantasies. After all, the English theater was restricted to male actors, and Shakespeare himself was a man. But as the Shakespeare scholar Stephen Orgel has pointed out, that interpretation isn't entirely correct.

"The theatre was a place of unusual freedom for women in the period," he writes. "[F]oreign visitors comment on the fact that English women go to the theatre unescorted and unmasked, and a large proportion of the audience consisted of women." Orgel goes on to argue (correctly, I think) that the success of any play or playwright at that time therefore would have depended on the endorsement of both genders. If women in the audiences did not enjoy Shakespeare's stories, his work could not have been a success.

PAIN IS NOT the opposite of pleasure. The opposite of pleasure is numbness.

In John's hands, I was never numb.

His hand cracked against my butt. He had been spanking me for about ten minutes, and I winced at the impact. I curled my fingers into the couch.

"This is for your own good, you know," John said. "How do you think your professors will react next year if you're late for a class?" He smacked me again.

"To be honest, babe, I don't think they'd react like this," I said. "Although if they did, I could probably blackmail my way into an A."

The joke broke John's focus. He stopped spanking me and laughed.

"That was cute, Jillian," he said, walking across the room. He went to his desk and opened a drawer. "I hope you think you're funny. The only thing your little jokes do is remind me that I don't have your attention."

He pulled a thick ruler out of the drawer.

"Maybe this will help you focus," he said.

A wave of adrenaline turned my stomach inside out.

"That's not one of those ones with a metal edge, right?" I asked, nervously.

"No, darling," he drawled. "I bought this one just for you. It's only wood." He tapped it, very gently, against my bottom. The gesture sent a thrill of anticipation up my spine.

"I should have sent you to the store to buy this," John mused.

"I wouldn't have gone," I muttered.

John grabbed a handful of my hair and pulled my head up.

"Did you just say something?" he asked.

"No," I squealed. (I can feel the weight of collective judgment from all the kinky people out there who are disappointed in me for saying "no" instead of "no, sir." But what can I say? John and I didn't play with the word *sir*. He never asked me to, and it never occurred to me to introduce it. That word is all over my erotica, but it's just not part of my real life.)

"That's what I thought," John said, letting go of my hair. I reached up to rub the sore spot on my scalp.

Then I heard the *swish* of something moving through the air and felt a sharp, broad smack. I squealed and reached back to wrap my fingers around my butt. I'm a masochist, but pain is pain.

John set the ruler on the edge of the couch, next to me. For a second, I wondered if we were done. Then I heard the familiar sound of silk sliding against cotton as he took off his necktie. (When he changed jobs and moved to Barcelona, the T-shirts and jeans of Seville had disappeared.)

"I've told you before to keep your hands away from there," John said. "I could hurt you if I hit your hand." He leaned forward and grabbed my wrists, binding them together in front of me with his blue tie. Then he stood up again. I frowned and moved my hands, adjusting to the fabric around my wrists.

"Why am I spanking you, Jillian?" John asked, from behind me. His voice was hoarse. He hit me with the ruler a few more times.

"Because I was late." I sighed.

"What are you going to do to make sure that doesn't happen again?" A few more smacks.

"I'm going to find a magical train that never, ever gets stuck in a tunnel," I snarked.

At that, John put his left hand on my back to hold me down and paddled me with the ruler, hard, thirty or forty times in rapid succession. My hands strained to reach back and stop him, but John's tie kept them locked in front of me.

"That's not the answer I wanted," he said.

The pain and surprise of that flurry of smacks overpowered my

last bit of resistance, and I started to cry. I pulled away from the
sofa and bent my knees, dropping my bottom to safety just below
the range of his ruler.

John gently tapped me with it.

"Where do you think you're going?" he said in a firm tone of
voice. "Stand up. We're not done."

I shook my head. A tear fell onto the carpet.

"No," I sobbed. "Please. I can't."

And I meant that. I really did.

Of course, if John hadn't done what he did next, I would have
been frustrated and disappointed the next day. The best translation
I can offer is that John was like a personal trainer, pushing me to
do one more set at the gym. (I'll never understand why pushing
through pain in pursuit of an athletic goal is praised as evidence of
mental strength, while pushing through pain in pursuit of a sexual
goal is stigmatized as evidence of mental illness.) And please don't
forget: by this point, John and I had established a safe word, and
"no, please, I can't," even when sincere, was not it.

"What did I just tell you?" John replied, unmoved. "You don't
want to make me ask again."

With a shuddering sob, I obeyed.

John reached out to touch me.

"Breathe, Jillian," he murmured in a soft voice.

I nodded.

"Do you want to try my last question one more time?" John
asked. The soft voice was gone.

"Next time, I'll leave fifteen minutes earlier," I recited, sniffling.

"That's better," John said.

He reached out and brushed the tips of his fingers against my
butt. I wasn't expecting the gentle touch and flinched, but then I
relaxed into it. I understood what he was doing. He was giving me
a break. I needed to ramp down before I could ramp up again.

"We're almost done," he told me. "You're being very good. I'm proud of you." His finger traced the edges of a bruise that was coming into focus, like a Polaroid photo, on my left butt cheek. I hugged my face into the couch cushion. My senses were so raw and active from the spanking that John's gentle touch felt almost unbearably intense, like the hypersensitivity of skin after an orgasm. I took a deep breath, released a quiet moan, and shuddered. At that, John pulled his fingers away. The contact high of his touch vanished.

"I'm going to give you ten more," he said, tapping my butt with the ruler to show me what to expect. "I want you to count them out loud. If you behave, we'll stop at ten. But if you feel like sharing any more clever remarks, we could go much higher than that. Is that clear?"

I nodded into the pillow.

In that moment, I understood my options: If I couldn't take much more, I'd "behave" during those last ten smacks and then it would be over. But if I wanted to go further, I could be argumentative or disobedient and the game would go on. Kink is more collaborative than it appears. I had control over the situation, too.

But I didn't need to use it. We'd only reached number four when John stopped spanking me and put his hand on my lower back. His touch felt tentative and uncertain. Something was wrong. I wiped some tears out of my eyes and looked over my shoulder at him.

John wasn't looking at me. His eyes were fixed on the wall behind us, which had a long, wide window. Although we were on the seventeenth floor, another apartment faced ours from the building across the courtyard.

"I think someone is watching us," John murmured.

"Oh, my God," I breathed, dropping to the floor, out of sight.

"She's gone now," said John, pulling our curtains shut. "It's okay."

"It is *not* okay!" I screeched. I jumped to my feet and ran—as best I could, with my pants and underwear twisted around my ankles—across the living room and into the bathroom. I locked the door.

"Oh, my God," I moaned again.

John tapped on the door.

"Let me in, bird," he said. "It's okay. She was probably just turned on."

He didn't sound convinced.

"I am going to drown myself in the bathtub," I announced. I could imagine exactly how we must have looked to the woman across the courtyard. John laughed.

"Don't laugh," I roared. "This is so not funny."

Outside, there was a muffled thud.

"I'm sitting against the door now," John said. "Warn me if you're going to open it. I don't want to fall back and crack my head open."

I ignored him and focused on unbinding my wrists with my teeth. Then I pulled some towels off a rack and began to build a towel nest with them in the bathtub.

"I don't know why you're freaked out," John continued. "I'm the one who's about to go to prison."

"That's true," I agreed. "But at least prison will improve your Spanish."

"Are you going to come out of there and vouch for me when the police show up?" John asked. It was only half a joke.

"No," I announced. I climbed into my towel nest and curled up. "Don't drop the soap," I added, helpfully.

On the other side of the door, I heard John sigh.

"Aren't girls like you supposed to be submissive and deferential, bird?" he asked.

I froze. That had struck a nerve.

"You're just lucky I'm willing to do this stuff for you," I finally said.

Another sigh.

"Okay, okay," he replied. I leaned my head against the edge of the tub and closed my eyes.

When I next opened them, Katherine was sitting on the edge of my bathtub.

"The door is locked," I said to her. "How did you get in?"

Kate shrugged.

"It's one of the perks of being fictional, I guess," she replied.

I leaned back into my towels.

"Some people don't like you," I told her. "George Bernard Shaw said that your relationship is 'disgusting.'"

Kate sighed.

"I know," she said. "But your reflection in another's eyes is just that—a reflection. It's as intangible as a word, and changes just as fast."

"We're not talking about my reflection, Kate," I replied. "We're talking about yours."

She stood up and quietly unlocked the door.

"Are you sure?" she asked, glancing over her shoulder at me as she left.

Twenty minutes passed. The police weren't coming.

"I wish you'd let me come in there with you, bird," John said from the hallway.

"It's been unlocked for almost half an hour," I replied from my towel nest in the bathtub. "You could've come in anytime."

The door cracked open. John looked tired.

"You unlocked it?" he asked. "Why didn't you tell me?"

I shrugged.

John pulled off his shoes and climbed into the tub, on top of me.

"Do you have a condom?" I asked.

John wrapped himself around my body and lifted me to the side. He slid to the bottom of the tub and I moved on top of him.

"That's not what this is about, Jillian," he said, as he settled in. "I just want to hold you for a minute."

"Oh," I replied.

"But, for future reference, I always have a condom," he said, with a weary smile.

I rolled my eyes.

"Does that mean you were a Boy Scout?" I asked him.

"What?"

"Their motto is 'be prepared,'" I explained.

"No," John said, in a soft voice. "I have never been a Boy Scout."

I snuggled into the crease between his body and the side of the tub, and rested my head on his shoulder. He wrapped his arms around me and closed his eyes. We stayed there, silently, for long minutes. Eventually John's hand slid down to my butt.

"Are you okay?" he asked.

"If I say 'I'm fine,' does that mean you'll feel free to use that *thing* on me again?" I asked, looking up at him. He smiled and pulled away, so that I slid back to the bottom of the tub, where I started. He was on top of me again.

"I, for one, enjoyed 'that thing,'" he drawled. "What about you?"

I ignored the question.

"My train did get stuck in a tunnel, by the way," I said. "That wasn't a lie."

John sighed. He seemed tired.

I reached over the edge of the tub and grabbed his blue necktie, which I'd left on the floor after I freed myself from it with my teeth. I wrapped it around his right wrist.

John looked at me. His eyes flickered with amusement.

"What are you doing, bird?" he asked.

"I'm giving you a bow," I replied, as I pulled the fabric to spread out the loops. "It looks nice."

In response, John slid his fingers through the hair at the base of my neck, leaned down, and kissed me.

"It looks better on you," he murmured.

We stayed there, on our platform of rumpled bath towels, for a long time. Long enough for the sun to set. By the time John climbed out of the tub, leaving me alone on my ruined former towel nest, it was night.

"Hey, little bird," John said, unwinding the fabric from his wrist. "Do you want to go to that place with the good tofu?" He reached down, scooped up the empty condom wrapper we had dropped on the floor, and deposited it into the trash.

I sat bolt upright in the tub.

"Are you serious?" I asked. The place with the good tofu was far away, and John had work the next morning.

"Sure," he said. "But I want to see you fifteen minutes early next time." He winked.

"Totally!" I replied. "*Thirty* minutes early." Tofu, like spankings, is a powerful motivator.

Spain had, and still has, a serious domestic violence problem. During the dictatorial reign of Francisco Franco from 1936 to 1975, wife beating was legal. Women who tried to flee abusive husbands could even be arrested and imprisoned for "abandoning the home." This laid the cultural groundwork for generations of abuse. In 1997, a brave woman named Ana Orantes had appeared on a Spanish TV show to describe the decades of brutal violence she endured at her husband's hands. Despite dozens of police reports, she said, Orantes was never able to get a restraining order. After the show aired, her husband attacked her one last time. He doused her in gasoline and set her on fire. Orantes's murder became a rallying cry for domestic-violence activists around the word.

Six years later, in 2003, while John and I lived in Spain,

violence against women was once again in every conversation and headline. Ms. Orantes was back in the news: that year, the Spanish parliament unanimously passed a bill that might have saved her life, called the Order for the Protection of Victims of Domestic Violence. It empowered victims to fast-track a restraining order against a violent partner. But despite the new law, domestic violence fatalities in Spain continued to surge. The year 2003 was on track to be the deadliest yet. That year, in Barcelona, the same city where John and I lived, an investigation was launched against a judge who ignored thirteen domestic-violence complaints from a woman named Ana Maria Fabregas. The courts finally paid attention only after her husband beat her to death with a hammer.

As John and I picked through tofu and vegetables in the downtown Chinese restaurant we loved, a depressing thought occurred to me.

"That sucked this afternoon," I said.

"I'll be more careful with the curtains next time," he replied. "It's my fault."

"That's not what I mean," I said. "It sucks that the woman who saw us didn't call the police."

For years, I had tried to convince myself that my personal life was *personal*. But set against the background of Spain's history of domestic violence, it was hard to ignore the possibility that my personal life might also be, as the second-wave feminist movement had insisted, political.

"Doesn't it make you feel guilty?" I asked John. "As if—well, it's as if what we do makes light of the real problem. As if we disrespect real victims. Don't you feel that way?"

John, frustrated, tossed his chopsticks onto the table.

"No, Jillian, I don't feel that way," he said. "And I don't think that's fair. Consent changes everything, doesn't it? Do women who enjoy sex 'disrespect real victims' of rape?"

"Of course not," I said, uncertainly.

"So why would you put that logic on us?" he asked.

I had no reply.

"You're not the only person in this relationship with feelings, Jillian," John continued. "When you compare what we do to abuse, you compare me to *those men*. How do you think that makes me feel?"

"You're nothing like that, John," I muttered.

"I just feel really alone in this sometimes," he finished. "Like it's only me."

I paused. He was right. I had been so fixated on my own insecurities that I hadn't noticed John's. He felt vulnerable about our sexuality, too.

I reached across the table to grab his hand.

Silence feeds fear, and makes it fat.

"It's not only you, okay?" I told him. "You're not alone in this."

"Say it, Jillian," he said. "I want to hear you say it. At least one time."

I swallowed and fixed my eyes on my plate.

"I like it," I choked.

"What do you like?" he pressed.

I looked up at him. My throat was tight.

"I like it when you spank me," I said. "I love it. I think about it all the time." It was the first time I had admitted such a thing out loud. I looked down and shook my head.

John pressed his lips together in a tight smile.

"And sometimes you're late on purpose, right?" he said.

I shifted under his gaze.

"Not today," I mumbled.

"But sometimes?"

With an embarrassed swallow, I admitted that it was true. My "brattiness" was purposeful: I used it to exert control over our game. John nodded. It was a slow nod, thoughtful and deliberate.

"Listen to me, Jillian," he said. "You can own this shit, too. If you want a spanking, just ask for one. Is that clear?"

I couldn't make eye contact with him. I scuffed my feet against the carpet and nodded at the floor.

John leaned back in his chair, satisfied.

"You can have the last piece of tofu, bird," he finally said.

"I was going to take it anyway," I muttered. He laughed.

Many people assume that the high-spirited "shrew" we meet in the early scenes of *The Taming of the Shrew* is the "authentic" Katherine. But what if that version of Katherine is a performance? What if Katherine's shrewishness, rather than being sincere, is a self-aware response to her circumstances before Petruchio enters her life?

Baptista, Katherine's father, sees his daughter as an object. At the time, daughters were the legal property of their fathers, to be sold or disposed of in marriage. Katherine can't control the fact that she is an object to her father and to her culture. But, by pretending to be "damaged goods," she *can* control the terms and timing of her own sale. As Stephen Orgel points out, "The idea of a rich man's daughter deliberately rendering herself unmarriage-able through antisocial behavior [would have had] a great deal of cultural resonance in the England of 1590." In other words, Kate's brattiness was like my own. She used it to seize ownership of her situation.

The Taming of the Shrew is, indeed, a play about misogyny and the subjugation of women. Someone does abuse Katherine. But we have the wrong villain in our sights. The abuser is Baptista—and, more to the point, the culture that produced him—not Petruchio. After all, Petruchio silences himself when Kate speaks. He encourages Kate to deliver the most memorable speech in the play. And he is the only person who sees through Kate's shrewish performance and defends the woman who hides behind it. "Yourself and all the world, that talk'd of her, have talk'd amiss of her," Petruchio tells Baptista.

Katherine isn't "broken" at the end of the play. She is broken at the beginning. In both *The Taming of the Shrew*'s fictional society and in our own real one, Katherine's real enemy is the ingrained cultural subjugation of women and children. There is a difference between the abuse inflicted on Katherine in her actual life and the performed abuse in her relationship with Petruchio. As I said, the scenes where Petruchio "tames" Kate do, and should, challenge us. But the feigned submissiveness that Katherine gives to Petruchio at the end of the play is nothing like the forced oppression that her father and her culture inflict. We can't let counterfeit suppositions blear our eyes.

Love is a country, with closed borders and a language no foreigner can speak. The only people who can understand its customs, traditions, and history are its citizens. A relationship doesn't have to make sense to all people. It only has to make sense to two people.

"If she and I be pleased," says Petruchio, "what's that to you?"

I couldn't put it better myself.

AT EIGHTEEN, AFTER many months in Spain, I flew back to Phoenix for the last few days before college. Away from the intoxicating physicality of Spain, I began to move back into my brain. Puzzle pieces I'd never noticed before came into focus. There was no dramatic moment of clarity. It was just a creeping awareness until, one day, I understood something.

Trust is a house of cards, and when mine fell, it fell as cards do: quietly. I picked up the phone and dialed long-distance to Spain.

John answered.

"It was a lie, wasn't it?" I said. "The reason you didn't want to help me pick a humanities course, the reason you wouldn't recommend classes—you didn't go to Stanford. You've been lying to me. Right?"

Through the line, I could almost feel John exhale.

"Yes," he finally said. "That was a lie."

I took a deep breath.

"Okay, okay," I said. I nodded as I spoke, although no one could see. "Was that the only lie?"

The pause was long. The pause was so long that seasons changed; the pause was so long that children were born, grew, loved and lost, and died; the pause was so long that flowers sprouted and bloomed over their tombstones; the pause was so long that those flowers died, too. My point is, it was a long pause.

"John, it's okay," I finally said. "I just want to know the truth. Was that the only lie?"

"No," he replied. "It wasn't."

I wrote before that kink is a trust fall. This is the moment when I hit the ground.

ACT THREE

Pain – has an Element of Blank –
It cannot recollect
When it begun – or if there were
A day when it was not –

—Emily Dickinson

3.1 Hamlet:

Nothing, My Lord

Dylan was so dreamy.

He had the mix of dark hair, dark eyes, and suave, confident sex appeal that inspires millions of fantasies. He was a twenty-two-year-old Honduran senior at Stanford, where he'd spent the previous four years studying Shakespeare and science. Dylan had the distant refinement of someone who grew up with jaw-dropping wealth, and he was brilliant.

And he was saying something to me. What was it?

I didn't care. I wasn't listening. I was thinking about the sound a belt makes when it slides through pant loops.

"Don't you agree?" Dylan said.

"Um," I said. "Sure. Yes, definitely. What?"

"Then how would you respond to Kahn?" he asked.

Oh, no. Was he talking about Coppélia Kahn? Joel Kahn? Michael Kahn? Victoria Kahn? Damn it! Why was every single person in academia named Kahn? I searched my memory for clues.

"Uh," I stalled. "Well—"

My cell phone rang and rescued me. I answered it.

"I'm here!" a voice announced through the phone.

"Great," I said into the receiver. "Come into the CoHo." (It was five months into my freshman year, and I'd absorbed the Stanford campus lingo: "CoHo" was short for "coffee house," "MemChu" was short for "Memorial Church," "MemAud" was short for "Memorial Auditorium," and so on. But despite my best efforts, and much to my disappointment, "PoOff" never caught on as an abbreviation for "Post Office.")

A minute later, I felt a hand on my shoulder. I turned around.

"Hi, honey," I said, standing up.

I turned back toward Dylan.

"You remember my boyfriend, right?" I asked him. "This is John."

"Of course," Dylan said, politely. "It's nice to see you again."

"Hey, man," John replied. They shook hands.

John turned to me.

"It was a long drive up here, bird," he said. "I'm exhausted. Can we head out?"

"Of course," I replied. "See you tomorrow, Dylan?"

When we got to his car, John didn't waste any time.

"I don't like that guy," he said.

"Come on, John," I said. "There's nothing to be jealous about. Dylan has a girlfriend. And I have a boyfriend." I poked John playfully in the arm. He replied with a reluctant smile.

When I first realized that John had been lying to me, a few months earlier, we didn't break up. We fought.

"You're being a snob," John had yelled, over the phone from Spain. "Why does it matter where I went to college?"

"It *doesn't* matter!" I'd yelled back. "What matters is that you lied! I trusted you!"

We went back and forth like this for almost an hour.

"I didn't mean to lie to you, bird," John finally said. "The lies were already out there before you showed up. I got stuck with them. I didn't expect to meet you."

I swallowed.

"You were in a different country," I offered. "You wanted to try on a different life for a while."

"Exactly," he replied.

I could understand the impulse. I sniffled and tried to regain my composure.

"What about the surfing?" I asked. My voice shook. "Was that true? Was Cloudbreak real?"

"No," he said.

A noise came out of my throat that I had never heard myself make before.

"Oh, bird," John said through the phone. "That was a joke! I was just trying to lighten the mood. Of course the surf stories are true. You've seen my scar."

I was sobbing.

"Jillian, Jillian," John said. "What's going on over there? Why are you crying now?"

I couldn't catch my breath to respond.

"This part is easy, bird," John was saying. "There are places in Northern California where you can watch me surf. This is the easiest thing to solve. I didn't mean to upset you. It was just a joke."

I gasped for air. My hands trembled.

"I thought I didn't know you at all," I wept.

"The surf stuff is true, Jillian," he said. "I swear to God, that part is true."

John did have that scar on his calf. (God knows I'd had plenty of opportunities to memorize it every time I was over his knee for some manufactured infraction.) But since I now required two-step verification for every detail of John's life, when he moved back to the United States and found a job in Southern California only a few months later, I flew down to Los Angeles to watch him surf.

He did surf—beautifully, and with obvious joy. So that, at least, was real.

It was also true that he had spent some time in law school. That's why he had been able to get the paralegal job in Barcelona. But he hadn't graduated.

He had also spent some time in jail.

"I don't want to talk about that." John brooded.

"No way," I replied. "That's not fair. I deserve the truth. All of it. I've earned it."

"I'm sorry, Jillian," he said. "I can't."

"Did it have something to do with Luce?" I asked.

John blinked.

"Wait—what?" he replied. "What about Luce?"

"You told me that things with Luce got out of control," I said. The coldness of my own voice surprised even me. "Did you do something to her? Is that why you went to jail? Is that what you meant when you said things went 'too far' with her?"

"What?" John said. "God, Jillian, no. I had a gun without a permit. Is that enough?"

"I don't know, John," I replied. "How can I believe anything now?"

This new detail about John's life—that he had been incarcerated—rewrote every memory. I remembered his heavy sigh when I joked at him to not drop the soap if the Barcelona police came to arrest him. I remembered the night we bought cocaine in Las Tres Mil Viviendas, and his furious fear when I left the car. I remembered a night in Spain when we had rented the movie *Wall Street*. At the end of the film, when Charlie Sheen's character gets arrested, he cries.

"He's crying?" I'd said, scornfully, at the time. John had bristled.

"A lot of people cry when they get arrested," he replied.

Did that mean John had cried at his own arrest? I had never seen him cry. I couldn't picture it.

"I can get over this," I finally told him. "But you can't lie to me ever again."

"I'll work to earn your forgiveness for as long as you'll let me," he said.

"Oh, please," I replied, rolling my eyes. "Don't do that Catholic guilt thing with—wait! We didn't go over that! Did you really go to Catholic school? That part had to be true, right?"

"Unfortunately, yes," John said, with a smile. "That part was true."

And so we tried to get over it. He got a job at a construction company in Los Angeles. I stayed in Palo Alto, five hours north. We were close enough to visit almost every weekend. But something irreparable had broken. In BDSM, we talk about "headspace"—a frame of mind that is far more important in kink than anything physical. When I'm in the right headspace, it feels like there's no degree of physical pain I can't savor. But after I learned about John's lies, my headspace was all messed up. I just couldn't submit to him as fully as I could before.

I went through the motions, but it wasn't the same. Pain started to feel, of all things, *painful*.

"Stay there," John said, as I knelt next to a bed in the Quality Inn on El Camino Real in Palo Alto. "Keep your eyes on that painting. Don't turn around."

I wasn't blindfolded. In our whole relationship, actually, John had never blindfolded me. It would've been easy to turn around and see what he was doing. But I kept my eyes on the painting.

Cold metal touched the back of my neck. I flinched.

"What is that?" I asked.

John didn't reply.

The painting was a landscape scene. Green trees stood in the horizon beyond a field. Behind some distant mountains, there was a pink sunset. It was bright, like strawberry lemonade.

The metal rolled down the length of my spine.

I didn't want to look at that prefabricated motel painting: I *wanted to want* to look at it. I wanted to feel what I had felt in Spain. I blinked, and, for a second, the landscape disappeared.

"Is that . . . is that my *curling iron?*" I asked. John paused.

"Yes," he finally confirmed, in a blunt, matter-of-fact tone. Its metallic tongue stopped licking my back. I heard the shuffle of movement behind me.

"What are you planning to do?" I said. I could hear a hint of anger in my voice.

"Does it matter?" John replied.

My eyelids fluttered with my breath. If I were inside that strawberry sunset, I decided, I'd have lunch. I wouldn't pack much: grapes, a baguette. But I worried my basket might sink into the soil. The painted grass looked too thick and wet, like marshland, to support my picnic.

"Lean forward," John said.

"Just tell me whether it's plugged in," I begged, pressing my hands against my stomach.

But John was right: it didn't matter. Either way, the next time metal grazed my skin, I gasped.

SPAIN, AND MY relationship with John, had pulled me away from the fears and neuroses inside my head, but at college, they returned. I reincarcerated myself in my own mind. I knew I wouldn't fit in at Stanford: I was too dumb, too different, and, although I was the same age as my classmates, somehow too old. I remember that once, during the first week, a new friend cheered in the dining hall that the best part of college was the freedom to skip her vegetables.

I felt like I was talking to an alien.

When I arrived at Stanford, I hadn't read *Hamlet* and wasn't particularly interested in it. Pop culture had appropriated the play and stripped it of any insight it had once had. "To thine own self be true" and "To be, or not to be," felt as rote and useless to me as "How many licks does it take to get to the Tootsie Roll center of a Tootsie Pop?" *Hamlet* was, at once, too distant and too familiar.

Nevertheless, college was a good time to get to know that guy everyone talks about. After all, Hamlet is a college student, too. At the beginning of the play, he's just come home from university to attend his father's funeral. It's not a pleasant homecoming. Although his dad has been dead for less than two months, Hamlet's mother, Queen Gertrude, has already married his uncle Claudius—her own brother-in-law. Empowered by this marriage, Claudius has assumed the throne of Denmark. Hamlet suspects foul play.

Those suspicions are reinforced when the ghost of Hamlet's father appears to him one night. The ghost says that he was murdered by Claudius (who poured poison into his ear), and urges Hamlet to seek revenge. Hamlet agrees to avenge his father's murder.

But he's the kind of guy who overthinks things. He's a talker, not a doer. He sinks into a deep depression and—perhaps—even insanity. For the rest of the play, Hamlet hesitates to kill Claudius, even as that equivocation, and Hamlet's resultant frustration, leads to many deaths, including that of Hamlet's girlfriend, Ophelia.

Hamlet is a douche bag. In his 1930 essay "The Embassy of Death," G. Wilson Knight wrote, "that Hamlet is originally blameless, that the King is originally guilty, may well be granted. But, if we refuse to be diverted from a clear vision by questions of praise and blame, responsibility and causality, and watch only the actions and reactions of the persons as they appear, we shall observe a striking reversal of the usual commentary." Yes, Hamlet is smart. Yes, he's got a flair for wordplay. But he's also an entitled, self-important, compassionless jerk. *Hamlet* is magnificent, but Hamlet is an asshole. He shows no remorse for accidentally killing

Ophelia's father, Polonius, or for intentionally sending his friends Rosencrantz and Guildenstern to their deaths. When his mother dies, his only remark is: "Wretched queen, adieu." (Apparently Hamlet is the kind of guy who returns from a semester abroad eager to remind everyone of his newfound multiculturalism by dropping words like *adieu*.) In both Shakespearean and contemporary literature, we have the unfortunate tendency to obsess about whether female characters are "likable." Hamlet, meanwhile, gets away with mountains of unlikable crap and remains, for the most part, critically and popularly unscathed.

I see no reason to love Hamlet as a person, but there are plenty of reasons to love him as a character. He's a fascinating example of performative self-awareness—that is, he is an innately theatrical figure, whose soliloquies might be more for our benefit than for his own. But Hamlet also has an internal life so vast that we can only guess at it. When he says, "I have that within which passeth show"—that is, that there is more in him than what is publicly apparent—he could be speaking for any of us. We all have things within which passeth show—dreams or details of our personalities that simmer beneath the surface. But in the entire Shakespearean canon, only Hamlet has an inner life so rich with detail that we forgive his considerable shortcomings.

"I NEED YOU to spank me this weekend," I wrote to John, in an email. I was stressed out. (Fetishists have as many varieties of spankings as a chef has knives, and one is for stress relief.) But by the time I made it to Los Angeles that weekend, I was way behind on an assignment for my required first-year humanities course.

"We can't," I moaned, when John reminded me of my request. "I have to finish reading this." I held up Thucydides's *History of the Peloponnesian War*. It was thick, and I was some two hundred pages behind where I needed to be.

"Maybe we can do both at once," John suggested.

I giggled and rolled onto my stomach.

"If we can pull this off," I joked, "I deserve extra credit."

In that apartment, John didn't have a bed frame—just a mattress sitting on the floor. He jogged over to my purse, pulled out my hairbrush, then plopped onto the ground and began to paddle me over my underwear.

The Spartan King Archidamus—

The hairbrush landed low, on the sensitive "sit spot" near the tops of my thighs. I winced. I was not even close to being in the right headspace to take wood on my sit spots.

The Spartan King Archidamus, who led this expedition—

John hit the same spot again.

"Hey," I accused. "You're doing that on purpose. You know I hate that."

John tossed the brush onto the mattress.

"It's gone, then," he said. "This one is for you to relax." He resumed spanking me with his hand.

The Spartan King Archidamus, who led this expedition, summoned the generals of all the states—

Now it didn't hurt enough.

"I don't feel anything now," I complained.

"Nope," John groaned, flopping onto his back on the mattress. "I can't spank you while you're focused on Thucydides."

I turned my head to look at him.

"Well, I can't focus on Thucydides while you're spanking me," I retorted.

John sat up.

"Maybe you shouldn't have left your homework for the last minute," he pointed out.

His face shifted into an expression I knew well: serious, controlled, penetrating. Kinky people call it "Dom Face." You've seen Dom Face before. It's the expression cops have when they ask for your license and registration. It's the expression your parents had when you played ball in the house.

"Don't look at me that way," I scolded John. "I'll never get through this if you're looking at me that way." He chuckled and flopped back down onto the mattress. I picked up my highlighter and pointed my face at *History of the Peloponnesian War.*

Follow your leaders, paying the strictest attention to discipline and security, giving prompt obedience to the orders which you receive, it read.

I folded down the corner of that page to revisit later. Maybe I hadn't given Thucydides enough credit.

WHAT STRIKES ME most about *Hamlet,* and Hamlet, is nothing.

No, really—nothing.

Whenever Shakespeare repeats a word, I think it deserves special attention. In *Hamlet, nothing* comes up thirty-one different times. The play begins when a night watchman declares that he has "seen nothing." Ophelia claims to think "nothing." Hamlet spends most of the play doing nothing—which might be okay, depending on your opinion, since there is "nothing either good or bad but thinking makes it so."

I think "nothing" is a fair way to describe Hamlet's sexuality, too.

Hamlet is sexually indifferent. He tells us as much when he says, "Man delights not me—no, nor woman neither." Despite that, I suspect that Hamlet and Ophelia slept together; near the end of the play, when Ophelia goes mad, her comments seem to hint as much:

OPHELIA
Then up he rose and donn'd his clothes,
And dupp'd the chamber-door,
Let in the maid, that out a maid

Never departed more.

. . .

Young men will do't if they come to't,
By Cock, they are to blame.
Quoth she, 'Before you tumbled me,
You promis'd me to wed.'

If Ophelia lost her virginity to Hamlet before the play begins, imagine how terrorized she must feel when her father and brother both lecture her on the importance of preserving her chastity. They tell her that she will become worthless without her virtue, but what if that "virtue" is already gone? The possibility makes Hamlet seem that much more cruel when he taunts Ophelia with lewd sexual allusions and tells her to get herself to a "nunnery," which was Elizabethan slang for a whorehouse. If Hamlet is sexually indifferent, his disgust for sexuality—and contempt for women who display it—seems like a logical (if unforgivable) outlet of that frustration. Hamlet fears that his sexual indifference makes him worthless, so he cruelly punishes Gertrude and Ophelia for their lack of indifference.

After Hamlet mocks Ophelia's makeup, her flirtations, and other indicators of her sexuality, he says once again that she should go to a nunnery and leaves. Left alone, Ophelia says: "O, what a noble mind is here o'erthrown! The courtier's, soldier's, scholar's, eye, tongue, sword." I have never seen this moment portrayed as anything but sincere and straightforward: Ophelia, we are told, is sad to see such a "noble" mind descend into madness.

Why do we so often take that sentence at such face value? Something is wrong with it! Hamlet has a courtier's *eye*? A soldier's *tongue*? And a scholar's *sword*? Those parallels are mixed up. If Ophelia means to praise Hamlet (or bemoan his loss) it'd be more apt to say that he has the flattering tongue of a courtier, the powerful sword of a soldier, and the sharp eye of a scholar. But that's not what she says. Is the mix-up a first indicator of Ophelia's descent into madness? Or is it, like the bold retort she shoots at her brother, Laertes, when he lectures her about virginity, a sarcastic hint that this woman has more vinegar than we realize? I don't think Ophelia's comment seems insane—I think it seems clever. Hamlet does have the shallow, superficial eye of a courtier. He has a tongue that can wound, just as a soldier can.

As for the *sword* of a scholar? Well, well. Perhaps murder is not the only occasion to which Hamlet cannot rise. Nothing kills sex like overthinking it.

The word *nothing* has another meaning, too. In Elizabethan slang, *nothing* was a term for female genitalia. (Men have a "thing" between their legs; women have "no thing.") When Hamlet taunts Ophelia in Act Three, he sexually harasses her with this slang.

I read *Hamlet* for the first time in the Stanford Coffee House, and could picture the scene so easily. Hamlet could be any one of the men on campus—some douche bag in a pink polo shirt, no doubt. He strolls into the CoHo, trailed by a string of friends and wallowing in his own prideful pain.

He spots Ophelia, the pretty freshman he made out with last week at Exotic Erotic. He can't attack his mother for remarrying so quickly after his father's death; she's still a majority shareholder in his late father's company, after all, and could revoke his trust fund. Worse, he embarrassed himself in front of the freshman at the smuttiest party on campus all year. Maybe he spilled his beer. So he rips into Ophelia.

"Lady, shall I lie in your lap?" he says. The jibe prompts a round of cruel guffaws and high-fives from his entourage of bros. Ophelia, hurt and humiliated, can't reply as she would like. (Her sassy side is reserved for her brother, Laertes—the only man who gets to see behind Ophelia's façade of respectful obedience.) Hamlet is the president of Sigma Nu, and Ophelia wants to pledge Pi Phi. She knows better than to piss off the most powerful asshole in the Greek system. So she swallows her rage and tries to end the conversation.

"No, my lord," she replies.

Hamlet keeps going.

"I mean, my head *upon* your lap," he exclaims, raising his hands in mock horror, as if Ophelia had imagined him *inside* her, rather than upon her. The Sigma Nu bros snort with laughter. Ophelia shifts uncomfortably in her seat.

"Ay, my lord," she replies. Her eyes are fixed on her latte. But Hamlet won't let it go.

"Do you think I meant country matters?" he says, emphasizing the first syllable of *country* so loudly that heads turn across the room.

Ophelia turns white.

"I think nothing, my lord," she mutters. By now, her protestations are almost inaudible.

Hamlet bends over the table. His face is close to her own.

"That's a fair thought to lie between maids' legs," he snarls.

"What is, my lord?" Ophelia replies. She doesn't realize it, but she just set up Hamlet's big punch line.

"Nothing," he says.

It's a timeless coup de grâce. Ophelia's sexuality is, at once, both "nothing"—nothing valuable, nothing real, nothing worthwhile—and something used to terrorize and humiliate her. It's no mistake that later, when Ophelia becomes insane and incoherent, Gertrude remarks that "her speech is *nothing*" (emphasis mine).

Elaine Showalter, an academic rock star, nailed Ophelia's place within the world of *Hamlet*. "Deprived of thought, sexuality, language," Showalter writes, "Ophelia's story becomes the Story of O—the zero, the empty circle or mystery of feminine difference, the cipher of female sexuality to be deciphered by feminist interpretation." (*The Story of O*, of course, is the landmark 1954 erotic novel about sadomasochism, dominance, and submission.) As I looked across the campus coffee shop at Ophelia that day, I finally understood, for the first time, that my own story of O could just as easily become a story of zero: one of emptiness, dissatisfaction, and nothing.

At the far end of the coffee shop, a door opened. A man walked in and ordered four shots of espresso. My face was pointed at my book, and I didn't see him.

I wish I had looked up. If I had, I would've seen a handsome face obscured by a baseball cap.

STANFORD SEEMED SO damn normal. I longed to fit in on campus. But I feared that the Quality Inn that John and I disappeared into every time he came to town was the place where I truly fit.

"Carolyn and I broke up," Dylan mentioned one afternoon.

"Oh," I replied.

As physical distance and cognitive dissonance chipped away at my relationship with John, my friendship with Dylan only strengthened. I wanted to set him in porcelain. He seemed so perfect—luminous and unfathomable, like the moon. Dylan was handsome, but that wasn't the point. He seemed so *whole,* a shot of organic wheatgrass to John's rotgut whiskey. I had never seen anyone love Shakespeare the way Dylan did. He could devote hours to a single break in iambic pentameter. In that collegiate temple of intellectualism, Dylan's unblemished exterior reflected the version of myself I wanted to see.

But John was the one, wasn't he? If he could understand my dark side so effortlessly, surely he would come to see my light side, too.

Once, when I flew down to Los Angeles for a weekend, I found something unexpected in John's apartment.

"Is this *Twelfth Night*?" I asked, picking up a book and a thin edition of Cliffs Notes from where they'd been scattered on a table.

"You've been talking about it so much lately," John said, with an embarrassed shrug. "I figured I should read the damn thing."

My heart swelled, like Cloudbreak cresting toward the shore. At that moment, holding that thin yellow-and-black bumblebee book, I couldn't imagine my life without John.

And yet, two months later—no, not even that much, not two— there I was in Dylan's dorm room.

"You haven't read *Henry V*?" he said, incredulously. "You haven't even *seen* it?"

"I haven't gotten to that one yet." I laughed.

"Oh, we're taking care of this right now," he said, seriously. He took my wrist.

I looked down at his hand. God, he was so gentle.

We rented a copy of the Kenneth Branagh film at the library, then headed across campus to the history corner of the quad—one of the classrooms there had a large screen that could be used like a private movie theater at night.

"How are things with John?" Dylan asked, as we walked.

I stuffed my hands into the pouch of my sweatshirt and looked down.

"I don't know," I admitted. "The truth is, I have a little crush on someone else."

"Really?" he asked. "Who?"

I shook my head.

"No way," I said. "I'm not telling you."

"Is it a freshman?"

"Wouldn't you like to know," I teased.

"Come on," Dylan said, playfully bumping into my shoulder. "Just tell me one thing about him and I'll leave it alone."

I sighed theatrically.

"Fine," I said. "I like listening to him talk about Shakespeare. Happy?"

I thought I was being subtle. I would've been less obvious with air-traffic-control lights and a runway.

Dylan had stopped walking and fallen behind me. I turned around to look at him.

"Is it . . . me?" he asked. His eyebrows were furrowed.

I laughed and kept walking.

"You promised to leave it alone if I told you one thing," I said. "So leave it alone."

Dylan ran to catch up with me.

"Jillian, is it me?" he said again.

I rolled my eyes.

"It's Stephen Orgel," I said, referring to Stanford's legendary Shakespearean scholar. (At seventy-something years old, Professor Orgel and I would have made an unlikely couple.) "We're star-crossed."

Dylan ran to stand in front of me and put both of his hands on my shoulders.

"Stop walking, Jillian," he said. "Is it me?"

The highlight of *Henry V* is Shakespeare's famous Saint Crispin's Day speech. In the film, Kenneth Branagh, who plays King Henry, stands on a hill and inspires his troops (and his audience) with some of the most stirring lines in the Shakespearean canon. "This story shall the good man teach his son; and Crispin Crispian shall ne'er go by, from this day to the ending of the world, but we in it shall be remembered," he cries. Violins climax in the background.

But I didn't see it. Some things can pull attention away from even the Saint Crispin's Day speech.

Kissing Dylan is one of those things.

The next morning, he appeared at my dorm room with a bouquet.

"You brought me flowers?" I said.

"Of course." Dylan shrugged.

I looked at them.

"They're beautiful," I said. The last thing John had given me was a welt. I was supposed to prefer the flowers.

I leaned over to sniff them.

"Mmm," I recited. "Beautiful!"

And just like that, I was cheating on my boyfriend.

With John, who reminded me of myself, I was free to be raw and uncensored. But Dylan reminded me of the person I longed to be. He seemed as smooth and sweet as refined sugar. I couldn't inflict my real identity on Dylan, so I tried to be someone else—someone normal.

My apparent ability to compartmentalize was frightening. I could spend a week with Dylan at Stanford and a weekend with John in Los Angeles without missing a beat. My brain had one boyfriend and my body had another. I tried to excuse the inexcusable by telling myself that it was just a fling; Dylan would graduate in a few weeks, and I would fully recommit to John. If I were ever to experiment with a more socially normative relationship dynamic, Dylan might be my only chance.

There was one hitch: I had accepted a summer internship in Nicaragua a few months earlier.

"I thought you were going to spend the summer with me," John had said.

"I know," I'd replied. "But I just—well, I feel like I have to see as much of the world as I can before—I mean, you know things might get bad with my disease, right?"

At that, John crumbled like feta.

"Of course, of course," he had said. "You're right. You should go." He was a good man.

I had rationalized my on-campus infidelity in so many ways. I didn't have sex with Dylan, so it didn't count; John had dated me for almost a year under a fabricated identity, so I deserved a big mistake of my own; I had never dated anyone else, so I was entitled to a sip of experience.

But how could I rationalize the fact that only a few weeks into my summer internship, I quit that job and took a bus from Nicaragua to Honduras?

"Happy birthday," Dylan said, with a smile, when I arrived in Tegucigalpa, his hometown. I had turned nineteen a few weeks before.

"It's good to see you," I replied.

Eight days later, in a cheap motel on the Caribbean coastline, I tasted vanilla for the first time. It was safe and sweet, like cotton candy—and like cotton candy, it left me empty and unsatisfied.

Dylan and I went through the motions in Honduras—we watched movies, we went to a play, we hung out with his friends. But something was off.

"My eyes itch," I said once.

"Doth that bode weeping?" Dylan asked.

"What?" I said, annoyed.

"*Othello*," Dylan reminded me.

I had to resist the urge to roll my eyes.

Once, as Dylan and I hiked in the Honduran rain forest, I farted. The accidental display of human biology was humiliating enough by itself, but Dylan's unamused reaction made it worse. It confirmed my suspicions: Dylan wasn't interested in anything that deviated from his script. It was obvious to both of us that, although we valued our friendship and had enjoyed our Stanford fling, we didn't click.

"Did John ever hit you?" Dylan asked me one afternoon as we sat in a café.

I blinked. I had no idea why he'd asked me that. But, knowing me, I'd probably dropped hints.

"What do you mean?" I asked.

"What do you mean, what do I mean?" he said. "It's pretty binary: Did he ever hit you?"

I pulled my legs up onto my chair and stirred my latte with a spoon.

"There's the kind of hitting that's violent, and the kind of hitting that's . . . not violent," I said. "John was never violent. Does that make sense?"

Dylan let that sink in. Then he asked: "Was this a dynamic he wanted, or a dynamic you wanted?" It was a moment of truth.

Of course, Hamlet had to butt in. He took a seat at the table.

"This above all: to thine own self be true," he said, with a smug grin.

"What the hell are you doing in Honduras, Ham?" I asked, rolling my eyes. "And that's not even your line."

"In this play," he smirked, "they're all my lines."

Dylan looked at me, expectantly.

"It was a dynamic I wanted," I admitted.

Dylan's expression changed.

"Honestly, Jillian, that makes me feel sad," he said.

It was a simple remark, said kindly and with compassion. But I bristled. It was my first confrontation with the fact that my sexuality might be judged not on whether it was satisfying to me, but rather on whether it was palatable to men. God forbid my sexuality make Dylan "feel sad."

In *Hamlet*, Shakespeare was right: sexual indifference is a beast. My experiment with vanilla romance had failed. I couldn't survive on food that disappeared so effortlessly on my tongue.

I turned back to Dylan.

"Who cares about John?" I said. "It's not even worth talking about."

Dylan nodded and sipped his coffee. Our fling was over. I knew it; he knew it.

An hour later, I picked up the phone and called California. I hadn't talked to John in a few days.

"Where have you been?" John asked. I shuffled my feet against the floor.

"I've been on a bus," I lied. "From Managua to San Miguel. I'm in El Salvador now."

"El Salvador?" he asked. "Why?"

"I just wanted to see it," I muttered.

"Is *that guy* in El Salvador or something?" John asked. He had been jealous, and suspicious, of Dylan since the beginning of freshman year.

"Do you mean Dylan? He's Honduran, not Salvadoran," I replied. "You know that."

"You didn't answer my question, Jillian," John said.

John and I liked to play with punishment and discipline. But I was never going to tell him why I deserved to be punished for real this time.

"I haven't seen Dylan," I lied. "I assume he's in Tegucigalpa, where his parents live."

"And you're in El Salvador?" John repeated.

Apparently I'm a gambler.

"I'm in a restaurant right now," I said. "I can give the phone to a waitress if you'd like her to confirm it."

I held my breath. Could I convince the barista to validate my lie? What if I paid her?

"That's not necessary," John said. "I'm going to come down there."

"What?" I asked, blinking.

"I'm going to buy a flight and come down there," he repeated. "I want to see you."

My stomach fluttered. I wanted to see him, too.

"I've missed you, John," I told him.

The next day, I wished Dylan good luck with his Ph.D. program, gave him an awkward kiss good-bye, and left Honduras.

There's a beach in El Salvador called La Libertad. It's one of the best right-hand point breaks in Central America. As John surfed there, cutting through the water like a rattlesnake in desert sand, I sat on the rocks and watched him. I had made a mistake.

I would never make that mistake again.

When he finished surfing, John and I bought *pupusas* by the side of road and ate them next to the water.

"I should punish you for quitting your internship so early," John said, wrapping an arm around me. "It's all I thought about during the flight."

I rested my head on his shoulder.

"But if you were still in Managua, we wouldn't get to be here now," John continued. "So I'll cut you some slack—this time." He pressed his lips to the top of my head in a hard, fierce, kiss.

We got back to our hotel, and I stepped into the shower to wash away the saltwater in my hair.

"Where's your aloe vera, bird?" John called from the other room.

"In my backpack," I replied, from the shower. "Check the outer pocket."

"Found it," he said.

I turned off the water, pulled on my underwear, and stepped out of the bathroom, tousling my wet hair with a washcloth. John was standing next to my backpack. His face was pointed away from me. The room felt oddly still and silent.

Then I noticed my passport in his hand.

I froze.

John turned to look at me. His face was still and hard, cut in ice in a way I'd never seen before. Without saying a word, he walked across the room and handed me my passport. It was open to the page where my Honduran entry and exit stamps were clearly marked.

I gazed down at it. I couldn't bring myself to meet John's eyes.

John grabbed my jaw, hard, and forced my face up to look at him. This time, no one was playing.

"What do you have to say for yourself?" he asked. His voice was quiet, but cold.

I heard myself reply, as if from across the room, in a voice I did not recognize:

"I guess this makes me a liar, like you."

I didn't see it happen. I felt it. A second after I spoke, a hard blow flashed across the side of my face. I fell back a few steps, holding my hand to my cheek. The back of John's hand was red.

I was stunned. John had hit me a hundred times before. But this time was different.

He brought his fingers up to his eyes and pressed them into the sockets, as if he had a headache.

"Damn it," he said. "I shouldn't have done that."

I sat on the edge of the bed and stared at my knees.

"I'm sorry," John said, sitting next to me. "Are you okay?"

I shook my head.

"I don't think it matters anymore," I said.

Minutes passed in silence.

"Did he hold you?" John finally asked. His voice was thick and hoarse, just as it had been the first night our better angels gave way to worser spirits.

I looked at John. Did Dylan "hold me"? My heart curled up into itself. Of all the questions John could have asked, that's what he wanted to know.

"Yes," I admitted. "He did."

John nodded.

The death of Ophelia happens offstage. We will never know for sure exactly why she dies. In defiance of artists, readers, academics, and even the other characters in the play, Ophelia simply slips beneath the water: we cannot follow her.

John once told me that when a person drowns, there is a moment of peace before the end. When he was trapped under the water at the Banzai Pipeline, John experienced it himself. He looked up toward the surface, at the oxygen he couldn't reach, and thought how beautiful the sunlight looked as it reflected through the waves.

"I love you, Jillian," John said. "I'll love you forever. You're the love of my life."

His jeans were ripped. There was a big tear over his knee. I picked up a pen from the nightstand and drew a heart in the hole, on his skin.

"No one will ever understand me like you do," I said, pressing my forehead into John's shoulder. He intertwined his fingers with my own, and we locked hands.

The next evening, we flew back to California on separate planes.

When John dumped me, over the phone, three weeks later, I sobbed. I begged him to change his mind. I begged him to give me another chance. I suggested we try an open relationship. I tried every humiliating, degrading tactic I could imagine in my tearful campaign to make him stay.

He refused. He didn't want to be with me. He wanted to be with someone else. Apparently I wasn't the only one who had explored other options that spring.

When pleasure and pain disappear, there are no feelings left. John ended the call, and I stopped crying. I tried to guess how many showers John had taken since the last time I saw him. More than twenty, probably. I thought about the little heart I had drawn on his knee. I wondered how many showers it survived before it washed away in all that water.

3.2   Twelfth Night:
What Should I Do

At the beginning of *Twelfth Night*, Viola survives a shipwreck and washes ashore in a foreign land.

"What country, friends, is this?" she asks, and learns that she is in Ilyria.

"And what should I do in Ilyria?" she replies.

What she does is disguise herself as a male castrato, seemingly devoid of sexual impulses, named Cesario. Her sexuality poses a risk in this foreign country, so Viola tries to get rid of it.

She can't, of course. Behind her disguise, she's still a woman. She's still herself. She is still able to fall in love—and she does.

Almost a year had passed since John had dumped me.

For the first few months, I disappeared. I buried myself in night shifts as an Olive Garden hostess. Between work and classes, I had little time to think or feel anything at all.

"Welcome to Olive Garden. How many in your party?"

"Welcome to Olive Garden. How many in your party?"

"Welcome to Olive Garden. How many in your party?"

The highlight of every day was just before bed. That's when I got to write "NJ" on the corner of my calendar, as a reward for resisting the temptation to call John for another day. "NJ" meant "No John," but it could have stood for "No Jillian." For those months, I just wasn't there.

After my calendar had filled with almost a hundred tiny "NJs," I tried to wake myself up. I went on first dates with classmates (both male and female; I'd known since high school that either was fine with me) but rarely a second. I spent enough time at a dungeon in San Francisco to realize that although BDSM is a broad term that includes spanking obsessives, like me, we also belong to different subcultures, with different aesthetic styles and mind-sets. I fit in at that dungeon only as well as a gay man might at a lesbian bar: we could relate, but it wasn't my place. For a brief phase, I wondered if I might be asexual, since spanking mattered to me so much more than anything formally recognized as "sex." I even hooked up with a classmate and her boyfriend one night, hoping that the triumvirate might remind me how feelings felt. But I discovered only that three scoops of vanilla interest me no more than two.

So, just as I had done at seventeen, I fled. First, to Oxford, where weekly twenty-page essay assignments for that Shakespearean cartographer helped me pass the time in a numb fog. Then, when Stanford gave me a grant to do honors thesis research abroad, I "stopped out" of college (albeit with the full intention of someday going back) and moved to Oman.

Oman, like Arizona, is a desert. It's hard to see the water in its earth.

I wanted to dry out, too. Over the previous year, the wounds from my twin failures—my failure to find vanilla satisfaction with Dylan and failure to find sadomasochistic sanity with John—had cauterized. Obviously, I was fucked up. I was a toxic person fishing for love in a radioactive pond. I felt hard and indifferent.

Love was shit. Sex was shit. Shakespeare—well, Shakespeare was too wrapped up with sex for me to separate the two, so Shakespeare was shit by association.

And spanking? Good grief, fuck that, forget that, forget me. Forget all of it. I'd be a castrato, too.

Besides, I had a new dominant in my life.

"No," Sabihah snapped, when she saw me in the hallway one morning on my way to Arabic class. "You can't wear that."

I looked down at myself. I was wearing a black abaya, just like almost every other woman in the country.

"What's wrong, Auntie?" I asked.

"Those sunglasses," she replied. "They are *ugly*. Go put on the other ones."

I suppressed a grin.

"Yes, Auntie," I replied.

Oman has close ties to Tanzania: in fact, the capital of the Omani empire used to be the Tanzanian island of Zanzibar. To this day, there is a huge Swahili-speaking Zanzibari community in Muscat. My apartment was in a predominantly Zanzibari neighborhood called al-Azaiba, where a few words of basic Swahili would be more useful than my broken Arabic. One afternoon, on a mission to better understand my neighbors, I went with two friends to a bookstore to pick up a Swahili-to-Arabic dictionary to supplement my Arabic-to-English one.

As I browsed the shelves, a large group of young Omani men walked into the store and headed for the stationery section. The two women I was with, both Omani, pulled black niqabs over their faces to conceal themselves from the men. Laughing, they began to quiz me to see if I could tell them apart with their faces covered.

I chuckled with them, but I was startled past genuine mirth. There is a scene in *Twelfth Night* in which two women, Olivia and Maria, cover their faces to confuse and tease a messenger. In Oman, I thought I could hide from Shakespeare, and every other part of myself. But he had tracked me down in this accidental Omani performance of *Twelfth Night*.

Shakespeare exists everywhere on earth. It was futile to resist him.

In Muscat, there's an upscale neighborhood called Shatti al-Qurm. It has a restaurant with beautiful *nargile* pipes and, most nights, live music. I slid into a seat at a table next to a familiar face.

"Welcome back," Duke Orsino, Viola's crush from *Twelfth Night*, said.

We ordered some mint-flavored *shisha* and settled in for the night. Orsino listened to the music, nodding with approval.

"If music be the food of love, play on," he said. "Give me excess of it, that, surfeiting, the appetite may sicken, and so die."

I nodded and slid the hookah across the table to him. Orsino inhaled a long stream of smoke as the musician's song reached a tragic crescendo. Its effect on Orsino was immediate: his eyes teared, his cheeks flushed, and he sat up straighter.

"That strain again!" he called out to the musicians.

"It had a dying fall," Orsino explained, turning back to me. "O, it came o'er my ear like the sweet sound that breathes upon a bank of violets."

"Slide the hookah back over here," I replied.

And that's how I entered my twenties: languishing with Orsino in a haze of sexual dissatisfaction, self-pity, and hookah smoke.

Until one night when I wandered into the desert and met a goat and a girl, and the fog began to clear.

Twelfth Night is so hot.

If Shakespeare was determined to derail my mission to unsex myself in Oman, he could not have chosen a better play than *Twelfth Night*. It touches my specific erotic quirks to an absurd degree.

After Viola washes ashore in Ilyria and disguises herself as a man named Cesario, she gets a job as a servant to Duke Orsino.

It's the relationship between Orsino and "Cesario" that slays me. I can't get enough of it. They have such an immediate connection that after only three days, Orsino tells Cesario: "I have unclasp'd to thee the book even of my secret soul."

As I mentioned, I've always been *seriously* drawn to platonic relationships between men that include a disciplinary element of power imbalance. It's a problem: there is no clear stand-in for me in my own fantasies! So it makes sense that I adore *Twelfth Night*. In Orsino's relationship with Cesario, Shakespeare solved my dilemma: it's a platonic male-male relationship—in which a woman gets to participate!

On top of that, she's his servant! At one point, *he scolds her*! And—

Excuse me, I need to go . . . run a bath.

But behind *Twelfth Night*'s amazing (and, I concede, very specific) erotic potential, there is an undercurrent of tragedy. Viola is mourning the presumed death of her twin brother, Sebastian, from whom she got separated during the shipwreck. Duke Orsino is in love with a woman named Olivia, who is mourning a dead brother, too. Romantic affection in *Twelfth Night* is, for the most part, unrequited: Viola wants Duke Orsino, who wants Olivia. Malvolio, a steward in Olivia's household, also longs for Olivia. And if you ask me, Antonio, the sea captain who rescued Sebastian from the shipwreck, seems to have more-than-platonic affection for the man he saved. In *Twelfth Night*, everyone is longing for something.

I was longing for something, too. I just didn't know what that was.

I began to lurk around the English department at Sultan Qaboos University (SQU) in Muscat. I wanted to weasel my way into a Shakespeare class and listen to Omani students share their interpretations of some of Shakespeare's most famous plays. There was nothing innovative about my plan. People all over the world, from a wide variety of backgrounds, have found ourselves in Shakespeare. The Arab world is no different. Shakespeare made his Middle Eastern debut in 1884, when the first Arabic translation of *Othello* was performed in Cairo. That production sparked a widespread interest in the region in Shakespearean literature, and inaugural Arabic productions of *Hamlet* and *Romeo and Juliet* soon followed.

"In Shakespeare, there is doubtless something Arabic," wrote the celebrated Lebanese poet Khalil Mutran. "Has he read our language or was it transmitted to him in some accurate translation? I don't know. But between him and us there are puzzling and numerous common features. . . . On the whole, there is in the writing of Shakespeare a Bedouin spirit which is expressed in the continuous return to innate nature."

Mutran was not the only person to sense a "Bedouin spirit" in Shakespeare's work. Iraqi scholar Safa Khulusi argued for the "Arabness" of Shakespeare, and the Lebanese writer Ahmad Faris al-Shidyaq even claimed that Shakespeare was actually an Arab man named "Sheik Zubayr." The Algerian scholar Nasib Nashawi drew comparisons between *Othello* and a similar work by the Syrian poet Dik al-Jinn, and even questioned whether Shakespeare might have had access to al-Jinn's work. These connections were also recognized outside of the Middle East: Anthony Burgess, for example, theorized that an Arab woman was the "Dark Lady" of the sonnets, and Frances Yates argued that Shakespeare had read Latin translations of Arab science.

But although scholars in the Arabic-speaking world have drawn parallels between their own cultures and Shakespeare's literature for a long time, there is also a long history of white people stomping around the world on campaigns to culturally dominate the planet. One British colonial officer described the intent to suppress Indian culture by forming "a class of persons Indian in blood and color, but English in taste, in opinions, words and intellect." The world doesn't need more attention paid to yet another white guy from the most dominant colonial power in history, right? *The Complete Works of William Shakespeare* has been translated into more languages than any other book except the Bible; it does not suffer from underexposure, to say the least. Literature can empower, but it can also oppress and suppress. I worried that I was a virus, parachuting into a foreign country for a bit of literary-themed cultural tourism.

After I begged my way into the student body of an SQU Shakespeare class, more challenges emerged. Language differences were the first problem, of course. Shakespeare's English can be difficult even for native speakers to understand. The Omani students, all of whom spoke Arabic or Swahili at home and had learned English as a second or third language, struggled through Shakespeare's unfamiliar words. But the language barrier wasn't my biggest problem.

My biggest problem was that the women thought I was a spy.

Specifically, one woman, Khalila al-Khatib, thought I was a spy. She shared her theory with her classmates.

"The girls say it's okay for you to sit in on classes," their Shakespeare professor told me, with an apologetic smile. "But they won't talk to you. They don't trust you."

It was an intense time to be an American in the Middle East. The United States had invaded Iraq only three years earlier, and photos of torture at Abu Ghraib, reports of abuse at Guantánamo Bay, and the mounting civilian death toll in Iraq had provoked outrage around the world. Omani men and women are hospitable and friendly, and only one person ever questioned me about my political beliefs while I lived there. But no one forgot my nationality. I wasn't just a person who wanted to ask conservative Muslim women about their romantic lives: I was an *American* who wanted to ask conservative Muslim women about their romantic lives.

Therefore, of course, I was a spy. No one wanted to talk to me.

Then one afternoon, when I was leaving SQU to go home, I strolled into an elevator and hit the button to go downstairs.

The elevator reached the ground floor, and the doors opened.

Khalila was on the other side, leaning against a rail with her arms folded across her chest. She tipped her chin down to peer at me from above her black sunglasses.

"You do realize you've been riding the men's elevator all day, right?" she said.

Oh.

After that, the spy rumor disappeared. With Khalila's endorsement, I was no longer a threat; I was just a dumb foreigner.

It was easy to see why Khalila was so popular with the group. She had boundless energy, laughing and telling stories and joking about handsome boys on campus. Unlike most of the students in her Shakespeare class, Khalila's family was Zanzibari and spoke Swahili at home. She shrieked and clapped her hands with delight when I surprised her with some of the Swahili phrases I'd picked up in al-Azaiba.

"You want to know about love, I think," Khalila once teased me, smiling. "Maybe that is why you come here to talk about stories of love." With a grin, I reminded her that she was taking the same class about "stories of love." She laughed.

Every woman I interviewed gave me permission, in writing, to use her remarks both in my undergraduate honors thesis and in any subsequent writing I might do. I also protected each woman with pseudonyms. Gradually, my fears about the potential negative cultural impact of this work ebbed, more or less. The women who volunteered to talk with me were truly enthusiastic. Their love for Shakespeare was familiar and undeniable. More than once, text messages appeared on my phone in the middle of the night to report some midnight epiphany about incest in *Hamlet* or intercultural marriage in *Othello*. The Omani students and I were all citizens of Shakespeare's world; his was our shared language.

We focused on three plays: *Hamlet, Romeo and Juliet,* and *Othello.* From the beginning, it was obvious that Khalila and the other Omani women understood the major female characters— Ophelia, Juliet, and Desdemona—on a more intimate level than I could. For example, when Juliet must choose between the man she loves (Romeo) and the man her parents want her to marry (Paris), the Omani women could directly relate to Juliet's dilemma. Most of them had to choose between arranged marriages and "love marriages" in their own lives, too. I understood Shakespeare's English language with native proficiency, but the Omani women understood Shakespeare's *cultural* language with native proficiency. It was a perfect fit.

WHEN VIOLA FIRST decides to seek employment in Duke Orsino's court, she boasts that she will be able to "speak to him in many sorts of music"—and that's exactly what she does. Viola, still in disguise, can't describe her love for Orsino directly. So she invents a sister who doesn't exist to hum the love song Viola cannot sing:

VIOLA
My father had a daughter loved a man,
As it might be, perhaps, were I a woman,
I should your lordship.

DUKE ORSINO
And what's her history?

VIOLA
A blank, my lord. She never told her love,
But let concealment, like a worm i' the bud,
Feed on her damask cheek: she pined in thought,
And with a green and yellow melancholy
She sat like patience on a monument,

Smiling at grief. Was not this love indeed?
We men may say more, swear more: but indeed
Our shows are more than will; for still we prove
Much in our vows, but little in our love.

DUKE ORSINO
But died thy sister of her love, my boy?

VIOLA
I am all the daughters of my father's house,
And all the brothers too: and yet I know not.

Viola's body isn't the only thing that needs a disguise: her speech does, too. She can't tell Orsino that she loves him, so she describes her feelings through this made-up sister.

My Omani friends and I did the same thing. Shakespeare was a vehicle we could use to talk about love, sex, marriage, and romance—subjects which otherwise would have been taboo. Direct conversations were out of the question. Whenever I asked Omani friends a question about romance—or, God forbid, sex—they usually changed the subject. But Shakespeare was the perfect way to circumvent cultural norms and talk about sex.

And I do mean *sex*. Shakespeare was not born in a puritanical time. In *Twelfth Night*, Malvolio reads a letter that he believes was written by Olivia, the woman he loves. To prove his theory, he analyzes her handwriting. Imagine his words read aloud, as Shakespeare intended them to be heard (emphases mine):

MALVOLIO
By my life, this is my lady's hand. These be her very
C**'s, her **U**'s, a**Nd** her **T**'s, and **thus she makes her
***great P's**. It is, in contempt of question, her hand.*

In case anyone missed the joke, Shakespeare repeats it in Sir Andrew's next line:

SIR ANDREW

Her C's, her U's, aNd her T's: why's that?

Twelfth Night is not the only play with a Shakespearean cunt pun: as I mentioned before, when Hamlet speaks of "*count*ry matters," it's no coincidence. Shakespearean literature is so bawdy that in the eighteenth and nineteenth centuries, some critics tried to distance themselves from its dirty side. In fact, they even tried to distance *Shakespeare* from the dirty side of Shakespeare, claiming that his lewd jokes were mere concessions to the groundlings—members of Shakespeare's audience who couldn't afford a seat, but could afford to pay one penny to stand in the yard—as if low income somehow correlates with "low" taste. "Shakespeare should not be put into the hands of the young without the warning that the foolish things in his plays were written to please the foolish, the filthy for the filthy, the brutal for the brutal," wrote an early-twentieth-century poet laureate, Robert Bridges.

If there was any way for a masochistic self-declared castrato to swap cunt jokes with conservative virgins in the Islamic world, Shakespeare was it. Shakespeare is "safe." He's a way to talk about sex without talking about sex. Omani women, like young people everywhere, have strong opinions about love and romance. They just wanted a comfortable way to share them. And in Shakespeare, we had found a way to talk about everything.

"Okay," Khalila finally said, when she approached me one day after class. "Let's talk."

A FEW DAYS later, Khalila and I sat with Soraya, her best friend, in an SQU courtyard. I drank an iced coffee. Khalila and Soraya fought.

Does *Romeo and Juliet* prove the value of Western-style love marriages, as Khalila believed? Or does it prove the value of Omani-style arranged marriages—Soraya's take?

"You're wrong!" Khalila shouted, slapping her hand against the table for emphasis. "Love marriage is much better. Sometimes parents will pick the right husband for you, but sometimes they won't. How can we know whether Juliet would have loved Paris? We don't!"

"But Juliet dies!" Soraya screeched. "Everyone dies! How can you say it is right for her to choose Romeo when everyone dies?"

For Soraya, this debate was personal.

In many ways, Soraya resembled the other girls in the Shakespeare class. She loved fashion, and often wore the stylish embroidered abayas that were popular among young women our age. (My own abaya was embroidered, too.) Despite her devout modesty, Soraya chose not to cover her gorgeous face behind a niqab. Her glasses, she thought, would be enough to hide her beauty from men. Still, she was protective of her virtue, and even missed classes whenever her driver could not bring her to campus. (As a single woman, she refused to take public transportation.) But Soraya and I had a lot in common. We both loved to travel. We both loved theater. And we both loved *Othello,* the play in which Soraya saw herself more than any other in the Shakespearean canon.

When Soraya was twenty years old, a male acquaintance from SQU approached her father to ask for her hand in marriage. Soraya had never dated the man; in fact, she had never even been alone with him. Their only exchanges had been brief, at chaperoned coed university classes and events. But Soraya was eager to marry him. Many of her friends had already found husbands, and Soraya felt ready to enjoy the special privileges and freedoms reserved for married women in Oman. She wanted to go out to dinners with her husband, move away from her parents' house, and have a first kiss. Above all, she wanted to fall in love—an experience that Soraya, like many Omani men and women, believed is possible only *after* marriage.

But Soraya's father unequivocally rejected the proposal. Her suitor was educated, from a good family, and a Muslim; in other words, he satisfied most of her father's conditions. But he was Omani. Despite Soraya's similarities to Omani girls her age, she, like Othello, was originally from North Africa. Soraya and her potential husband shared a common language and religion, but Soraya's father insisted that only an Algerian compatriot could marry his daughter. Like Brabantio, Desdemona's father, he wanted a husband from his own culture for his only child. Unlike Desdemona, however, Soraya accepted her father's decision—and she didn't regret it. In *Othello*, she had seen conclusive proof that intercultural marriages can't work.

Soraya leaned back in her chair and glared at Khalila.

"You can't just pick your own husband," she said, in a serious tone of voice. "This is why Juliet ends up dead; Ophelia ends up dead; Desdemona ends up dead. What do they all have in common? None of them listened to their fathers. You can't marry someone if your family doesn't approve."

"Well, I can't marry someone if *I* don't approve," Khalila replied. "Love is dangerous, but I think that's how love has to be sometimes. Love is a miracle."

Soraya rolled her eyes.

"You sound like an American," she said, derisively.

I looked up from my notebook and protested. "Hey!"

Soraya pointed at me.

"I've seen your American movies," she said. "You people are too obsessed with sex, but you tell yourselves that it's passion. You don't think about the important things—family, home, life. You don't think for the future."

"What about love?" I asked her.

"What *about* love?" Soraya snorted. "Love is simple: you find a good man, and you love him for the rest of your life. Haven't you read any of these plays you're always talking about?"

"Sex matters, too, Soraya," I pointed out, fiddling with the straw in my coffee.

She shrugged.

"So find a good man and figure it out," she said. "You're not dead yet."

That was true. It's so easy to forget sometimes.

"You don't think love is a miracle?" I asked.

"I think love is a *choice*," Soraya answered, with a nod.

Did Soraya have a point? Had I missed a message in Shakespeare's love stories? Was love a choice—something that I could leap, not fall, into?

Khalila rolled her eyes.

"Choice, choice," she scoffed. "Who sounds like an American now?"

As I continued to discuss Shakespeare with Soraya, Khalila, and the other women in the class, a fascinating pattern emerged. Despite what Western stereotypes had led me to expect, most of the Omani students seemed to think that the female characters were superior to the male characters, specifically because of their gender. They praised Juliet, Desdemona, and Ophelia for their "feminine" qualities, such as intelligence, practicality, and foresight. (Juliet's insistence that an honorable "bent of love" wait for marriage, in particular, seriously impressed them.) Meanwhile, they dismissed Romeo, Othello, and Hamlet as stupid, impractical, impulsive, irrational, and emotional—in other words, they said, typically "male." But despite their praise and admiration for the female characters, and their disdain for the male ones, the students ultimately blamed the women for the tragic endings of the plays. Even Desdemona, who dies when her husband, Othello, strangles her in her bed, was held responsible for her own death.

"You must understand, Othello cannot control his jealousy. It is his nature as a man to be jealous," said Zahra al-Hassan, another student in the class, when I asked her who is to blame for the tragedy of *Othello*. "The question that occupies me is, why wasn't Desdemona more aware? She should have investigated more, noticed more."

In all three plays, the women agreed, the male characters—and men in general—are the victims of their inherent gender flaws. But their firm belief that women are "superior," to my surprise, didn't empower the female characters at all. It just put higher expectations—and therefore greater responsibility and culpability—in their hands. Almost all of them criticized the female characters for failing to capitalize on the gifts inherent to their gender. Khalila best articulated the judgment that fell on Juliet, Desdemona, and Ophelia: "She should have known better."

But there was one exception: Najla al-Shadi, a girl with sunken eyes who never spoke up during class.

It infuriates me when people paint all of Shakespeare's transvestite female characters with the same brush. Male clothing no more makes Viola the same as Rosalind, the fierce character who disguises herself as a man in *As You Like It*, than male clothing makes Falstaff the same as Romeo. Rosalind is a troublemaker. She's fierce and uninhibited. In disguise, Rosalind finds freedom and a voice. But Viola's disguise is merely a way to hide herself. (Anne Barton points out that, for Viola, the Cesario persona "operates not as a liberation but merely as a way of going underground in a difficult situation.")

Twelfth Night is a comedy, so I understand why so many actresses play Viola as if they were playing Rosalind: brash, energetic, and confident. But, someday, I would love to see Viola played as she describes herself: "patience on a monument, smiling at grief"—scared, suppressed, and, above all, as still as a statue.

People make the same absurd mistake with Omani women. Their clothing (the outer layers of clothing that we can see, that is) is alike, so those women are often described as if they were interchangeable. But Najla al-Shadi was as different from Khalila, in personality, experience, and literary perspectives, as Rosalind is from Viola.

For weeks, she had listened from a distance to my conversations with the others (which drifted away from *Hamlet* and toward recent episodes of *The O.C.* more often than I'm proud to admit). She never jumped in to contribute.

"You should talk to me," Najla finally said, one afternoon, in a low voice. "I'll tell you the truth."

Najla had grown up near Sur, a small fishermen's town on the eastern Omani coastline. Sur isn't as diverse as Muscat, and has a rural propensity toward conservativeness. While most women in Muscat only cover their hair and necks, most women in Sur cover their entire faces, even their eyes, with thin black fabric. Najla explained that this was how she used to be able to recognize other girls on campus from her home region, without even speaking to them. But after some boys disguised with face veils managed to sneak into the girls' on-campus dormitory, she told me, SQU prohibited female students from covering their faces, and Najla was forced to remove her niqab at school. Her face was expressive and serious as she told me about her discomfort during the first weeks after that rule was enforced.

Najla had come to SQU to study mathematics, a discipline that she told me runs through her veins "like blood." But the circumstances by which she had transferred from the math department to the Shakespeare seminar were not good. When her father learned that Najla shared her coeducational math classes with male colleagues, he forced her to switch to the all-female Shakespeare class. When Najla resisted, begging her father to let her stay in the math department, he whipped her.

"There is a proverb, 'love is blind,' and Ophelia is blind to what these men do to her," Najla told me. "My sister loves her husband even though he beats her. He doesn't care if she is pregnant or not, if she is sick or not. He tells her she cannot go to our parents' house. But she loves him, even though these things happen. She doesn't see that he is cruel and selfish. Do you see how love is blind?"

The expression "love is blind"—which Najla called a proverb, but also happens to be a line from *The Merchant of Venice*—is appropriate in Oman, where arranged marriages are so common. On rare occasions, the bride and groom are not able to meet even once before the wedding ceremony, so, in a sense, the betrothed couple is blinded by circumstance. Considering Najla's rural background, it was unusual that at twenty-three she was still unmarried. But given other details of her background, her reluctance to commit herself to a husband made sense.

"I relate to Ophelia, because she is a victim," she told me. "Ophelia is a toy in the hand of her father and her brother. I know I am giving you a bad story of our culture, but men abuse their wives and daughters. It is a fact. They abuse women."

I didn't know what to say. "I'm sorry, Najla," I murmured. "You deserve better."

"It's terrible that people can just beat your body, and there's no way to stop it," she muttered. "It's the worst thing. Do you know what that's like?"

My neck tightened.

"No, I don't," I replied.

It was a lie. I felt sick and uncomfortable.

Najla nodded.

"Oh," she said, simply.

I shifted in my seat.

"Najla," I began, and then stopped. My tape recorder was looking at us. I turned it off.

"You—you're so smart," I told her. I didn't know what else to say.

She shook her head.

"I'm afraid to get married," she said. "I don't want to live like my sister."

I swallowed.

"You said that love is blind, Najla," I replied. "But *you* are not blind. You see things very clearly. You will know what to do."

Najla nodded dispassionately.

"Do you want to go to a movie or something?" I asked. "Do you want to just forget all this and go have fun?"

"No," she replied. "I want to be heard. I want you to hear me."

I nodded. "I'm listening," I said.

She pointed at my tape recorder.

"Are you recording?" she asked.

"Oh," I said, looking down at it. "I turned it off just now. I thought—"

"Turn it back on," she ordered. "What's your next question?"

So it was only Najla, with the sad eyes and casual references to abuse, who refused to blame Ophelia when I asked her who is responsible for *Hamlet*'s tragic end. She considered the question for a long time—so long, in fact, that I was tempted to repeat myself when she suddenly spoke.

"Polonius," Najla declared—Ophelia's father. "Polonius makes the tragedy. But Ophelia, perhaps, should have freed herself more." When I asked Najla if she considered herself free, she sighed and did not answer.

Najla's passion for Ophelia, and the conviction with which she volunteered comparisons between herself and Shakespeare's undervalued heroine, were very powerful. But I want to stress that Najla was unique among the Shakespeare students at SQU; the experience she described fits many unfair and often inaccurate stereotypes about women in the Middle East. Unlike Soraya and Khalila, who loved their families and had huge amounts of self-confidence, Najla had endured an abusive past and steeled herself to accept an abusive future. She is *not* representative of the many fulfilled women I met in Oman. In the only photo I have of her, Najla is a small, unsmiling slip of hurt.

But Ophelia is as unique among her peers as Najla is unique among hers. She is not like Rosalind or Cleopatra or Lady Macbeth or Juliet: Ophelia exists only in the shadow of the play she inhabits. As uncomfortable as I am with anything that seems to support a stereotype, I can't ignore Najla any more than I can ignore Ophelia. Both women say something to me about the pain humans can bear. Even in the final moments of her life, before she disappears beneath the water, Ophelia shuts out the brutality of what she has suffered and gathers flowers.

Weeks after I finished my final interviews, Najla called and asked to see me again. When I returned to SQU to meet her, Najla said that she had been thinking about me and about our conversations. She said that, early on, she hadn't understood why I wanted to study Shakespeare in, of all places, Oman. She couldn't imagine why I traveled across the planet to join her Shakespeare class—especially since she never wanted to join the class herself. But finally, she told me, she had figured out the reason I came to Oman to talk about Shakespeare.

"Could you tell me why I did?" I asked, with a laugh. "I'm not sure I know myself."

"Write it down," she told me. "This is important."

I pulled out my notebook.

"In Oman, we are Ophelia. Our fathers and brothers do not hear us," Najla said, choosing her words deliberately. "I want to be Claudius. I want to utter more loudly. I want to face this world."

A few hours later, I sent Najla one last text message. It was a quote from Emilia, a woman in *Othello* who refuses to be silent even under threat of death:

> *'Twill out, 'twill out! I peace?*
> *No, I will speak as liberal as the north:*
> *Let heaven and men and devils, let them all,*
> *All, all, cry shame against me, yet I'll speak.*

—*Othello*, 5.2

"Yes," she wrote back. "We must remember those words, you and I."

IN MY LAST few weeks in Oman, as I geared up to return to Stanford and finish my degree, I got an email from the president of my college Shakespeare club.

"Some new members joined while you've been gone," she wrote. "Connect with them on Facebook, okay?"

I scrolled through the list of faces. They all seemed friendly enough, but one profile photo stopped me cold. In it, a handsome but unsmiling man flipped off the camera from beneath the brim of a frayed baseball cap. Next to his photo, in the status update section, he had written: "O God, I could be bounded in a nutshell and count myself the king of infinite space, were it not that I have bad dreams." It was from *Hamlet*.

I knew exactly how he felt.

"You and I haven't met yet, but I can already tell that you're a very good addition to Shakes," I wrote to him in a message.

"It'll be nice to finally meet you when you come back!" the man replied.

Flourish. Enter David, a man.

I would say that's how, in the same Internet café where I had broken my self-imposed prohibition on kink a few months earlier, I met the love of my life. But that's not quite true. In a sense, I'd met him years before. I just didn't know it yet.

"Journeys end in lovers' meeting," a love song in *Twelfth Night* declares.

Journeys begin that way, too.

3.3 Love's Labor's Lost:
Wonder of the World

In *Love's Labor's Lost,* the King of Navarre and his three men, Berowne, Longaville, and Dumaine, commit themselves to self-neglect in pursuit of scholarship. For three years, they vow to avoid food, sleep, and the company of women.

It's a doomed mission. Their oath of celibacy dissolves the second the Princess of France arrives to conduct business in Navarre, accompanied by three women of her own: Rosaline, Maria, and Katharine. The numbers (and attractions) are a perfect match. Soon, everyone is in love. In Shakespeare, affections overpower oaths. The play ends with a cliffhanger: a messenger arrives to tell the Princess of France that her father has died, and the women prepare to return home—with the expectation that their loves will find them again in one year.

Montaigne argued that "the good that comes of study (or at least should come) is to prove better, wiser, honester"—in other words, that the value of a person's education is measured by her character. Montaigne's writings are believed to have inspired Shakespeare: his essay "Of Cannibals" is seen as a major influence on *The Tempest*—so much so that some people believe *Caliban* is an anagram of *cannibal*. Perhaps Montaigne influenced *Love's Labor's Lost*, too, showing that the pursuit of scholarship is meaningless if it doesn't enrich our lives.

I decided to learn from the king and his men's mistake. I would not invest in scholarship and lose myself.

So when I returned to campus and ran into David, that handsome new guy in my Shakespeare club, outside the athletic center one afternoon, I knew exactly how I wanted to flirt with him.

"Nice belt," I teased, pointing at the red canvas accessory around his jeans.

"I have a leather one, too," David replied.

What was that? Ever since I circled every *M* word in *The Tempest*, years before, I'd been searching for clues in Shakespeare's language. Perhaps it was inevitable that, when faced with a new question, I also searched for clues in sexual language. And something in David's words gave me pause.

I stopped moving and watched him. Was that a hint?

LOVE AT FIRST sight does exist.

I can't believe that I believe that. I'm not a mushy romantic. I've never seen *The Notebook*. I've forgotten my own anniversaries more times than I've remembered them. I don't believe in ghosts. I don't believe in Bigfoot. I don't believe the Earl of Oxford wrote the plays attributed to William Shakespeare.

But I do believe in love at first sight. How the hell did that one slip through?

I can only defend this lapse of pragmatism with the fact that some of my favorite friends agree. Aristophanes, in his theory of love from the *Symposium*, wrote that in the miraculous event that a person finds his or her other half—the same half she was ripped away from when the gods split every essence into two bodies— she knows it. "When one of them meets with his other half, the actual half of himself . . . the pair are lost in an amazement of love and friendship and intimacy, and one will not be out of the other's sight, as I may say, even for a moment," Aristophanes argued. "These are the people who pass their whole lives together, and yet they could not explain what they desire of one another." And Dostoevsky, in the first of his novels that I read—*Crime and Punishment,* of course—wrote: "We sometimes encounter people, even perfect strangers, who begin to interest us at first sight, somehow suddenly, all at once, before a word has been spoken."

Many of Shakespeare's characters give themselves up to love in less time than it takes me to order in restaurants. In *As You Like It*, Shakespeare, quoting Christopher Marlowe, asked: "Who ever loved that loved not at first sight?"

The most fascinating moment in *Love's Labor's Lost* hints at a mystery of love at first sight. Rosaline and Berowne, the most prominent pair of the play's four sets of lovers, apparently have a history that predates the timeline of the play. (Shakespeare often hints at intriguing yet indecipherable backstories to his plays.) How do they know each other? Shakespeare gives us only small clues. Here's their first conversation:

BEROWNE

Did not I dance with you in Brabant once?

ROSALINE

Did not I dance with you in Brabant once?

BEROWNE

I know you did.

ROSALINE

How needless was it then to ask the question!

I have no idea what to make of this moment. Berowne and Rosaline know each other—and on such an intimate level that they can banter this way—but how? Shakespeare teases us with this riddle, but leaves us few clues with which to answer it. Earlier, when the Princess of France asks about the men who accompany the King of Navarre, Rosaline tells her that Berowne is a great guy:

ROSALINE
Another of these students at that time
Was there with him, if I have heard a truth.
Berowne they call him, but a merrier man,
Within the limit of becoming mirth,
I never spent an hour's talk withal.

It seems as if they know each other well. But later, Berowne asks a nobleman, Boyet, about Rosaline, as if he doesn't know her name:

BEROWNE
What's her name in the cap?

BOYET
Rosaline, by good hap.

BEROWNE
Is she wedded or no?

BOYET
To her will, sir, or so.

If Berowne "danced" with Rosaline "in Brabant once," why does he not know (or remember) her name?

It's possible that "dance with you in Brabant" is a sexual double entendre, referring to a one-night stand. According to Gordon Williams, an authority on sexual language in Shakespearean literature, "dancing schools" may have been slang for brothels at the time. And during Shakespeare's life, Brabant was located in the Netherlands. (The *nether lands*. Get it?) There's something rather romantic about the possibility that Berowne and Rosaline had a torrid one-night stand. He didn't even learn her name—which would explain why he asks Boyet for that information—but each was so struck by the tryst that they remembered each other, and hungered to meet again. That said, as much as I love the dirty side of Shakespeare, I've always been reluctant to see this moment as something carnal. I prefer the notion that Berowne and Rosaline shared a (literal) dance in the (literal) Netherlands.

In either case, I love that exchange. I love its implication that some people, even without effort, always circle back into one another's lives.

Did not I dance with you in Brabant once?

A few weeks after I returned to Stanford, I invited some friends from the Shakespeare club back to my dorm room for a nightcap.

To be honest, I just wanted an excuse to hang out with David.

From the first second we had met, I had a crush on him. As we became friends, I learned the basics of his background: David had grown up on a sunflower farm in rural North Dakota. He wanted to be a doctor. He had joined the Shakespeare club at the encouragement of his roommate, Kyle, who worried that David never had fun, because on top of his premed classwork, David had four part-time jobs.

David and I flirted every time we hung out. (Certainly, the comment about his leather belt had intrigued me.) But he was dating a girl named Alex.

Anyway, I insisted to myself, David was all wrong for me. I couldn't stay in one place; David had never applied for a passport. Even the small details didn't align: I loved tofu; David had never tried it.

That night, as we all drank our beers, we launched into a conversation about past relationships. Everyone was twenty or twenty-one years old, so none of us had much experience, but we liked to think we did. At eighteen months, my relationship with John seemed long.

"Actually, my longest relationship was four years," David said.

"Wow," someone exclaimed. "That's amazing! What's the story there?"

David shrugged.

"It's not amazing," he said. "It was a weird situation. Her father was my high school principal. And after my mom died, he became—well, he became my foster guardian. Small towns, you know. So that relationship lasted a lot longer than it would have otherwise."

My throat closed.

I remembered sitting on a stoop outside an apartment complex in Seville, waiting for John. I'd just left an Internet café, where I had read a story that I couldn't forget. A boy in rural America was living in foster care with his high school principal, after his mother died of MS and his alcoholic father became violent. He worried about paying for college. I had imagined him with a baseball cap.

Did not I dance with you in Brabant once?

The conversation had moved on.

"You wrote that thing," I said to David, interrupting the others.

"What?" he asked.

I shook my head. "Nothing," I said, too loudly. "I'm tired. You all have to leave."

It was rude and abrupt, but I didn't care. Adrenaline was rushing through my veins. My heart pounded. I wanted to run, and I never run.

I stood up and opened my door.

"Bye," I said. My friends looked confused.

"Bye," I repeated, as they filed out. My hands shook.

I closed the door behind my friends and leaned against it. I didn't understand the reaction that my body was having. David, my crush, that handsome guy in my Shakespeare club, was also the boy with the baseball cap I had imagined three years earlier, in Spain. So what? It wasn't a big deal. It was a weird coincidence, nothing more.

If I didn't do something to release the energy in my body, and soon, I'd throw up.

I really, really needed to move. I grabbed my iPod, pulled on a coat, and went downstairs.

There is a four-mile road at Stanford called Campus Drive Loop. That night, I walked the Loop, listening to the same song on repeat, over and over again, until dawn. And then I kept walking. I wasn't tired at all.

Did not I dance with you in Brabant once?

At 11:00 A.M., I slowed down. I had been walking nonstop for about twelve hours.

David's dorm was to my left. That's where I needed to go.

I knocked on his door. In the second before he opened it, it occurred to me that I should have gone back to my room first. I should've put on some makeup. Or at least brushed my hair. God knows how I looked after that night walking around campus.

"Hi," I said.

"Hi," David replied, ushering me into his room. "Thanks for having me over last night."

I nodded.

"That's why I came by," I told him. "I know the way I said good night was abrupt."

David nodded.

"Was everything okay?" he asked.

I laughed to relax my nerves, and sat on the edge of his futon.

"The truth is, that was about you," I told him. He sat next to me.

In the few weeks that we had known each other, I'd already come to understand that David was a closed-off guy. He didn't talk about his past with anyone. David had told his story exactly once—anonymously, and online. On the other side of the world, I had read it. It was the kind of coincidence that is impossible to fake. I knew details about David's life that no one else at Stanford (indeed, no one else in the state of California) could have told me. As I told David his own story from my point of view—how I had lived in Spain, read his words, and remembered them—a potent charge electrified the conversation. I mentioned that I had MS myself. I told him that I'd been rooting for him.

"I wondered a lot if you ever got that scholarship," I said. "It's so cool to see that you did."

David looked stunned.

"Wow," he said.

"It's weird, huh?" I agreed.

David shook his head.

"It's really something to think—" he broke off.

"What?" I asked. David looked at me.

"It's just something to think that a person cared about me back then," he said.

My heart lurched.

"I would have sent you a message in the forum," I said, trying to lighten the mood. "But I'm so bad with technology, I couldn't figure out how to make an account."

David was somewhere else.

"Do you think that sometimes people who are meant to meet just . . . do?" he asked. I shook my head.

"I don't believe in things like that," I admitted.

"Neither do I," he quickly replied.

He pressed his lips together in thought. Then he smiled.

"This will be interesting, I think," he said.

I laughed with relief.

"You don't look the way I pictured you," I said.

"Oh?" he said. "You didn't expect me to be so damn handsome, right?"

I giggled. *Giggled*. And, let's be honest, probably ran my fingers through my hair.

"I imagined that you were—smaller, I guess," I said. "Although I did picture you with a baseball cap. I was right about that."

David's hat is legendary. It has the logo of his beloved football team, the Atlanta Falcons, and was such a regular presence on David's head that people in the Shakespeare club pretended not to recognize him without it. When David had bought that hat five years earlier, back when he was sixteen, it was black. But by the time I met him, daily sun exposure had bleached it almost white. The brim was frayed.

My long night finally caught up with me. I was hit with a wave of exhaustion.

"I should go," I told David. "I need to get some sleep."

"Oh," he replied. "Yeah, of course."

I said good-bye and stood up to leave. As I walked toward his door, I looked over my shoulder to smile at him—and plowed directly into the doorframe.

David laughed.

"You weren't kidding," he said. "You do need to sleep!"

I blushed with embarrassment, waved good-bye, and fled.

I ran downstairs and left his dorm. The door swung closed behind me, and I stopped in the courtyard.

Something big had just happened.

For only the second time in my life, I was filled with uncharacteristic confidence. Something very important would happen between this man and me. I was certain.

It didn't take long.

"IAMBIC PENTAMETER IS fun," I explained as David and I picked through a salad bar a few days later. "When you understand it, you can hunt for clues in the rhythm. It's like a puzzle."

"Uh-huh," David murmured, skeptically, as he reached for the cherry tomatoes.

"Like trochees," I said. "Trochees are my favorite. You know how regular iambic pentameter is a bunch of feet that make a heartbeat? Ba-*bump*, ba-*bump*, ba-*bump*, ba-*bump*, ba-*bump*? If *mu, sic be, the food, of love,* play *on*?"

"Sure," David replied.

"Well, a trochee is an inverted foot," I said. "Like, *ba*-bump instead of ba-*bump*."

"Oh my goodness," David teased. "How have I lived for twenty-one years without inverted feet?"

I made a face.

"It's *fun*, David," I insisted. "Trochees are Shakespeare's way of letting us know when a character's heart skips a beat."

"Well, that explains it," David joked. "My heart is a metronome. It doesn't skip anymore. I have no use for trochees."

I used the salad tongs to grab a bunch of radicchio leaves and dumped them on his plate.

"There you go," I teased. "Some bitter leaves to match your bitter mood."

David smiled.

"Can you blame me?" he asked. "Who isn't bitter on Valentine's Day?"

I blinked.

"Is it Valentine's Day?" I asked.

David nodded.

"It's February fourteenth," he said. "How come you never know the date?"

I sprinkled croutons on my salad.

"Don't you have plans with Alex?" I asked, trying to sound casual.

David shook his head.

"I broke up with her last week," he said. "I'm interested in someone else, actually."

After lunch, I ran back to my dorm, unscrewed a lightbulb from a lamp in my room, and tied a small note to it.

"Here's something to make this Valentine's Day *brighter* than the rest," I wrote. I congratulated myself on the joke and, a few hours later, left it outside David's door.

That night, on the balcony of the Italian-language dorm, he wrapped his hands around my neck, leaned forward, and kissed me.

"I mean, you gave me a literal lightbulb," David said.

I laughed.

So David and I started to date: burritos at Taqueria Cancún in San Francisco's Mission District; midnight movies in Santa Clara; brunches in Palo Alto. While John had intoxicated me with giddy physicality, and Dylan had excited me with intellectual theories, David just made me laugh. He made me laugh more than anyone ever had.

A few weeks after our first kiss, David announced that we were going on a "fancy" date.

"Didn't you call Red Lobster 'fancy' the other day, farm boy?" I teased.

"Compared to Tater Tot hot dish, Red Lobster is damn fancy," he insisted.

I frowned.

"Do I want to know what Tater Tot hot dish is?" I asked.

David considered the question.

"No, you don't," he concluded. "But I'm serious. This date will blow your mind. I can out-fancy any of these big-city folk."

And he did. That weekend, he picked me up wearing a suit and, for the first time, no hat. My boy with the baseball cap was a man, too.

"Who are you?" I joked. "The guy I'm waiting for doesn't have a cranium. A hat grows out of his face."

"Get in the car, woman," he said. "We're being fancy now."

I had teased him, but in truth it was just a cover for my nerves. I'd changed my dress some fifteen times that afternoon, agonized over every detail of my hair and makeup, and even made the risky choice to switch out the studs in my newly pierced ears for pretty earrings.

"Actually, it's good you didn't wear your hat," I said, deadpan. "We need to find out whether I like *you*, or if I just like the fantasy of some dude I read about one time." (I didn't say it, but I also needed to find out whether David liked me, or was just on some quest to "save" a woman with the same disease that killed his mother.)

"That's it," David said, as if he'd read my mind. "Fancy Night, like Fight Club, has some rules. The first rule of Fancy Night is: No psychology on Fancy Night."

"Psychology is not fancy?" I asked.

He laughed.

"Psychology is *not fancy*," he agreed.

I smiled.

"I couldn't agree more," I said. "Any other rules?"

David looked at me.

"We'll start with that one," he said.

All night, throughout the restaurant and post-dinner jazz club (which were, as promised, fancy), David's last remark gnawed at my mind. He *must* be kinky. He had to be, didn't he? Who jokes about "rules" and hints that there are more to come? Who makes a point to tell someone that he has a leather belt?

Maybe I was a magnet for kinky men. Maybe my compatibility with John wasn't the coincidental rarity I'd thought it was.

"Before you picked me up tonight, I was nervous," I told David, as we drove back to Palo Alto at the end of our date. "I had a mental list of things that could go wrong."

"And nothing did go wrong," he cheered. "I nailed it! I'm fancy!"

I giggled.

"Well, one of the things I was afraid of did happen," I admitted. "Have you not noticed me dabbing at my ear all night?"

"What?" David said, craning his neck to look. "What are you talking about?"

"I got my ears pierced for the first time last week," I told him. "I wasn't supposed to take the studs out until next Thursday. But I wanted to wear cool earrings tonight, so—"

"Wait," David interrupted. "Are you about to tell me that you've besmirched my fancy date with *earlobe blood*?"

I laughed again.

"I had to confess," I replied, with a shrug. "You deserve to be forewarned if you're getting involved with the kind of girl who takes her studs out too early."

David clicked the turn signal and pulled onto the exit ramp. It wasn't our exit.

"This is how the story ends? You're kicking me out of the car?" I joked. "We can work through this! It's just one lobe!"

David pulled into an empty suburban parking lot, turned off the ignition, and turned to face me.

"There's a word for girls like you, Jillian," he said.

"Oh yeah?" I asked. "Is it *bootylicious*?"

David smiled.

"No," he said, suddenly serious. "It's *keeper*."

I blinked. I hadn't expected that.

"Because . . . my ear is bleeding?" I said.

David laughed again. "No," he replied. "I just like you a lot. I want you to know that."

I didn't know what to say. I was so disarmed by his candor. David was unlike anyone I'd ever met.

And the truth was that I liked him a lot, too.

"But I'm also bootylicious, right?" I finally joked.

He laughed.

"Sure," he said. "You're bootylicious, too. Just my type."

My stomach tightened. I looked out the window.

"You don't really know what type of girl I am yet," I admitted.

"I want to find out," David muttered, his lips inches from my own. We kissed.

I was falling for this boy too fast. Although I had a few reasons to hope that David might be kinky, I still hadn't smoked out his sexuality for sure. And if David was vanilla, I needed to know as soon as possible so I could nip things in the bud. I was not going to let myself get involved with another vanilla guy. That was a recipe for disaster. A relationship with someone who didn't share my sexuality seemed just as unappetizing as a relationship with someone who did not share my species.

There's a scene in *Love's Labor's Lost* when the Princess of France and her ladies hear that the men are coming, in disguise, to see them. They decide to turn the tables. They put on masks and swap the tokens of love that the men had previously given them. If the men used the tokens to identify them, each man would flirt with the wrong woman.

"Hold, Rosaline, this favor thou shalt wear, and then the king will court thee for his dear," the Princess says, handing her own token to Rosaline. "Change your favors too," she encourages the others, "so shall your loves woo contrary, deceiv'd by these removes." Katharine asks the Princess to explain the purpose of this gambit, and the Princess replies: "The effect of my intent is to cross theirs: they do it but in mocking merriment, and mock for mock is only my intent."

It works. The men identify their loves with physical tokens and woo the wrong ones.

It's a silly idea—in real life, of course, any true lover could recognize the object of his affection with or without a mask. But I saw a serious message in the silliness. Masks turn love into a farce. My first relationship, with John, had been marred by the mask he had worn for nearly a year. And when I tried to mask my sexuality and elevate myself to Dylan's seemingly unblemished level, it hid our mutual incompatibility.

"We, following the signs, woo'd but the sign of she," says Berowne, after the men realize they had each pursued the wrong woman in disguise. I refused to make the same mistake with David. He was falling for me, that much was clear. But I wanted him to fall for more than just the sign of me.

Not that my tactic was much more mature than that of the Princess and her friends. I went to a dorm party, pretended to be drunk, and sloshed up to David's roommate, Kyle.

"Hi, Skyle," I slurred.

"Hi, Jillian," he said, smiling. "It looks like you're having fun."

"Mm-hmm," I said, nodding into my cup. "I like David."

Kyle laughed.

"That's good, because David likes you," he said.

"I'm also kind of into S&M," I blurted. "So I hope David is into it, too."

Kyle blinked.

"Whoa," he said. "For real?"

I made my eyes as wide as possible and nodded.

"Yeah," I drawled.

"Interesting," Kyle replied. (Kyle was the first of many, many, *many* people who would use the word *interesting*—always followed by a literal or vocal period, never an exclamation point—to respond to my sexuality in the years to come.)

A few nights later, as David and I sat in a bar near University Avenue, I learned that my efforts had paid off.

David swirled the scotch around in his glass.

"So, Jillian," he asked. "Are you, like, into pain?"

I blushed.

"Um," I replied. "Yes?"

It wasn't quite true. But it seemed close enough—and definitely less embarrassing than the whole story.

"Interesting," David said.

"Kyle told you, right?" I asked.

"He said you mentioned it at the party," David confirmed.

I smiled with an embarrassed cringe.

"I told him that for your benefit," I admitted. "I wanted it to get back to you."

David picked up his scotch and took a sip. Then he leaned back in his chair and eyed me.

"Well then," he said. "You'll be hurting tomorrow night."

My stomach clenched in the best way. I excused myself and hid in the bathroom to call Peng, who had recently moved back to the United States after spending a few years in China. (At this point, she'd only heard the same "S&M" euphemism that Kyle did; she didn't know the details of my fetish.)

"That settles it, right?" I whispered to her over my cell. "He wouldn't have said that if he weren't into it, would he?"

Peng humored me. She's been humoring me since I was ten years old.

"Sure," she said. "That makes sense."

"I mean, I don't think he's had a chance to explore it yet," I added. "But it seems like the underlying impulses are there, don't you think?"

"Mm-hmm," Peng replied.

I went back to the table. In the dim light of the bar, David had never looked better. Was it possible for one man to be so perfect for me? I slid back into the booth.

"You seem too good to be true," I told him. "I'm waiting for the other shoe to drop."

David smiled. He stood up and leaned over the table to kiss me.

"There is no shoe," he said.

THE NEXT NIGHT, David took me out to a movie. It was a kids' movie.

"What was that?" I joked, after we had returned to his dorm room. David turned red.

"I didn't know it was a kids' movie!" he protested. "It had a high rating on Rotten Tomatoes."

"It's a unique way to set the mood." I giggled.

"We don't have movie theaters where I'm from," David joked, with a mock groan. "I'm not used to these big-city contraptions."

I laughed.

"That's what I get for dating a farmer," I said.

David grinned.

"I'm straight out of *Oregon Trail*," he agreed.

"I didn't pay attention to the movie, anyway," I admitted. "I was thinking about what you said last night."

David's hands slid around my waist.

"You were, huh?" he asked, with a wicked grin.

"Yeah," I replied. "Do you still want to . . . ford that river?"

David laughed.

"Of course," he said, leaning down. As we kissed, he pulled my dress up, over my shoulders. I was in my underwear.

"Should I blindfold you? Is that what you want?" David asked. He was so cute.

"You can if you want to," I replied. "But that's not quite what I have in mind." As we continued to kiss, my fingers moved to his waist and unbuckled his belt.

David smiled.

"Are you trying to get me naked, young lady?" he teased.

I swallowed and shook my head.

"No," I said.

I pulled his belt off and folded it in half.

"The other day, you kind of smacked my butt," I told him.

"I did?" David replied.

No, he didn't. But cut me some slack—this was my first time topping from the bottom, and there's no script.

"Mm-hmm," I hummed, nodding. "You did. And I like that kind of thing. So I thought this time, you could do *that*, but with *this*." I handed him the belt. (The more direct tactic of asking him to spank me was out of the question. I would not be able to bring myself to say that word out loud to him for another six years. That's how potent some words—for me, that word—can be.)

"Oh," David said, jerking his head back—either with excitement or surprise, I couldn't tell. "Yeah, totally."

"And if there is anything you really like, we can do that, too," I rushed to add.

"I really like *you*," David replied.

"Very clever," I teased. "Ten points for that one."

"Hey, I play basketball," David said. "If you set me up for a shot like that, I'm going to take it."

I laughed.

"The point is, if you have any fantasies, I hope you feel free to tell me," I said. "I won't judge anything. I want to make you feel comfortable."

"Duly noted," David said. "For now, I just want to make you feel *un*comfortable."

"Yay!" I cheered, softly clapping my hands together. "I'm so glad you're into this."

"Cool," he said.

"Cool," I replied.

Then we just stood there, looking at each other. I had no idea what to do or say. John had always taken charge in these situations.

I pressed my lips together and squinted.

"Um," I said.

David and I both burst into embarrassed laughter.

"Okay," I continued, nervously bouncing up and down on the balls of my feet. "It's not awkward."

"Why would it be awkward?" David agreed, with an awkward smile.

"So I'm going to lie down," I said, as I climbed onto his futon and lay on my stomach. "And we'll figure it out."

"Should I—should I pull down your underwear?" David asked.

"Oh, so sexy," I teased. "Am I blushing?"

"Shut it, Keenan," David said, yanking my panties off my hips. "I'm going to hit you now."

"Bring it," I said.

"I'm bringing it," he replied.

The leather of his belt slapped against my skin.

"Like that?" David asked.

I stretched out along the futon. It felt—well, "good" isn't quite right, because it hurt. But it felt satisfying. Very satisfying. I'm a spanking fetishist, and I had just been single for a year. Some sexual activities can be enjoyed solo, but spanking is not one of them. Like trying to tickle yourself, it just doesn't work. (Yes, I had tried. No, we will never speak of this again.) After such a long drought, it felt amazing to play. It was obvious that David didn't have the same kind of hardwired fetish that I do. But maybe he had a seed of sexual deviance that I could coax into bloom.

"That was great," I said. "Exactly like that."

"So this is how you get down, huh?" David asked.

I cringed.

"You could say that," I replied, embarrassed.

He hit me again.

And again. That time, I gasped at the sting and pressed my face into the futon.

"I'm not hurting you, am I?" David asked.

I looked over my shoulder and tried to smile reassuringly.

"You don't need to worry," I told him. "I like it."

David hit me one more time, then dropped the belt. He knelt down on the futon and ran his hands across my shoulders. I reluctantly flipped onto my back and let him kiss me.

"You broke my metronome, Jillian," David said that night. "You're my trochee."

Later, I sat alone in my dorm room.

It was—

You know, it's important to consider—

Well, it was definitely—

I left my room and walked to the edge of campus, and beyond, to the base of a hill with a satellite dish at its crest. At day, the hiking trail that leads up to the dish is popular with students. At night, the hill is closed off by a locked fence to separate students from the mountain lions that roam the area.

"Fuck it," I thought.

I climbed over the fence and hiked up the hill. As I approached the dish, I heard a chatter of happy voices. A cluster of drunk students I didn't know were drinking beers and shots of liquor.

"Hi," I said, walking over to them.

"Hey!" they yelled. "Who are you?"

"I'm stressed out," I told them. "Who are you?"

"We are done with the LSAT!" one of them yelled, to a chorus of cheers.

I laughed.

"Congratulations," I said. "Mind if I join you?"

"No problem!" one of them replied, handing me a shot. "The more, the merrier. And the less likely we'll be mauled by a mountain lion." The others laughed.

"So why are you stressed out?" someone asked.

I took the shot and winced. It was tequila.

"Why else?" I said. "Sex."

The group cheered and clinked bottles.

"Sex!" one shouted.

"Hey, do you guys want to do something with me?" I asked.

"Sex?" another man asked, laughing. I squinted at him in the dark.

"Berowne?" I said. "Is that you?"

"You know it!" he called.

I shook my head with amusement and turned back toward the group.

"I want to scream something, okay?" I asked them. "Scream with me."

Everyone agreed, and staggered to their feet. I told them what we were going to yell.

"That dude from *A Midsummer Night's Dream*?" one guy slurred.

"Exactly," I said. "One, two, three!"

His name, screamed by a dozen voices, echoed through the hills. Berowne wrapped his arm around my shoulders and handed me another shot.

"What fool is not so wise, to lose an oath to win a paradise?" he asked, with a wink. "Bottoms up, oath breaker."

I sighed.

"Bottoms up, buddy," I replied. We clinked glasses, and I threw the tequila down my throat.

Two things were certain: I was in love with my boy with the baseball cap.

And he was as vanilla as a Snack Pack pudding cup. There wasn't even a sprinkle in sight.

3.4 Antony and Cleopatra:

Here Is My Space

I gasped and sat up in bed. To my left, on his side of the mattress, David was still asleep. He hadn't noticed me move.

It was our senior year of college. I was twenty-one, and David was twenty-two. We had been dating for more than a year and living together almost as long. We both recognized the recklessness of moving in together so fast, but, as Shakespeare points out in *Antony and Cleopatra*, "there's beggary in love that can be reckoned"—in other words, love that can conform to reason is stingy love indeed. So we had submitted to our less practical impulses and signed the lease.

Besides, I was suppressing enough impulses.

In our shared apartment, our things, like our lives, blended: David's biochemistry books mingled on the shelves with my Kafka and Edith Hamilton; we used each other's laptops all the time; I stole his comfortable T-shirts more often than I wore my own.

Wait—we used each other's laptops *all the time*.

It was a terrifying realization. My search history felt like a crime scene. I could only imagine what David would think if he were to discover that journal articles and fantasy travel itineraries weren't the only things I looked up online.

David already knew that I had an interest in "edgy" sex play, of course. But it was a far cry from that trendy euphemism to the graphic spanking stories I read to lull myself to sleep whenever I had insomnia. (Trust me, it's more fun than counting sheep.)

After that first awkward experience, David did spank me sometimes—if slapping my ass a few times during foreplay or sex counts as spanking, which, to me, it doesn't. But it was enough to keep my physical needs *almost* satisfied. I filled in the holes with capsaicin cream, a medication that produces a painful burn when applied to skin, and with the Internet.

I also joined an exercise class.

"Stand up!" yelled Marcus, the instructor, standing over me with a weight bar. "We're not done!"

"No, please, I can't," I moaned, shaking my head. "It hurts."

"It's for your own good," Marcus replied. "Ten more!"

And figging, of course. How shall I explain figging?

Figging, let's say, is "the act of using peeled raw ginger root for anal stimulation." In other words, you peel a finger of raw ginger into the shape of a butt plug and stick it where God and Julia Child never advised.

According to the Internet, figging began life as a disciplinary tactic in ancient Greece, and was widely used in Victorian England to dissuade spanking victims from clenching their butt cheeks during their punishments. (That's probably apocryphal; I can't bring myself to make the phone calls necessary to confirm the historical origins of anal ginger play.) For years, the BDSM communities have embraced figging, often as a supplement to spanking. It hurts. The ginger oils warm up and then burn. It's painful and amazing. I regard this paragraph as a public-service announcement. It's not fair for the BDSM communities to keep figging to ourselves. It's just too good. (If there was ever a hope that my sexuality might be merely a "phase," I'd say it died the second I began to pervert arthritis cream and East Asian produce aisles for masochistic masturbatory purposes. Never assume the girl next door doesn't have a knobby rhizome up her butt.)

David was almost everything I had ever wanted in a partner: curious, strong, sexy, and smart. Unfortunately, he also had no apparent desire to beat me to tears at my request. I hadn't planned for that one.

There's a moment in *Antony and Cleopatra* when Cleopatra, perhaps the most fully realized sexual character in the Shakespearean canon, talks to a eunuch.

"Hast thou affections?" she asks Mardian, a member of her entourage.

"Yes, gracious madam," he replies.

That takes Cleopatra by surprise.

"Indeed?" she asks.

"Not in deed, madam, for I can do nothing but what indeed is honest to be done," Mardian replies, punning on Cleopatra's question. "Yet have I fierce affections, and think what Venus did with Mars." (Venus, the goddess of love, and Mars, the god of war, were legendary lovers; in fact, according to myth, Cupid was their son.)

Even when sexuality sleeps, it's never gone.

So I panicked. I had been drifting into sleep, midway through an excellent fantasy about naval insubordination and the captain from *Master and Commander,* when the vulnerability of my search history occurred to me with a jolt. Had I missed anything else?

It took me almost an hour, but that night, frantic in our living room, I learned to hide my tracks. I erased my search history, reset my computer preferences, and consolidated my favorite spanking stories into one folder. I titled it: "David, If You Find This, Please Don't Look Inside."

Then I walked back into our bedroom and looked at my boyfriend. He was still asleep.

I exhaled with palpable relief. My secret was safe. It ached to be so grateful for an empty history.

I would stay in this lonely sexual purgatory—hiding, sneaking around, sticking ginger up my butt in the isolation of locked bathrooms—for the next five years.

DAVID ONCE SHOWED me a satellite image of the United States at night. On most of the map, lights from the major cities make the geography familiar and identifiable. But there are black holes in the middle.

"That's where I'm from," David said, pointing at a black hole.

"This reminds me of satellite pictures of the Korean peninsula at night," I told him.

During Shakespeare's life, maps weren't taken for granted. In fact, they were a popular new fad. Maps adorned walls in homes, appeared in art and literature, and fascinated the intelligentsia. Many of Shakespeare's plays tapped into the global interests they provoked; he wrote often, of course, about countries other than his native England. But nowhere does Shakespeare explore the globe with more exuberance than he does in *Antony and Cleopatra*.

In both figurative and literal senses, *Antony and Cleopatra*'s central lovers come from very distant places.

Mark Antony is one of three rulers of the Roman Empire. Cleopatra is the Queen of Egypt. Despite the dramatic differences between the Roman and Egyptian cultures and outlooks, Antony and Cleopatra fall in love. But after the death of his Roman wife, Fulvia, Antony leaves Egypt to return to Rome and marry Octavia, the sister of one of his fellow rulers, in the hope that the marriage will ensure political stability.

It doesn't work. War breaks out among the three Roman rulers, and Antony returns to Egypt—a move that drags Cleopatra into the war as well.

The Roman forces follow Antony to Egypt, and, despite the fact that Antony is better prepared for a land conflict, Antony chooses to fight at sea, in what is known as the Battle of Actium. Cleopatra's ships turn and flee, and Antony follows her, leaving his own ships to destruction. Later, after a series of political shenanigans, Antony becomes convinced that Cleopatra has betrayed him, and vows to kill her. To prove her loyalty, Cleopatra sends word to Antony that she has committed suicide and died with his name upon her lips. Antony decides to join his lover in the afterlife and falls on his own sword. The wound doesn't immediately kill him, however, and Antony dies in Cleopatra's arms. When the Roman army takes Cleopatra prisoner, she kills herself as well.

The differences between Rome and Egypt are obvious and endless. As literary scholar Rosalie Colie wrote, "Rome is duty, obligation, austerity, politics, warfare, and honor. . . . Egypt is comfort, pleasure, softness, seduction, sensuousness (if not sensuality also), variety, and sport." Cleopatra is sexual; her "passions are made of nothing but the finest part of pure love." Antony, for his part, finds himself pulled from the "holy, cold, and still conversation" of Roman culture and into the warm, overflowing Egyptian waters of the Nile.

But my favorite geographic detail from *Antony and Cleopatra* is that, as Antony dashes from place to place, we never see Cleopatra in Rome. In fact, the threat of being taken to her boyfriend's hometown is what drives her to suicide at the end of the play.

Cleopatra had the right idea.

David's hometown, in the black hole of central North Dakota, has a population of about five hundred people, if you round up. I'll call it "Credence."

There are no stoplights in Credence. The nearest supermarket is an hour away by car. There are six Protestant churches, but no bookstores. There is one paved road, Main Street, which has a handful of small businesses and a bar.

It is listed in the county phone book as "Bar, The."

The first time David brought me to Credence, the local news

section of the county newspaper reported: "On Saturday, Bob and Deena Smith called their cousin Jerry, who lives in Omaha. He said it was cloudy there." (Really. That's an actual article from the newspaper, in its entirety, although I changed the names.) The same newspaper announced my visit in a subsequent issue, complete with a photo-illustration.

Credence doesn't get a lot of visitors.

"Do you want to see our crops?" David asked.

I blinked.

"What?" I said.

"The wheat crop is out," he explained. "Do you want a tour of the farm?"

I suppressed a grin.

"I like it when you talk about *crops*, babe," I said, sharing the inside joke with myself.

"You're interested in farm stuff?" David exclaimed. He was flattered.

"Sure," I replied.

I tried to focus on David's tour of the tractor shed, but it was easy to get distracted. If I had known how much potential for sadomasochistic fantasy there is in farm culture, I'd have rustled up a farm boy sooner.

"This is the machine we use to *thrash*—" he said.

"What?" I interrupted.

"I was saying, this is the machine we use to thresh wheat," David explained.

"Oh," I replied.

"Damn, girl, be cool," said Cleopatra, lounging in the driver's seat of a tractor. "In a minute, he's going to show you how to tie different kinds of knots, and I don't want your head to explode."

I blushed.

"But you see what I'm seeing, right, Cleo?" I asked.

Cleopatra stretched out and ran her fingers through her hair.

"Oh, yeah," she replied, eyeing a swivel carabiner tie-down. "This is some perverted farm porn right here."

"I'll show you how to tie a tension hitch," David said.

Geography is destiny. It influences our personalities, histories, interests, and even our politics. Roman Cleopatra wouldn't be Cleopatra; Egyptian Antony would be unrecognizable. Geography shapes us in ways we can understand and in a million more ways we can't.

But I wanted to understand. North Dakota was a culture shock unlike anything I had ever experienced. It made Oman feel as familiar as a Starbucks menu. Credence was part of my country, but it wasn't part of my world. I wanted to understand how this place had produced a man like David.

I'd known the basics of David's story from the beginning of our relationship, of course. As we dated, he filled in the details I hadn't read online.

In 2001, David had gone to high school with bruises on his face. (David's older sister had recently graduated and moved away.) The school principal called North Dakota Child Protection Services, which sent a social worker to Credence and ultimately placed David in informal foster care. For the next three years, David, for the most part, didn't talk to his father, C.J. David didn't talk to C.J. when he graduated from high school as valedictorian or when he got accepted to college. When he moved to California, he flew there alone.

In the year before I met him, however, David had tried to reconnect with his dad. They talked on the phone sometimes—usually when C.J. drunk-dialed David at 2:00 A.M., on the dot, because that's when the bar ("Bar, The") closed. During my last few weeks in Oman, David had even gone back to North Dakota for Christmas. At the end of that trip, C.J. had punched David in the face (for no apparent reason) and then, to apologize, bought David a lap dance at a strip club several hours away. The stripper was in her late forties and introduced herself as an "old friend" of C.J.'s.

As she performed, she asked David maternal questions about his coursework and career aspirations.

There was the story about the time C.J. got high and had a violent fistfight with an air conditioner on Main Street. There was the story about the time C.J. violated a restraining order to break into David's foster home, and the story about the time C.J. took nine-year-old David to a makeshift golf course just outside of Credence and tried to shoot golf balls with a Colt .45. (There were many other people on the golf course at the time, scurrying from the bullets; no one called the police.)

David and I had been on the farm for three days, but we hadn't yet seen his father. C.J. had agreed to pick us up at the airport, but when we got off the plane, a voice mail on David's cell phone instructed us to "find the rental car with a cigarette box behind the back tire" and drive to Credence ourselves. We wandered around the airport parking lot until we found the cigarette box, which had the rental keys inside. When we got to Credence four hours later, C.J. was nowhere. He stayed gone for the first two nights.

C.J. had apparently not paid his bills in some time, because neither the Internet nor the lights in the house worked. By candlelight, David's childhood home was a circus tent. Dead animals, posed in taxidermy as if alive, decorated every single room; so did framed pencil portraits of Native Americans and Jesus. Guns were everywhere: in closets, on shelves, under a mattress. Drugs and condoms were everywhere, too.

There was a full-size suit of silver armor in the basement.

Above the bed in David's childhood room, someone had hung a mirror. There was a mirror next to the bed, too.

"Did my father turn my bedroom into a fuck pad?" David said, his forehead in his hands.

"I might need to be celibate this week, honey," I replied.

David rubbed his eyes.

"I might need to be celibate for the rest of my life," he said.

To escape, David and I explored the farm.

"What do you want to do after graduation?" he asked me on our third evening in Credence, as we sat atop a thirty-foot grain bin, waiting for sunset.

I shrugged.

"I like living in different places," I told him. "I'd love to get a job abroad."

"You move around too much, Jillian," David replied. "A rolling stone gathers no moss."

I had no idea how to respond to that.

"Well, I'm not . . . trying to gather moss." I laughed, confused.

David shook his head.

"It means that if you move around too much, you won't make any money," he insisted. "I learned that in high school. Moss is green, and money is green, so that expression is about money." He said a teacher had explained this, and the students had written essays on the subject.

I blanched. Squinting into the distance, I chose my words with care.

"Honey, all literary interpretations have value," I said. "Even that one. Authorial intent doesn't necessarily matter."

David looked at me.

"Okay," he said.

"But that proverb is from, like, sixteenth-century England," I said.

"That sounds about right," he agreed.

I rubbed his knee.

"Okay," I said. "In what countries, and for how long, has money been *green?*"

David's eyes widened.

"Oh, my God," he breathed. From our perch on the grain bin, David looked down at Credence. "What the hell is wrong with this place?" he said.

I laughed.

David shook his head. "No, I'm serious," he said. "What the hell is wrong with this place?"

I shrugged. "So why do you come back here, babe?"

"I keep hoping things will change," David said. "But they never do."

I squeezed his knee and frowned at a water tower in the distance.

Scarlett, David's mother, was diagnosed with multiple sclerosis when David was five. Her health deteriorated fast, and by the time David was ten, Scarlett was in a wheelchair. C.J. decided this was a good time to abandon his family and move to Ohio to live with a woman he had met online. One year later, after that other woman filed a restraining order against him, C.J. crawled back to Credence.

Scarlett had two children and a serious disease. She told David to make a "welcome home" banner for his father.

When David was placed in foster care, he didn't trust C.J. to take care of Scarlett. So one evening, when David noticed C.J.'s truck parked outside the bar, he realized it was a chance to check on his mom.

Inside the house, David's fears were realized. Scarlett was sitting on the couch, alone. David had no idea how long she had been there, but it had been hours, at least. It was clear that she'd been sitting there all day. Maybe all through the previous night, too.

At that point, Scarlett couldn't move without help, so there was no way for her to leave the couch to get food, move into bed, or walk to the bathroom. Mercifully, David told me, she didn't seem upset or scared. Mostly confused.

And cold. The windows in the house were open, and it was winter. Scarlett was shivering.

That night, fifteen-year-old David put his mother in a car and drove her to her parents' house, in another city. She died a few months later.

Why does Antony love Cleopatra? He has so many reasons not to be with her—political, personal, geographic. Today, readers adore Cleopatra, but there are reasons (some valid, some not) that readers despised her for a long time, too. Cleopatra is often moody, insincere, or manipulative. She'd be a fabulous person for a fun night on the town. But how many people would want to be in a long-term relationship with her?

Oh, she's a sexual firecracker, sure. That's a given. Shakespeare makes it clear. But that can't be the only reason Antony loves her, can it?

Although *Antony and Cleopatra* stands alone, it's useful to remember that it is a kind of sequel. Shakespeare wrote *Julius Caesar* in 1599; *Antony and Cleopatra* premiered eight years later, in 1607. Mark Antony is a character in both plays, and details of his personality are consistent in both. In *Julius Caesar*, Antony already has a reputation as "a reveller," who "is given to sports, to wildness, and much company." When Caesar describes to Antony why he prefers him to the more austere, classically Roman Cassius, he says: "He loves no plays, as thou dost, Antony. He hears no music." These moments hint at the untamed Egyptian personality that Antony later tries to embrace in *Antony and Cleopatra*.

In the context of both plays, Antony's filial admiration for Julius Caesar raises interesting possibilities about his affection for Cleopatra. Cleopatra was previously in a relationship with Caesar; in fact, she bore his son, Caesarion. (Shakespeare also found ripe potential for sexual innuendo in farm culture, since he summarized Cleopatra's history with Caesar with the phrase "He plowed her and she cropped.") Antony hasn't forgotten Cleopatra's history with Caesar. In one moment of fury, he snarls at her: "I found you as a morsel cold upon dead Caesar's trencher."

It's enough to make a girl wonder if Antony's devotion for

Cleopatra is inspired, in part, by an unresolved need to fulfill Oedipal impulses by sleeping with his father figure's spouse.

Over the previous year, David and I had joked a few times about how the fact that I share a disease with his mother cast unfortunate Oedipal shadows over our relationship. But we had never confronted the fact that I could die exactly as Scarlett had.

The water tower was the tallest structure in my line of sight. Nothing scrapes the sky in Credence.

David had said he kept hoping for things to change.

"Is it cruel for me to be with you, babe?" I asked him. "Is it cruel to risk putting you through the same shit all over again?"

David put his hand on mine. "I don't care about that," he said.

I shook my head.

"That's the *right* thing to say," I told him. "But you're saying it too quickly."

"I'm not," he insisted. "I've given this a lot of thought."

I swallowed. "You've thought about this a lot?"

David nodded.

I looked at the ground, thirty feet below. We were so high up. I touched David's hand.

"You know I'm not your mom, right?" I said uncomfortably.

David laughed.

"Trust me," he said. "I know you're not my mother."

"And you're not C.J.," I replied. "If you need to protect yourself and walk away from this relationship, it's okay. I'll understand."

David's jawline tightened.

"You worry that I stay with you because I don't want to be like my father?" he asked.

"Do *you* worry about that?" I replied.

David let go of my hand and ran his fingers through his hair.

"No, I don't," he said. "The risk of pain is part of the deal. Love isn't love if it never hurts."

I looked at him.

"I'll try to stay healthy for as long as I can," I promised.

David wrapped his arm around my shoulders and kissed my temple.

Somewhere beneath our feet, as the sun inched toward the horizon, a pickup truck pulled onto Main Street.

For three days in Credence, David and I had puzzled over a grand mystery: Where was C.J.? We had only one clue. The first time I stepped into David's childhood home, I found it almost immediately. C.J. had left a note on the staircase. It was at once ominous and childlike. It read [sic]:

> *Jillian Welcome To N. Dak.*
> *Hey, you play Pocahonta's +*
> *DAVe will play Capt. John Smith*
> *+ I will play the Villian!*

So I can't say he didn't warn us.

SHAKESPEARE PLAYED JAZZ music with words. Every time the English language failed him, he invented new terms and phrases. He coined words as familiar as *hurry* and phrases as seemingly modern as *skim milk*. When the perfect color wasn't on his palette, he mixed paint and invented new shades.

For the rest of us, language often fails. If the Sami people, who live in the northern parts of Scandinavia and Russia, can create more than a thousand different words to describe reindeer, a more loving culture could produce more words for love. But we are not that culture, so we have only one: I "love" my cat. I "love" New York. I "love" tacos. No wonder the word so often rings hollow.

Pain suffers the same linguistic famine. There is pain that empowers; pain that arouses; pain that frightens; pain that motivates; pain that discourages; pain that encourages; pain that recalls; pain that predicts; pain that breaks; pain that heals. There is the pain that Cleopatra describes, "which hurts, and is desired."

For all those pains, we have only one word.

David and I climbed down the grain bin and walked back into his dark house. We lay on the bed in his basement, talking, until I drifted off.

Hours later, something loud startled me out of sleep. I blinked awake and squinted at my cell phone. It was almost 3:00 A.M.

Cleopatra was standing at the foot of the bed. There was no one else in the room.

"Where's David?" I asked her.

"I don't know," she replied coolly.

I sat up and rubbed my eyes. Why had David left?

I sighed.

"Cleo, is Antony's love for you just an Oedipal thing?" I asked.

"That's none of your business," Cleopatra snapped. "If you want to know why David is attracted to you, ask him yourself. Stop displacing your fear onto us."

I crossed my arms in front of my chest.

"I'm not 'displacing' my feelings onto you," I replied. "I'm processing them *through* you. That's how people experience literature."

Cleopatra scoffed.

"Are you sure there isn't something more?" she asked. "Something you're unwilling to face?"

I bristled.

"Hey," I said, pointing my finger at her. "I faced it. I was honest with David about that shit from the beginning."

Cleopatra's lip curled with contempt.

"Good grief, I'm not talking about your 'kink,'" she said. "This incessant whining doesn't impress me at all."

There were angry shouts upstairs. I slid off the bed and stood up.

"Is there a point to any of this?" Cleopatra pressed, her voice rising to a yell. "Or are you just *wasting our time*?"

The muffled sound of glass shattering echoed above me. I looked up toward the ceiling.

"What's going on up there?" I asked.

Cleopatra stepped back to the corner of the basement, almost invisible in shadow.

"I fled from Actium, but I know when and why to go to war," she said. "Do you?"

I turned my back to her and ran upstairs.

As a child, I was scared of the dark. David's house, still illuminated by candles, flashlights, and other battery-powered sources of light, came straight from my nightmares.

I stepped into the living room.

In his earlier years, C.J. had been a bodybuilder. His muscle mass had long since disappeared into rolls of alcohol fat, but it was easy to see the formidable man he had once been.

"What the fuck is wrong with you?" David was shouting. "Why can't you hold it together for one goddamn day?"

C.J. shook his head, stumbling around the room.

"Meth makes a man think different," he slurred. His eyes, wide and insane, shifted in their sockets.

"Meth makes a man fucking worthless," David snarled.

I picked up a flashlight and turned it on.

David turned his head to look at me.

"Go back downstairs, Jillian," he said, in an even tone of voice.

I scanned the room.

David looked furious. His eyes were fixed on his father, who was wearing—good Lord—a Native American Halloween costume. (It wasn't Halloween.) C.J.'s eyes bulged from his head. Drool dripped from his mouth, like from a dog's. There was broken glass on the floor.

"Hi, C.J.," I said. "We met a few months ago in California. Remember?"

C.J. blinked at me with obvious confusion. He hadn't realized there was someone else in the house.

"Go downstairs, Jillian," David said, again.

I shook my head.

Something was wrong.

A handgun, I've decided, is like a typo: you don't notice it until you do.

But then it's the only thing you see.

The gun was hidden in the thick flesh of C.J.'s paw. Only a hint of barrel betrayed its transformative presence in the room, but it was pointed in David's direction.

I reflexively put both of my hands in front of me. All the muscles in my body were tight. I wanted to claw C.J.'s face off with my fingernails.

"That's a cool gun," I said. "Can I see it?"

C.J. swung around to face me. Now the gun was pointed at my stomach.

"What?" he slurred. He had already forgotten I was there.

I nodded.

"I'd like to see it," I said, taking slow, cautious steps toward him. "Can you teach me about guns? I'd love to learn from someone with your expertise."

C.J. blinked, waving the gun around. He was confused. He turned to look at David.

"Okay," he slurred.

I nodded again.

"But I'm not brave like you," I continued, inching forward. "Can we take out the bullets first?" I forced a giggle.

C.J.'s hands shook as he tried to remove the magazine. Finally, it slid out with a click. He pointed the gun at David.

"Empty now," he said with a laugh.

By now, I was right next to C.J. I put my hand on his wrist

and pushed his arm down. The barrel of the gun redirected from David's torso to his legs.

"Are you sure there isn't one more round in the chamber?" I asked. (I had learned a few things from John.)

C.J. roared an odd, terrible laugh and pulled the slide back on the top of the gun. The last bullet leapt out and skittered along the carpet. I picked it up, put it in my pocket, and exhaled.

"Okay," I said, shooting a glance at David. He was looking at C.J. with murderous eyes.

C.J. stumbled into the kitchen, still holding the empty gun. David and I followed. When we found him, he had the gun in one hand and a bottle of whiskey in the other.

I scanned the room. There were two kitchen knives on the countertop.

"I thought you were going to teach me about your gun," I said. C.J. nodded and pointed at David with the bottle.

"Scarlett, Scarlett," C.J. mumbled. "David will take care of you."

My fingers curled up into the palms of my hands.

"I'm Jillian," I said, my neck tight.

C.J. pointed at me.

"If some fucker rapes you," he roared, stumbling around the kitchen, "David will—" C.J. cut himself off. He began to hump the end of his kitchen counter. "If some fucker rapes you," he repeated, still thrusting his pelvis against the counter, "David will— *Bang! Bang!*" C.J. fell on the kitchen floor, humped the ground, and performed an elaborate pantomime of David shooting my imaginary rapist. He dropped the gun, and it clattered against the linoleum.

I looked at C.J. rolling on the floor.

I picked up the gun. I had a bullet in my pocket.

Did I mention there is no police station in Credence?

I gave the gun to David.

He had seen C.J. remove the magazine and empty the chamber,

but still confirmed that the gun was unloaded before he slipped it into the back of his pants.

This continued nonstop through the night, and past dawn, until eleven the next morning. David and I were exhausted.

"Do you remember the first crop you farmed?" C.J. slurred, pointing at David with a cue from the pool table in the basement.

David was leaning against a wall with his arms folded over his chest.

"Yes," he replied.

C.J. nodded. For a second, he looked gentle. Then his voice changed again. "You think I never did anything for you," he snarled, shaking the cue. "But I taught you to farm."

David didn't move. He kept C.J. fixed in the crosshairs of his sight and did not say a word.

C.J. stumbled across the basement, toward the suit of armor in the corner.

"We went out and saw the sunflowers when they bloomed," he slurred. "You couldn't see the end of 'em. Do you remember?"

David looked at me. I was sitting on the pool table.

"Yes," he said. "I remember."

C.J. dropped the cue, satisfied.

"So don't say I didn't do anything for you," he snarled, stumbling up the stairs. "I taught you the only thing you're good for—putting your seeds in *dirt*." In case anyone had missed the joke, C.J. shot a pointed glance at me and guffawed. Then he tripped out of the house and disappeared.

Shakespeare did not write monsters. He always hints at some drop of humanity in his characters, even at their worst. They have complex histories and nuanced human motivations. They have scars in their own stories. Even Iago, one of the most evil Shakespearean characters, has glimmers of humanity. As Gertrude puts it in *Hamlet*, "one woe doth tread upon another's heel:" pain begets pain. The people who cause harm are the ones who have been harmed. Shakespeare knew that. Shakespeare doesn't just show people at their worst and leave them there. Shakespeare is better than that.

I am no William Shakespeare.

David sank into a chair. I walked over to him.

"Are you okay?" I asked. David glanced up and gave me an exhausted smile.

"I'm fine," he said, shaking his head. "I'm fine."

He reached up, put his hands on my hips, and pulled me toward him. He pressed the crown of his head against my pelvis. I ran my fingers through his hair.

"What do you need?" I asked. "We can fly back to California tomorrow. We can go to one of your friend's houses. We don't have to stay home."

With his head still pressed against my body, David spoke to the ground.

"You are my home, Jillian," he said, as his fingers tightened around my hips.

Years later, a friend of mine remarked that this moment must have been frightening. "You see a guy's blasted home life, and then he tells you that you are his home?" he said. "Scary."

But it didn't scare me. I understood. My mother and I had more or less stopped talking a few months earlier, after she "washed her hands of me" yet again because I had ended a phone call, as she put it, "abruptly." Her love was like her money: hers to spend. I had understood ever since I was nine, when she threw me out of her house the first time, that I wasn't entitled to anything. And it's true. I knew that.

But it's an odd thing, not being loved. The possibility that my mother didn't, or couldn't, really love me was exactly like my disease. For months, or even years, I'd feel fine. I'd forget. But these things relapse. Sooner or later, I'd end up back in the same place: on the floor of some bathroom, frozen, waiting out the pain.

I loved. I had so much love: Caliban, Katherine, Hermione, Juliet, Orsino. Even Hamlet, although he annoyed me. Even that damn Friar, although he was always right. But I wanted to love someone who could love me back. I wanted to love someone who could hold me back. It doesn't surprise me that Juliet, the girl whose father threatens to hit her ("My fingers itch") and whose mother washes her hands of her ("Talk not to me, for I'll not speak a word / Do as thou wilt, for I have done with thee"), is also the girl who drowns herself in Romeo.

I had found David once before. And now that I had found him again, I wasn't going to let mutual interdependency scare me off. So I bent over David's body, wrapped my arms around his torso, and pressed my face into his hair.

When I think about it, Freud's Oedipus complex was built on a flaw—or, at least, a lazy misread. In *Oedipus Rex,* the Greek tragedy that inspired the psychoanalytic theory, Oedipus's parents, Laius and Jocasta, hear a prophecy that their son will kill his father and marry his mother. In fear, Laius orders that the baby be killed. His plan fails, of course. Oedipus survives to grow up and fulfill the prophecy. But the tragedy would have been avoided if, at the beginning, Laius had not tried to kill his son.

Shouldn't there be a "Laius complex"? Why is a parent's willingness to murder his child undiscussed, while the child's inevitable response to that original sin is pathologized?

I think Antony's love for Cleopatra comes back to geography. Antony is a leader of an empire, but a man without a country. He doesn't quite fit in Rome, and he doesn't quite fit in Egypt. In fact, there is no place for him anywhere on the globe. So Antony pulls Cleopatra close to him and plants his seeds in the soil of the only place where he belongs. "Here is my space," he tells her.

When people have no place, we find our place in people.

I slid my hands down the back of David's neck.

"Should we try to sleep?" I asked.

He shook his head.

"No," he said. "Let's get out of here."

We walked out his back door, into a field with tall grasses that stretched up to my waist. Abandoned farm equipment spotted the landscape, a metallic graveyard of old tractor parts. David sat on the rim of a six-foot-tall discarded tire. Tired from the long night's ordeal, I just stood there in front of him. A cool breeze tickled the back of my neck.

"What kinds of diamond rings do you like, Jillian?" David said after a while.

A cold weight settled in my stomach. It was not the right time for this conversation.

I sank to my knees in the dirt and rubbed David's calves.

"I don't wear much jewelry, babe," I said. "And I don't like the ethics of the diamond industry."

He sighed.

"I know," David said. "I just ask for future reference." I put my hand on his face. His stubble was rough against my hand, like the boar bristles on my favorite hairbrush.

"Okay," I said. "For future reference, I want to date for at least five years before we have that conversation."

David pulled me toward the tire, and into its space inside.

Maybe Aristophanes was right. Maybe once, a long time ago, before the gods interfered, David and I really were one person. Maybe that's when I learned to crave pain. Maybe when Zeus reached down to cut us apart, I turned my half of our body toward the blade, so that it cut into my flesh and ripped through my nerves, leaving David, for once, unhurt.

ACT FOUR

Therefore, good Brutus, be prepared to hear;
And since you know you cannot see yourself
So well as by reflection, I, your glass,
Will modestly discover to yourself
That of yourself which you yet know not of.

—Julius Caesar, 1.2

4.1   Macbeth:

Double, Double

I was in a bar on the top floor of a skyscraper in Singapore.

And I was drunk. Very drunk.

And I was standing on a table, loudly reciting act 1 of *Macbeth*, as people in nearby booths looked on with irritation.

I'd love to say this only happened that one time, but I can't.

"How much of *Macbeth* have you memorized?" a colleague at the Singaporean theater company where I worked had asked, minutes earlier, as she slid me another drink across our table. I grabbed the cocktail and hoisted it into the air like Yorick's skull, staring at it through bleary eyes for long seconds.

"The whole thing," I declared, infused with vodka and false confidence.

"Really?" she said. "Prove it."

And so I found myself atop the table, swaying as I struggled to maintain my balance and ruining act 1 of *Macbeth*.

"Doubtful it stood," I slurred. "As two spent swimmers that do cling together and choke their art." Some of my drink sloshed over the edge of the martini glass and onto my shoe. I frowned at the unexpected wetness on my toe.

To the American taxpayers who funded my time in Singapore through the Fulbright program: I apologize. I do solemnly swear that sometimes I was sober.

After more than four years together, David and I had been pushed by circumstance to far points on the globe. We were still in a relationship—that point had never been in doubt—but David lived in New York City, where he was in medical school, while I lived in Singapore, where I'd landed a dream job working as the dramaturge for a fancy production of *Macbeth*. (That means, more or less, I was the theater's on-call nerd.) I edited the script with the director, Nikolai, defined words for the actors, and helped everyone understand the history, context, and interpretations of the play. I loved my job, and I loved Singapore. But I hated the 9,521 miles between David and me.

If the dull substance of my flesh were thought,
Injurious distance should not stop my way,
For then despite of space I would be brought,
From limits far remote, where thou dost stay.
No matter then although my foot did stand
Upon the farthest earth remov'd from thee,
For nimble thought can jump both sea and land
As soon as think the place where he would be.
But ah, thought kills me that I am not thought,
To leap large lengths of miles when thou art gone,
But that, so much of earth and water wrought,
I must attend time's leisure with my moan,
Receiving nought by elements so slow
But heavy tears, badges of either's woe.

—SONNET 44

Long-distance relationships demand effective communication. I grabbed my cell phone.

"Wheree [sic] are you???" I typed to David, in a drunken text. "Come over hrer [sic] and fruck [sic] me." (I didn't really want David to "fruck" me. You know what I wanted him to do. But I still couldn't say that word to him, even when drunk. Although it had been years since my last real spanking, the fervor of my fetish had not calmed. As Shakespeare wrote in *Henry IV Part 2*, "Is it not strange that desire should so many years outlive performance?")

I had forgotten one detail, though: when you send a sexually explicit text message to your boyfriend at 3:00 A.M. in Singapore, it's only 3:00 P.M. in New York.

"I would love to," David typed in reply. "But I'm in a gross anatomy lecture right now." A second later, he followed up with a helpful addendum: "Also, you're in Asia."

It's hard to be a world away from the person you love.

I'm not only talking about geography.

With David, I had stuffed my real sexuality into a secret space and called it "privacy." I saw no problem with this. In Oman, I had finally achieved some measure of inner peace. That was enough. Outer peace was too much to ask. David didn't need to accept this part of me. He didn't even need to *see* this part of me. He didn't need to know that every night as I fell asleep, or every time I gazed out the window during a car trip, I was thinking about my weird, perverted spanking stories. David could continue to believe that I flirted with the trendy fringes of BDSM, and never find out how deep into its core my identity was lodged. My secret life was my own.

Stars, hide your fires: let not my boyfriend see my black and deep desires, you know?

Macbeth is a play about doubles.

And it begins with a prophecy.

SCOTLAND IS AT war.

Macbeth, a general, is returning home from battle with his best friend, Banquo, when they are confronted by three witches. These "weird sisters" predict that Macbeth, the Thane of Glamis, has a grand destiny: he will be promoted to Thane of Cawdor, and then King of Scotland. When Banquo demands that they look into his future, too, the witches say that he will be "not so happy, yet much happier;" in other words, Banquo won't be king himself, but his descendants will be kings.

Who are these witches? Are they even witches at all?

Interestingly, the word *witch* actually only appears once in the play—and when it does, it's a recollection of something that happened offstage. ("Aroint thee, witch," a sailor's wife said, refusing to share her chestnuts.) More often, the witches refer to themselves as the "weird sisters." But even that isn't certain. The first folio, the earliest source text for many of Shakespeare's plays, describes the women as "weyward Sisters" or "weyard Sisters."

Today, *weyward* and *weyard* aren't words. *Weird* is. So is *wayward*. What's a modern editor to do?

Most editors choose *weird*, since *wyrd* is the Old English word for "fate" or "destiny." It seems appropriate for these sisters who speak of fortune and prophecy. But what about *wayward*? (Sometimes, we can figure out how to pronounce Shakespeare's words or names through iambic pentameter, since when in doubt, it's safe to assume Shakespeare intended to fill his meter. In this case, the witches speak in trochaic tetrameter, which is four feet of trochees, instead of five feet of iambs, but the point remains: the syllabic rhythm of Shakespeare's language is a clue. But since *weird* can be pronounced with two syllables, as can *wayward*, the meter doesn't solve this riddle.) What if Shakespeare intended to describe his three frightening prophets as the "wayward sisters," rather than as the "weird sisters"? Does that even matter?

It's "a simple vowel shift that effects a striking semantic one," write academics Margreta de Grazia and Peter Stallybrass. As "wayward sisters," rather than "weird sisters," the witches are transposed "from the world of witchcraft and prophecy . . . to one of perversion and vagrancy."

What a difference a word can make, right? In *Macbeth*, even language is double.

After the *weyard* sisters—modernize that word how you will—deliver their first prophecy, a messenger appears. He informs Macbeth that the Thane of Cawdor will be executed for treason, and that the title has passed to Macbeth. This development is enough to convince Macbeth that the prophecy is real.

Spurred on by his wife, Lady Macbeth, Macbeth murders King Duncan, implicates Duncan's sons and heirs for the crime, and becomes the King of Scotland. The *weyard* sisters' prophecy has come true—for now.

I wish I could say I found my own prophet on a foggy Scottish moor.

But I lived in Singapore, which means I found my fortune-teller in the most classically Singaporean of places: the mall.

Actually, it'd be more accurate to say she found me.

"Hey, you!" an old woman shouted from a plastic folding table as I walked through the top floor of VivoCity. "You want to hear your fortune?"

I looked around.

"Me?" I mouthed, pointing at myself.

"Yes, you," she shouted. "I will tell you your future!"

Her T-shirt said: BELIEBER!

I paused. I don't believe in fortune-tellers. But on the other hand, I was the dramaturge for a play about witches, prophecies, and phantasmagoria. It was my professional responsibility to have a brush with the mystic beyond, right? Maybe I could even write it off my taxes as a business expense! (Note to the IRS: I didn't.)

I sat down at her table.

"I can do a full palm reading of love, money, family, health, and career for one hundred dollars," she said, "or I can read one topic for twenty-five dollars."

I wasn't about to spend a hundred dollars on a prophecy.

"Love, please," I said.

I held out my palm.

Prophecies are tricky. After Macbeth assumes the Scottish throne, he becomes paranoid, obsessed with keeping his stolen crown. So he returns to the witches one last time. They give him three final prophecies. The first is that he must "beware Macduff," the Thane of Fife. The second is that "none of woman born shall harm Macbeth." And the last is that "Macbeth shall never vanquish'd be until Great Birnam wood to high Dunsinane hill shall come against him."

Macbeth laughs.

"Sweet bodements! Good!" he declares. Everyone is "of woman born," he reasons, and a forest can never uproot itself and march to a hill. Macbeth feels safe.

In VivoCity, the fortune-teller picked up my outstretched palm and squinted at it.

"You have someone," she said.

"Yes," I confirmed. "His name is David."

She nodded.

"You will marry him," she announced, with total confidence. "Your love line is very long. But—"

She frowned and leaned down.

"There is a problem here," she continued. "Do you want me to tell you?"

I nodded.

"Well, your love line is long and strong," she repeated. "But it has a cut."

"My love line breaks?" I asked, surprised. David and I had

never even come close to splitting up. But the fortune-teller shook her head.

"No, it doesn't break," she said. "But there is another line that cuts through it. This other line is very short, but deep. Whatever that line is, it is something that will hurt you."

My heart sank. My infidelity with Dylan had proven that I am capable of terrible things. What I had done to John was my greatest regret: not because John and I broke up—one way or another, that relationship needed to end, and I had no desire to re-create it in my relationship with David—but because that episode had shown me how far short I can fall of the person I aspire to be.

"Does that mean I'll have an affair?" I asked.

The fortune-teller shrugged.

"It could be an affair," she said. "But this intruder line doesn't trail off. Its end is very abrupt. It could also be an abortion."

That did not make me feel better.

"Now that I'm aware of the risk, I can just avoid it, right?" I asked.

The fortune-teller shook her head.

"No," she said. "There is something in your personality that put this line here. It is already written on your hand. This will happen, whether you like it or not."

I shook my head.

"Damn it." I sighed. "Damn it."

Belieber squeezed my hand.

"Don't worry," she said. "This intruder will hurt you. But not for long."

Behind me, in the mall, a little kid screamed. I twisted around in my seat to look, but there was nothing there.

I turned back to face the fortune-teller and gasped.

Her body hung limp, like a broken marionette. Six empty eye sockets stared at me from above three sets of cracked, lipless teeth.

Three rotting tongues crawled in and out of her face, like maggots on a corpse.

I covered my eyes.

"No," I begged, my stomach tight with fear. "I don't want witches. I want to talk to Lady Macbeth."

The mall's sound system, which had been playing Adele's "Rolling in the Deep," abruptly shut off. A loud, screaming static filled the room.

"Fair is foul, and foul is fair," the static shrieked, again and again.

Fair is foul, and foul is fair!
Fair is foul, and foul is fair!
Fair is foul, and foul is fair!
Fair is foul, and foul is fair!
Fair is foul, and foul is fair!

The static stopped. Fifteen fingernails scraped down my scalp.

Three voices, almost inaudible, began to whisper inches from my ear. I didn't breathe for fear an exhalation would drown out the words.

"Beware," they hissed.

"Beware the equivocation of the fiend—

"Beware the equivocation of the fiend that lies like truth.

"—The fiend that lies like truth.

"—Lies like truth."

Then it was silent.

"Rolling in the Deep" crackled back onto the loudspeaker. Laughter and shouts once again filled the mall.

I uncovered my eyes. The witches were gone.

"Do you want another reading?" said the fortune-teller, restored as the grandmotherly Belieber she was before. "Maybe career? Or health? Only twenty-five dollars!"

I swallowed.

"No, thank you," I said.

She nodded and patted my hand.

"When it comes, don't worry," she said. "Your love line won't break."

I walked out of the mall. I stepped into the sunshine, near the monorail to Sentosa Island, and started to feel better. I remembered that I don't believe in fortune-tellers.

"THERE'S NO ART to find the mind's construction in the face," King Duncan says.

Thank God for that, right?

Most nights, after work, I went out for drinks with Nikolai, the director of *Macbeth*. "You look distracted," he said one evening. "What's on your mind?"

I winced. I knew exactly what was on my mind. Ever since Oman, where some women in the Shakespeare class had introduced me to bootlegged DVDs of *The O.C.*, I'd been a huge fan of the pulpy teen drama. By the time I moved to Singapore, however, the show had been canceled and the Internet had given me something even better: *The O.C.* spanking fan fiction. It exists, it is awesome, and it, as usual, was on my mind that evening. Nikolai was innovative, artistic, and nonjudgmental. If I had been fantasizing about Angelina Jolie in a black leather catsuit—in other words, the "sexy" stereotype of BDSM—I probably would have shared the fantasy. Nikolai would have laughed. But it's one thing to be edgy; it's quite another to fantasize about Sandy Cohen, with the epic eyebrows, spanking Ryan Atwood. So, no, my boss didn't need to know what was on my mind.

"I'm not thinking anything," I said, too loudly. "Let's drink."

We did. We drank so much that, before long, we were drunk. Nikolai and I stumbled out of the wine bar and danced down a brick path near Robertson Quay, a posh stretch of restaurants, bars, and clubs along the river. A loose brick jutted out from the path.

"Get it!" Nikolai urged. "Pull it out!"

Giggling with the rush of being bad, I pulled the brick out of the path and threw it in the river. (I regret this. As a guest in Singapore, I had a responsibility to behave better.)

Then we ran.

"We're in trouble now," Nikolai joked. "They're going to cane us!" (As the world was reminded during the 1994 Michael Fay controversy, when an American eighteen-year-old was sentenced to receive four cane strokes on his bare buttocks, the Singaporean judicial system employs corporal punishment.)

"Not me," I teased. "Singaporean courts don't cane women. Only men."

"Really?" Nikolai said.

I nodded.

"Trust me," I slurred. "I know everything there is to know about judicial caning." (Remember all those middle-school book reports on corporal punishment?)

Nikolai grinned.

"Since we're being naughty tonight, shall we be *really* naughty?" he asked.

I nodded.

"Always," I replied.

Section 377A of the Singaporean Penal Code states: "Any male person who, in public or private, commits, or abets the commission of, or procures or attempts to procure the commission by any male person of, any act of gross indecency with another male person, shall be punished with imprisonment for a term which may extend to two years." In other words, the Singaporean penal code criminalizes homosexuality.

Nikolai is gay.

"Let's go to a gay bar," he suggested.

"Do you know where to find one?" I asked.

"Of course," he replied.

Nikolai didn't just know where to find *one*—he knew them all. So we went on a pub crawl that night, walking from nondescript bar to nondescript bar. The more I drank, the less it felt like we were breaking a law. What at first had felt naughty felt, in no time, normal.

"Are you scared the government will come after you?" I asked the owner of one club.

He shrugged.

"Not really," he said. "They leave us alone."

I imagine that with regard to unenforced prohibitions, Singapore is a bit like Shakespeare's England. During his life, homosexuality was technically punishable with harsh laws. But those laws were rarely enforced. As Bruce Smith pointed out, during the combined forty-five years of Elizabeth I's reign and the twenty-three years of James I's reign, there was only one sodomy conviction—and that was for sex with a five-year-old boy, so it would be more accurate to call it a rape conviction.

King James—yes, the same one who sponsored the King James Bible, and the patron for whom Shakespeare wrote *Macbeth*—may have even been gay or bisexual himself. (But it's important to remember that, at that period, those terms didn't exist. It's possible that people then understood sexuality as something more fluid. A lot of how we understand our identities is culturally and historically specific.) James had a wife and three children, but he also spoke quite candidly about his passionate love for men, especially George Villiers, the first Duke of Buckingham. "You may be sure that I love the Earl of Buckingham more than anyone else," said James to his Privy Council in 1617, in what some scholars believe was an early defense of same-sex love. "I wish to speak in my own behalf and not to have it thought to be a defect, for Jesus Christ did the same, and therefore I cannot be blamed. Christ had John, and I have George." And in 1624, during his last illness, James sent Buckingham a telling letter, begging him to come to his bedside:

> I cannot content myself without sending you this billet,
> praying God that I may have a joyful and comfortable meeting
> with you, and that we may make at this Christenmass a
> new marriage, ever to be kept hereafter; for God so love
> me, as I desire only to live in this world for your sake, and
> that I had rather live banished in any part of the earth with
> you, than live a sorrowful widow-life without you. And so
> God bless you, my sweet child and wife, and grant that ye
> may ever be a comfort to your dear dad and husband.

Although most surviving literary references to homosexuality from this period refer to same-sex attraction between men, writers were also aware of lesbian attraction. In one remarkable poem, John Donne—a poet and cleric in the Church of England—imagined sexual desire between women:

> *My two lips, eyes, thighs, differ from thy two,*
> *But so as thine from one another do,*
> *And, O, no more: the likeness being such,*
> *Why should they not alike in all parts touch?*
> *Hand to strange hand, lip to lip none denies;*
> *Why should they breast to breast, or thighs to thighs?*

Shakespeare's own possible homoerotic interests have also been the subject of debate. Although he married Anne Hathaway and fathered three children with her, some readers cite the sonnets as evidence of Shakespeare's bisexuality. Twenty-six of the sonnets are addressed to a married woman, who has often been called the "Dark Lady." But *one hundred* and twenty-six of Shakespeare's sonnets, including Sonnet 18 ("Shall I compare thee to a summer's day?") seem to be addressed to a young man, often called the "Fair

Lord" or "Fair Youth." (Sonnet 20 explicitly bemoans the fact that this young man is not female.) Some scholars theorize that this young man might be the same "Mr. W. H." to whom the sonnets were addressed. Maybe Shakespeare was bisexual. Others reject that theory; after all, there's no reason to assume the sonnets are autobiographical.

What the Singaporean bartender had told me that night seemed true. No one in the club acted worried about an imminent raid. Despite their clandestine nature, the bars we visited did not feel shrouded by fear. I glanced around the room, pausing to wave hello to Antonio from *The Merchant of Venice*. Patrons laughed and flirted. Everyone seemed to be having a good time.

Maybe this wasn't so bad.

Then I saw a familiar face.

One man wasn't having fun.

I had met Edwin, a Singaporean friend, at a mutual friend's beach party on Sentosa Island. We had bonded over our mutual long-distance relationships: my boyfriend was in New York; his girlfriend was in Kuala Lumpur. After that, Edwin and I ran into each other at parties or dinners every few months. He was smart and funny. I liked Edwin, though we didn't share political views.

"It's not biblical," Edwin told me once when same-sex marriage came up. "It's perverse."

Tonight, in a secret gay bar with no sign on the door, Edwin sat alone. He gazed around the room, both hands on a glass of beer. His eyes were hungry and sad.

"Double, double, toil and trouble," begins *Macbeth*'s most famous incantation. Everything in the play is double. Macbeth and Banquo are like "cannons overcharg'd with double cracks," who "doubly redoubled strokes upon the foe." When King Duncan stays at the Macbeths' castle, where he will be murdered, it is "in double trust," and Lady Macbeth promises that their care of him will be "in every point twice done and then done double." Later,

Macbeth tries to kill Macduff in an attempt to "make assurance double sure," only to discover that the witches have toyed with him in "a double sense."

Macbeth is a play about doubles. But there is a twist.

In Shakespeare's tragedies, the hero (or antihero) often has a "double," or voice—a secondary character who speaks for the central figure, linking him to the real world and to the audience. Marjorie Garber describes these sidekicks as "someone on the stage who encounters things and verifies [that what seems] impossible or unbearable [is], nonetheless, true." In *Hamlet*, Horatio fills that role: at the end of the play, Horatio is the one who promises to tell Hamlet's story. In *King Lear*, that voice is Edgar. ("I would not take this from report. It is, and my heart breaks at it," he says at one impossibly sad moment.)

Macbeth's obsession with equivocation speaks to this idea of double voices. The word *equivocation* itself comes from the Latin word *æquivocus*, which means "of equal voice." In *Macbeth*, where even the fundamental premise of the play demands verification— are the witches "real," or merely a product of Macbeth's imagination?—that double voice is more important than ever. At first, Banquo fills that role. He links *Macbeth* (and Macbeth) to the audience. Indeed, Banquo seems to speak for us. "Were such things here as we do speak about? Or have we eaten on the insane root that takes the reason prisoner?" he asks, after the *weyard* sisters first appear. We know Banquo saw the sisters, too. Unlike the dagger that Macbeth sees (or imagines) before he kills King Duncan, Banquo's voice verifies for the audience—and, indeed, for Macbeth himself—that these sisters do exist.

But *Macbeth* has a twist that sets it apart from every other Shakespearean tragedy: Macbeth murders his voice. Mad with fear that Banquo's heirs will seize the throne, Macbeth has Banquo killed. After that, our antihero is on his own. There is no one left to verify what is real and what is not. Macbeth sees—or imagines—Banquo's ghost at a feast, and from then on, there is nothing good left in his life. In fact, the night that Banquo dies is *the very last time* we see Macbeth and Lady Macbeth, who previously had the strongest marriage in the Shakespearean canon, speak to each other. When Macbeth's voice dies, everything else disappears, too. Macbeth is alone.

He can't survive that way. No person can.

In the bar, I lowered my face and walked over to Nikolai.

"We have to leave," I muttered. "My friend is here." I had invaded a safe space. Edwin didn't want to be seen.

Nikolai chugged the rest of his drink and hopped to his feet.

"Let's go," he said. We slipped out of the club.

Whenever Singaporean friends tried to defend 377A, they always emphasized the fact that it is rarely enforced.

"Homosexuals can do whatever they want," a colleague once told me. "They just have to keep it private."

But the look on Edwin's face that night told me a different story. I recognized the expression.

"Privacy" is one of the most potent and insidious weapons a sexual majority can use against people with nonnormative sexual identities. "Privacy" sounds good. It sounds responsible and mature. But "privacy" is tied up with isolation and shame. It drives people underground. It puts people in danger.

"Privacy" palters with us in a double sense.

Sexuality doesn't just appear at age eighteen. Like everyone else, kinky kids grow up with questions about our emerging sexualities. The difference is that, unlike people who grow up with normative sexual orientations, we can't turn to pop culture for answers. There are almost no books, TV shows, or movies that show people like us, or relationships like the ones I craved, in a healthy or positive light. Our fear and shame doesn't just come from negative messages; it comes from the lack of positive ones. When culture insists that people keep their "private" lives "private," those who fall outside the norm fall through the cracks. We have no way to learn how to explore our fantasies safely.

One thing we do have is the Internet. Sexual minorities feel "private" online.

Predators feel "private" online, too.

When my friend Beth was sixteen, she met a fifty-four-year-old sadist on an Internet message board. His name was Logan. Beth was exactly like me at that age: obsessed with spanking and desperate to connect. She talked to Logan because she had no one else. After a few months of emails, Logan drove to Beth's boarding school. She was nervous, but felt obligated to meet him. She didn't want to be rude. He had made hotel reservations. So Beth got permission to leave school grounds for the weekend.

Beth was a virgin. She had never even been kissed. (For obvious reasons, her story hits close to home with me.) She didn't want to have sex with Logan; she just needed to explore her masochistic impulses. But Beth was a good girl. She knew that she was supposed to keep her private life private. So she didn't tell any of her friends where she was going that weekend. She didn't tell anyone whom she was going to meet. Her only safety precaution was to leave a sealed envelope on her desk, with all the information she knew about Logan, just in case.

It was Friday. No one expected her back at school until Sunday night. If Beth disappeared, her friends would not find the envelope until a few days later.

"I was a rational, levelheaded kid," Beth told me. "But the desire for *it* was more important than not getting murdered."

To respect Beth's privacy, I'll leave out the rest of her story. Rest assured: no one had to open that sealed envelope. Beth went on to graduate school, became a top professional in her field, and eventually found healthy, safe, loving ways to explore her fetish with wonderful partners. In the end, things worked out. But the point is that when a kink is lifelong, innate, and unchosen—as it is for people like me and Beth, and many others—it mixes with stigma and "privacy" into danger.

We take risks because the isolation and emptiness of the alternative is worse.

I was lucky. I met John. He and I made mistakes—big ones, in some cases—but I stayed, for the most part, safe. Stories like Beth's are common, but I was the safe one.

Think about that: I dropped out of high school, moved to a foreign country, and let a drug dealer whip me bloody before I had even learned about safe words—and compared to dozens of other stories I've heard, mine was the "safe" path.

Without sexual privacy, discretion suffers. Without sexual transparency, people suffer.

My "privacy," unlike Edwin's, was, for the most part, not the product of institutionalized government oppression. (That being said, fetishists can and do lose jobs, security clearances, or child custody battles because of our consensual orientations; in some places, consensual kink is explicitly illegal.) The biggest thing choking me was me. I'd been force-fed stigma for so long, I had lost the gag reflex to resist. If the men and women of Pink Dot, a grassroots Singaporean movement for LGBT equality, could challenge their government, I had no excuse to cower behind my own shame.

Nikolai and I said good night and I walked home. I lived on the forty-fourth floor of a skyscraper on Cantonment Road, in an apartment I shared with three flatmates. One entire wall of my bedroom was a huge window. I sat on my bed and remembered the expression on Edwin's face. The city skyline sparkled before me.

I thought I'd been so honest with David, but that wasn't true. I had doubled myself up so many times that I was more tightly folded than any origami crane. It would be impossible for anyone to read what had been written on my page. I was so repressed I couldn't breathe.

The façade of honesty is more dangerous than a lie.

I was that equivocator. I was the fiend who lies like truth.

The two spent swimmers that do cling together and choke their art both had my face.

I MOVED BACK to New York.

"Will you marry me?" David said, sitting on the green couch in our living room. We were a few months shy of the five-year minimum I had imposed years earlier, but I was flattered that he jumped the gun. I said yes.

The deadline was clear: I had to out myself—really out myself—to David before we got married. It wasn't fair that I had concealed so much from him for so long. I couldn't let him marry the woman he thought I was.

But how?

"Let's have a long engagement," I said. "Why rush?"

The Macbeths' marriage fascinates me. Harold Bloom argues that "with surpassing irony Shakespeare presents them as the happiest married couple in all his work," and, with a possible challenge from Portia and Brutus in *Julius Caesar*, they win the contest for me, too. In the beginning, at least, no couple communicates better than or is as strong a team as the Macbeths. They are deeply in love with each other; their partnership is ahead of its time. Macbeth doesn't just include his wife in his politics; he turns to her for advice. If I could mimic the dynamic of any Shakespearean marriage, I'd choose to mimic the Macbeths—before the murder, ruthless ambition, and torturous descents into madness and death, that is. Macbeth and Lady Macbeth share honesty, communication, and mutual respect. They have each other's backs. It is only after Lady Macbeth lets political ambition supplant every other ambition, famously declaring that she will "unsex" herself, that she and her husband stop communicating. The last time we see her,

Lady Macbeth furiously tries to wash imagined bloodstains off her hands, in a midnight bout of guilt and madness.

In *Macbeth,* the breakdown of communication is the breakdown of the whole world.

"So how do I tell David about this spanking thing?" I asked Lady Macbeth over oysters and wine in the Financial District. (Lady Macbeth lives in Manhattan, of course. She knows where real power is.)

She squinted.

"Do you worry that you belittle Shakespeare by appropriating us into your reductive little narrative like this?" she asked, drizzling mignonette onto an oyster.

"Every day," I replied. "But the only alternative is to unsex myself. How'd that work out for you?"

Lady Macbeth laughed.

"Touché," she said.

"So what do I say?" I pressed. "Where do I start?"

Lady Macbeth huffed with impatience.

"It's obvious, isn't it?" she said. "Where does my story start?"

I raised my eyebrows.

"Oh," I said, as her implication dawned on me. "Macbeth writes you a letter."

Lady Macbeth's lips stretched out into a wide, toothy smile.

"So write it down," she said.

I went home and googled "spanking fetish."

I read that I'm mentally ill. I read that I've been brainwashed. I read that I've internalized patriarchal oppression. I read that I was spanked too much as a child, so I eroticized that trauma; ironically, I also read that I was spanked too little, so I eroticized the idea of "discipline." I read that I feel guilty for my success and therefore want to punish myself (as if professional guilt explains the masochistic impulses I had by age five). I read that I've been "fooled" (as if my own sexual and intellectual agency are irrelevant). I read that women fundamentally want to submit to men (as if dominant women and submissive men don't exist).

"If [your sexuality] entails wanking to women being tortured, it might be best to leave it unexplored. Or kill yourself," one "feminist" blog declared.

"Sick motherfuckers!" the very first comment agreed. "Absolutely fucking sick!"

In my entire life, I'd never had a single orgasm that didn't revolve around the thought of a woman being "tortured." Or—why lie?—Ryan Atwood being "tortured." Or, more to the point, *me* being "tortured." Even at age eight, when the girl across the street and I had accidental orgasm races with the water jets in her swimming pool to see who could withstand the "tickling" the longest, the fantasies in my head had always been about punishment.

I sighed. The suggestion that I leave my lifelong and unchosen sexual orientation "unexplored" had, of course, never been an option. As for the suggestion that I just kill myself—

I opened a Word document.

Over the next three days, I unfolded myself as best I could. I wrote down things I should have told David five years earlier.

The hardest part of "coming out kinky," if such a thing even exists, isn't coming out to other people. Beyond sexual or romantic partners, coming out to others isn't even necessary. The hardest part is coming out to ourselves. Many never do. I didn't share my obsession publicly in the hope that other fetishists would do the same. I did it in the hope that, despite our national epidemic of sexual repression, a few others might feel empowered to confess their desires to *themselves*.

I passed my laptop, with a draft of what I'd written open on the screen, to David.

"This is hard to show you," I said. "Also, I'm worried that my paragraph structure is confusing."

In that essay, I wrote that coming out of "the closet" isn't the right expression, for any sexual identity. The rooms in which we hide our sexual selves never have only one door. Shame is a labyrinth, with a dozen doors. And every one is heavy.

For me, one door was heavier than the rest.

"I've been exposed to enough pop psychology to recognize the obvious first question: yes, I was spanked as a child, but infrequently and never to an extreme degree," I had written.

Like the *weyard* sisters' prophecies, it was only factually true. Just as they promised, at the end of the play Macbeth is not harmed by someone "of woman born:" Macduff, who eventually defeats Macbeth, was "untimely ripped" from his mother's womb because he came into the world by cesarean section. And Macbeth, as promised, is not vanquished until Birnam Wood comes to Dunsinane hill: Macduff's army cuts down its branches and carries them to disguise their numbers. And I really was spanked "infrequently and never to an extreme degree." But although everything the witches say is factually true, the *truth* is a far different story. At the end of the play, Macbeth is still dead.

I was so afraid to perpetuate the incorrect—and damaging—stereotype that kink is caused by childhood trauma that I had clung to a factual technicality at the expense of truth. The truth was too much. Too painful. Too difficult to face. The truth didn't fit into a thousand words of newsprint.

MACBETH
How does your patient, doctor?

DOCTOR
Not so sick, my lord,
As she is troubled with thick-coming fancies,
That keep her from her rest.

MACBETH
Cure her of that.

Canst thou not minister to a mind diseas'd,
Pluck from the memory a rooted sorrow,
Raze out the written troubles of the brain,
And with some sweet oblivious antidote
Cleanse the stuff'd bosom of that perilous stuff,
Which weighs upon the heart?

DOCTOR
Therein the patient
Must minister to himself.

"Is there a point to any of this?" Cleopatra had asked me. "Or are you just wasting our time?"
There is a point.

4.2   King Lear:
Speak

My hometown was named for a bird that burns itself to death and is reborn. That's how the city itself survives. Each summer, Phoenix explodes into a heat that forces drivers to touch their steering wheels and seat belts only through the protective padding of oven mitts. People call Phoenix "the Valley of the Sun."

What I'm saying is, it gets hot. Very hot.

"Yes, but it's a *dry* heat," Phoenicians reply, as if that matters past 120 degrees.

In my neighborhood, we used the summer heat as a chance to play a vaguely masochistic Phoenician game: we walked barefoot down the street, as our feet burned against the pavement, to see how long we could withstand the heat. One by one, kids would yelp with pain and rush onto the grass for cool relief until only one person, the winner, remained. It's a weird game. I hear kids still play it.

At night, I played another game. From time to time, someone came into my room, when I was four years old or so, to practice naming body parts in the dark. I don't remember this person's face—or even a gender—but I remember our game. The person would touch my nose and say, "Is this your ear?" And I would giggle because it was so silly. That wasn't my ear! And then the person would touch my elbow and say, "Is this your chin?" And I would laugh again. That wasn't my chin! The game always ended the same way, with "Is this your belly button?" But the person was never touching my belly button. That made me laugh, too. It was silly. My belly button was on my stomach, not between my legs.

This chapter is the low point. You could say we're at the nadir. We can only go up from here.

Or I could be wrong. As Shakespeare scolds me, "The worst is not so long as we can say 'This is the worst.'"

But I hadn't read *King Lear* yet.

YOU CAN ASSUME a lot about a person by how he or she reacts to *King Lear*. (At least, I assume a lot.) I assume that people who sympathize with the elderly King Lear, whose ungrateful daughters take advantage of his creeping dementia to push him out of power, were the happy kids. And I assume that people who are more inclined to look for reasons to understand Lear's daughters and Gloucester's bastard son, Edmund, were the unhappy kids.

We don't really *read* literature. We only read ourselves, and each new book is another chapter.

As *King Lear* begins, Lear, the elderly king of Britain, wants to split his kingdom between his three daughters—Regan, Goneril, and Cordelia. But there's one condition: before they receive that inheritance, the daughters must describe their love for Lear. Regan and Goneril flatter their father with obsequious declarations of love, and their father rewards them each with a third of his kingdom. But when it's time for Cordelia, Lear's youngest and most beloved daughter, to speak, she resists. She tells her father that although she loves him as a daughter should, it would be insincere for her to pretend, as her sisters did, that she loves him more than she will love her future husband.

"What can you say to draw a third more opulent than your sisters?" the king urges his youngest daughter. "Speak."

"Nothing, my lord," Cordelia replies.

To me, the fact that Cordelia refuses to humor her father's request for words of love is the most fascinating mystery in the play. Why won't she just tell her dad that she loves him? He's an old man. He wants to hear that his daughters love him. What's wrong with that? Cordelia's refusal to comply seems especially ungrateful when we remember that, according to sixteenth-century philosophies of kingship, Lear wasn't even obligated to divide his kingdom between his three daughters. In fact, to split his kingdom this way would have been considered counter to divine law, which said that kingdoms should pass undivided to the eldest child after the reigning monarch's death. With that in mind, Cordelia's refusal to describe how much she loves her father, despite the fact that he's circumventing God's law on her behalf, seems cruel.

King Lear recoils with surprise.

"Nothing!" he says.

"Nothing," she confirms.

"Nothing will come of nothing," the king warns. "Speak again."

But Cordelia doubles down. She refuses to play this game. At that, her father flies into an uncontrolled rage. He disinherits and banishes her.

Adults forget what it's like to be a child. I think that's why we don't extend more sympathy to Lear's eldest daughters, who, after Cordelia's banishment, treat their father with cruel disregard as he descends into madness. But Regan and Goneril are not that old. At the beginning of the play, they're most likely in their late teens or early twenties. How terrifying must it be for Regan and Goneril to watch their father's abrupt and violent banishment of Cordelia, knowing, as they do, that he values them even less? In

sixteenth- and seventeenth-century England, daughters were the
literal, legal property of their fathers. I think they've been twisted
into something hard and heartless after years under their father's
powerful heel. I know exactly how destabilizing it is to grow up
under the total control of someone so powerful yet so unpredictable and easily enraged.

I was ten years old. My mother woke me up early one summer
morning. She was erratic and inconsistent with everything, and
the educational choices she imposed on me were no different. By
then I had attended at least six different schools.

Yet again, it was time for a change. This time my mom hoped
to enroll me in a public school in a different, wealthier district. I
was exhausted. I didn't want to get out of bed. It was supposed to
be my summer vacation. But since we didn't live in that school's
neighborhood, we had to meet with the principal to see if I could
charm my way into one of the few spots reserved for out-of-district
students.

I don't remember much of that meeting, other than how tired
I felt. I must have thought it had gone fine, though, because I
was stunned to learn as we left that my mom was furious. She
thought I had been rude. She screamed at me through the parking
lot, dragging me toward her car, while I begged her to yell more
quietly and not make a scene in front of any future classmates who
might be lurking on the playground.

When we got to her parked car, she pulled a flat hairbrush out
of her purse and told me to lie, facedown, on the backseat. My
mom's outbursts of physical violence were usually too uncontrolled
to call them "spankings," but she had targeted my butt enough
times that I knew exactly what she intended to do. I was crying
and scared, but I thought maybe we could negotiate. I suggested a
compromise: "Not with the brush," I begged, in tears.

"No," she said. "Get on your stomach."

The human response to fear, they say, is to fight or to fly. But there are moments when neither is possible. For me to get on my stomach and offer up the sexual center of my body against my will, I had to choke down the human inside me until she stopped my breath.

I lay, facedown, on the backseat of my mom's Volvo.

I had been playing kinky games with neighborhood friends for at least five years by this point. Given how early I can pinpoint the origin of my kink, some people have, incomprehensibly, asked me whether it's easier to be spanked by a parent when you're developing a spanking fetish. Of course it's not easier. It's worse. It felt like the most erotic part of my body was being violated against my will, in a way that was profoundly sexual to me—because that's exactly what was happening.

Then it was over. My mom returned to the driver's seat and began to drive home. I remained in the backseat, furious. I almost never talked to myself—to this day, my thoughts process in feelings or images, not words—but in that moment I decided I should. I could comfort myself.

Hey, I thought to myself gently, *at least it's over.*

From the front seat, my mother announced: "I'm going to do it again when we get home."

Twenty minutes later, I was sitting on the floor of our kitchen, my butt pressed into the three-way protection of the corner and floor, while my mother beat me with her hairbrush on my arms, which I had wrapped around my head, and the sides of my body.

That was much better for me, by the way. At least my butt, that big clitoris on the back of my pelvis, was safe.

Several hours later, my mom told me to come out of my bedroom, where I had been crying, sulking, and indulging in maudlin revenge fantasies. She was sitting on a couch in the living room.

"Take down your pants," she said coldly. "I want to see if you're bruised."

"No," I said. "It's *my* body."

"Do what I say, or I'll spank you again," she replied.

That was the shibboleth; the magic words that overpowered my fierce declaration of bodily integrity and self-determination. Simmering with rage, I pulled down my pants and underwear and showed her my butt.

She touched one cheek with the tip of her finger.

"You have a bruise there," she said.

She moved her finger to the other cheek.

"And there."

I would not speak about this memory—not to anyone, not even to myself—for more than a decade.

But for the next eighteen years, when I was alone, I would have flashbacks to this day, usually in cars. For no apparent reason, I'd start to cry: violent, choking sobs that always forced me, for safety's sake, to pull my car onto the side of the road. Then a fist of nausea would punch up through my stomach, and I'd spill out of the driver's seat, throwing up onto the asphalt. What couldn't come out in words came out in vomit.

Roughly a year after that incident, when I was eleven, I found a text brochure in a doctor's office. It listed, in titillating words like "bruises" and "welts," the warning signs for child abuse. I took it home and tucked it into a space between my bed and the wall.

That brochure didn't stay in the dark space. It came out—a lot.

I was a masochist, but didn't know it yet. I was confused. The closest reference points for my emerging sexual identity were things that had happened nonconsensually, and at my mother's hands. I was a child. I spoke to myself in the only language I'd been taught.

When I was twelve or thirteen, I went to a pool party. I hadn't done a good job putting on sunscreen, and my back and thighs burned fire-engine red in the sun. When I got home, my mom was, as usual, furious.

"Get on your stomach," she ordered. It's a loaded phrase.

"Please, no," I begged, in that tone of voice exclusive to scared kids in trouble.

She left the room. I thought she was getting something to spank me with, but she returned with a bottle of aloe vera. She just wanted to put it on the backs of my thighs, where the burns were worst. She wanted to help. But to this day, I can still recall the sickening crush of fear that washed through me when she told me to lie down.

As I entered early adolescence, my mother went through a phase where she sometimes patted my butt, lightly, while we were walking. It disgusted me. Every time she did it, I seethed with rage and growled at her to keep her hands off me. Once, when I was roughly thirteen, she did it while we were walking in a mall.

I spun around to face her. I grabbed her wrist and squeezed it, as tight as I could, in my fist. It felt small and vulnerable. I was getting bigger. Suddenly, I was the one with some physical power.

I let go of my mother's wrist.

"Never touch me there," I roared.

"What?" my mom said—laughing, I presume, at what she perceived to be the adolescent extremity of my reaction. "It's just a love pat!"

I felt nauseous.

That night, I dreamed I was kicking her in the face. I kicked until I felt the bones give way and the tip of my shoe crashed into wet, bloody tissue. I woke to discover I had been crying in my sleep.

As an adult, when I confronted my mother with those memories, she cried. That reaction surprised me.

"Why are you upset?" I asked her.

"Because it's gruesome," she said.

I felt cold and compassionless. This story has two victims.

None of this caused my fetish, but I've learned to tolerate skepticism of that fact. What I do know is that these memories left me

vulnerable to a self-defeating fear, which would haunt me for years
to come, that my sexuality was "sick." What could have been—
should have been—a source of pure pleasure had been poisoned.

I felt, in the pit of my stomach, that my fetish was *not*, as conventional psychiatry would have me believe, the result of childhood trauma. But how could I deny that theory with such certainty
when my own life seemed to confirm it?

When Cordelia refuses to tell her father how much she loves
him, she puts her own life in danger. What would have happened
to the newly disowned and disinherited Cordelia if the King of
France hadn't rescued her with a marriage proposal? (If France
hadn't offered Cordelia that domestic lifeboat, then she, not her
father, would be forced out onto the stormy heath. How would
that story end?) Shakespeare did not write stupid women. So why
does Cordelia refuse Lear's demand that she perform love for him,
even at the risk of dangerous banishment?

Something is very wrong with this family.

When Lear orders his daughters to display their "love" for him
in a perverse competition for land, it's obvious that he misunder-
stands love. (The King of France, an outsider to the situation and
to the family, points out that "love's not love when it is mingled
with regards that stands aloof from th' entire point.") Lear thinks
that love can be purchased—and his eldest daughters, Regan and
Goneril, are familiar with this transaction. They don't hesitate.
Lear snaps his fingers, and they perform for him on cue. They declare that they love their father more "than eyesight, space, and lib-
erty," and that their love for him is so paramount that it is, in fact,
"enemy to all other joys." Regan and Goneril are often criticized
for the gushing insincerity of these replies, but I think that's unfair.
They're only doing what their father has ordered them to do.

Cordelia, on the other hand, tells her father: "I love your Majesty according to my bond, no more nor less." Then she zeroes in
on a specific objection to her sisters' speeches:

Why have my sisters husbands, if they say
They love you all? Happily, when I shall wed,
That lord whose hand must take my plight shall carry
Half my love with him, half my care and duty.
Sure I shall never marry like my sisters,
To love my father all.

In Cordelia's rebuttal, and indeed throughout this first scene, Shakespeare draws uncomfortable parallels between the kind of love that Lear expects from his daughters and the kind of love that exists between spouses.

It's important to consider that in Cordelia's famous first reply, she doesn't actually say nothing. She says, "Nothing." She makes a firm declaration of her unwillingness to participate in this forced demonstration of love. Why does Cordelia feel the need to be so explicit in telling her father about the fact that her love is nothing more than natural filial affection? Why doesn't that go without saying?

The interpretation that most fascinates me is also the darkest. What if Cordelia suspects that the kind of love her father demands is unnatural? What if she believes that her father has sexually abused her two older sisters, and she fears that the same gruesome fate awaits her? (I am not the only person to sense an ominous sexual edge in *King Lear*: the idea is perhaps best explored in Jane Smiley's 1991 novel *A Thousand Acres*, which transplants Lear and his abused daughters to an Iowa farm.) The possibility that King Lear is a sexual predator transforms almost every aspect of the play and all of the characters in it. From this perspective, the insincerity of Regan and Goneril's forced declarations of love seems more like self-defense—and Cordelia's refusal to obey, even at the risk of her own safety, makes sense.

A number of textual clues hint at this possibility. The King of France is immediately suspicious of Lear's motivations and behavior toward Cordelia:

This is most strange,
That she, whom even but now was your best object,
The argument of your praise, balm of your age,
The best, the dearest, should in this trice of time
Commit a thing so monstrous, to dismantle
So many folds of favor. Sure, her offense
Must be of such unnatural degree
That monsters it, or your fore-vouch'd affection
Fall into taint; which to believe of her
Must be a faith that reason without miracle
Should never plant in me.

The King of France recognizes what so many people miss: this is not healthy parental love. The words that he chooses— *monstrous, unnatural, offense*—paint a dark frame around the entire scene. Did Lear, perhaps, organize this strange test of love in the specific hope that Cordelia would fail it, lose her dowry, and therefore lose all of her marriage prospects? Was this scenario designed to remove any rivals for Lear's most prized daughter? Is that the "darker purpose" Lear hints at in his second line of the play?

In *King Lear,* Shakespeare uses phallic and sexual language to an extent that seems extreme for a political and domestic drama. When Kent, a nobleman, tries to intervene to protect Cordelia from Lear's wrath, for example, the King warns him: "The bow is bent and drawn, make from the shaft." (*Shaft* seems to have been a favorite phallic pun of Shakespeare's; he also described "Cupid's fiery shaft" in *Midsummer.*)

There are ominous sexual innuendos in Regan and Goneril's conversations, too. After Cordelia's banishment, Goneril approaches Regan to discuss "what most nearly appertains to us both"—that is, a secret they share that cuts close to the bone—as they list which nights they expect Lear to spend with each daughter. Goneril confides in Regan that she fears their father, empowered with a band of knights, will "hold our lives in mercy." She concludes, "Let me still take away the harms I fear, not fear still to be taken. I know his heart." Soon after, she tells Oswald, a servant, to deliver a letter to Regan, which will "inform her full of my particular fear."

As I've said, whenever a word appears multiple times in a single scene, it's worthy of consideration. In that scene, the word *fear* appears six times. Goneril is scared.

With good reason. Earlier in the play, Lear makes an ominous threat to Goneril that he might "resume the shape which thou dost think I have cast off for ever." Later, when Lear tries to talk his way into Regan's house, he warns her, "'Tis not in thee to grudge my pleasures." He adds that she shouldn't try to "oppose the bolt against my coming in."

But the most damning lines of all are the ones Lear speaks in a fit of madness:

> *Tremble, thou wretch*
> *That hast within thee undivulged crimes*
> *Unwhipt of justice! Hide thee, thou bloody hand;*
> *Thou perjur'd, and thou simular man of virtue*
> *That are incestuous!*

In this moment of vulnerability, is Lear speaking to himself? Is the "bloody hand" Lear describes a manifestation of his own guilt, as a similar vision is for Lady Macbeth? Is he the "incestuous" man who breaks under the weight of "undivulged crimes?" At the end of the play, Cordelia tries to heal her ill father with a kiss, saying: "Restoration hang thy medicine on my lips." Why do those words—and that kiss—feel so similar to Juliet's final kiss with Romeo, when she tries to suck poison from his lips, saying, "I will kiss thy lips. Haply some poison yet doth hang on them, to make me die with a restorative?"

CAN SPANKING CHILDREN be a sexual violation?

Of course it can. In 2006, a businessman in Tennessee was convicted of sexual battery for spanking employees without their consent. Why would the same nonconsensual physical act cease to be sexual battery merely because the target is a child?

For obvious reasons, there isn't much funding for scientific research into the origins of fetishism. But it really doesn't matter what causes it. It doesn't matter whether I was born with my sexuality intact, as I believe, or whether my fetish was imprinted early in life by events I can or can't remember. What does matter is that sexuality—even nonnormative sexuality—exists in children far earlier than most people want to admit. By the time I was three years old, I was a fetishist, and spanking, to me, was a sex act more penetrative than sex. From that point on, for me, nonconsensual spankings were unintentional sexual assaults. I experienced them as such.

Winston Churchill supposedly said: "If you have an important point to make, don't try to be subtle or clever. Use a pile driver. Hit the point once. Then come back and hit it again. Then hit it a third time—a tremendous whack."

So I have three things to say.

Children have emerging sexual identities.

Children have emerging sexual identities.

Children have emerging sexual identities—and if even 1 percent of them perceive spanking as a sex act, *we are sexually violating too many kids.*

Not every child feels that the butt is the most erotic part of his or her body, as I did. But bottoms are widely understood to have sexual potential. That's why if most adults saw a teacher patting a child's ass, for example, they would react *considerably* differently than they would if they saw that teacher patting a child's shoulder. Our widespread cultural denial of the fact that the same body part that is so erotic for many adults might also be sexual for many children is not only willfully obtuse, it's dangerous.

My opinions on the relativity of sexual assault do not come from a position of inexperience. I have those memories of being molested as a toddler—it's how I learned to name my body parts—but I also acknowledge that memories from early childhood can be unreliable. I have felt frustrated and confused by these memories, but I have never felt traumatized by them. They've never caused a nightmare, let alone a flashback. Years later, when I was a teenager, a man held me down, as tears ran down my face and I said, "I don't want to have sex," and had sex with me. That upset me.

But that did not traumatize me, either.

Many other people, without a doubt, would have, and have had, traumatic reactions to the same events. Their reactions are fully justified—but so are mine. Just as there is no "correct" way to be a sexual creature, there is no "correct" emotional response to sexual assault. And there is no easy definition of what sexual assault can be. The fact that most people with normative sexual identities did not feel sexually violated by childhood spankings no more disproves my experience than the fact that I was relatively unbothered by being forced to have vaginal sex against my will disproves the experience of traumatized rape survivors.

Most smokers don't get lung cancer. That doesn't make cigarettes safe.

As I've said, my butt has always been, by far, the most erotic part of my body. (I've wondered if that might explain why I wasn't nearly as shaken by those nonconsensual violations of my vagina.) If being nonconsensually assaulted on an erotic body part doesn't qualify as sexual assault, what does? Parents have to touch their children's bodies, of course. But there is a big difference between the kind of touch that keeps a child healthy, like putting on a diaper, and the kind of touch that is explicitly nonconsensual and makes a child scream.

PEOPLE WILL INSIST that childhood spankings have no sexual intent. (My mother, of course, did not imagine that being repeatedly hit on a "private" body part might make me feel sexually violated.) I have two responses to that. The first is that intent doesn't matter. The man who had sex with me while I begged him to stop, for example, did not intend to sexually violate me; according to him, he merely intended to show me how "irresistible" I was. Intent is irrelevant.

My second response to the claim that childhood spankings can never be sexual assault because they have no sexual intent is: Are you sure? Are you *certain* there are no repressed spanking fetishists out there—working as principals in schools that administer corporal punishment, for example, or writing books about why parents should dare to discipline their kids? How much would you gamble on that certainty?

But things change slowly, most of all minds. The best thing I can do—the only thing I can do, really—is talk about my experience so that people who also felt sexually violated by childhood spankings will know, at least, that they weren't alone.

Two years after I first started to write about spanking, I described the physiological reasons that spanking children is sexually problematic in an article I wrote for *Slate*. The reaction from readers was immediate and overwhelming. I got emails with subject lines like "Thank God someone finally said it!!!!" and "You Just Saved Me."

A few emails came from people who aren't fetishists, but still felt damaged by the sexual perversity of childhood spankings, such as this one:

> I suffered physical and sexual abuse as a child and that act
> [spanking] was a part of both. And in fundamentalist Christian homes, like mine, there is more than a little sexualizing

in those acts. That's part of the draw of it. They love it
and it turns them on in a big way. It took me a long time
to untangle this. Thanks for articulating what I felt. I do
not have that fetish, but I know it is sexual behavior.

I got emails from fetishists who told heartbreaking stories
about otherwise good parents who left them with decades of
trauma symptoms, such as this one:

> When I was 7 years old, my dad lost his temper with me and
> spanked me—and because he lost his temper, he hit me very,
> very, very hard. I had never been spanked before. My dad was
> not a bad man at all; he loved me very much. He also never
> spanked me again. Sadly, that one time did a great deal of
> damage. My best friend knows this. She also knows I have had
> a spanking fetish (that I can't engage in at all) since I was five
> years old. (It started with a dream.) So she sent me your two
> articles on spanking. I read the one about not using spanking as
> a punishment first. Learning about the physical aspects—such
> as the nerve tracks and the artery in the butt/groin—caused a
> profound revelation in me. My entire life, I have carried about
> 40% of the markers of a rape victim—uh, survivor—but I
> have never been raped. As a result of this great mystery, of
> my inability to explain or make connections, no therapist has
> ever been able to help me. But now I finally, finally, finally
> understand what happened. Or rather I understand what my body
> experienced. . . . You just enabled one suffering adult to finally
> make the right connection to go get help and take back her life.

One spanking fetishist, who has served several tours in combat
zones with one of the most elite branches of the U.S. military,
raised an interesting possibility.

"My shrink thinks my PTSD is from combat," he wrote to me.
"Ha ha."

It was the first time someone had suggested a label for the vomiting "episodes" that had plagued me for seventeen years.

"Is that what this is?" I replied. "PTSD?"

"That's what I think it is," Toby wrote. "I see a lot of it over here."

After Toby raised the possibility, I read a lot about post-traumatic stress disorder—both medical descriptions in David's textbooks and Shakespearean descriptions in *Henry IV, Part 1.* The symptoms were familiar: flashbacks, avoidance, nightmares, depression, sleeplessness, angry outbursts.

Every single day from age ten to age twenty-eight, I wrestled with one question: How could I be so viscerally certain that fetishism is *not* caused by childhood trauma when my own trauma seemed to contradict that? For eighteen years, I poked at that question like a loose tooth. Then one day, just like that, the tooth gave way and blood flowed out:

Trauma doesn't cause kink. But kink can cause trauma.

In other words, if a child's innate sexuality is nonconsensually inflicted on her, trauma is a natural response.

Most of my rage, which had been the product of my inability to understand what had happened to me, went away. In the chicken-and-egg question of which came first, I suddenly understood, with perfect clarity and absolute certainty, which did.

I haven't had a single flashback or nightmare since.

Different ideas aren't easy to swallow. There are more popular ways to interpret *King Lear.* When Lear tells Goneril that he will resume a prior shape, he might only mean that he'll regain his former kingly power and authority. It's important to acknowledge, too, that after Lear bemoans "undivulged crimes" and a seemingly virtuous man who is "incestuous," he goes on to claim that he, in contrast, is "more sinned against than sinning." And despite the sexual implications of shafts, bolts, and "coming in," double entendre alone can't convict Lear of sexual predation.

As Lear says, "How sharper than a serpent's tooth it is to have a thankless child." It's easiest to dismiss Regan and Goneril as ungrateful monsters.

But Shakespeare encourages us to resist that impulse. "Let them anatomize Regan; see what breeds about her heart," Lear also says. Regan and Goneril are cruel, but much is lost if we don't even try to ask ourselves in what garden those hearts have grown.

The problem with a sexually abusive reading of *King Lear* is that it develops a terrifying new tragedy at the expense of the more traditional one. It's impossible to empathize with a predatory Lear. That version of the character would deserve everything he suffers throughout the play, and more. How can we rob ourselves of the chance to weep for Lear when he rips his clothes on the heath or finds Cordelia's body?

An explicitly abusive version of the play robs us of the ability to feel for Lear. But an explicitly sympathetic Lear robs us of the ability to feel for his daughters.

So I think that the best version of *King Lear* is exactly the one that Shakespeare wrote: ambiguous. It's the only version in which each character is frustratingly, but fascinatingly, complex. Cordelia loves her tyrannical and mercurial father, but she can't bring herself to say it. It's a paradox—and a question—so rich and sad that Shakespeare required a whole play to explore it.

I LIKE TO think Cordelia and I would be friends. We'd find a wine bar in Manhattan, someplace decorated with wood and candles, and settle into a quiet table at the back. I'd order a South African shiraz and pour us each a glass.

"What's the secret to forgiveness?" I would ask her.

Cordelia would think for a minute, then open her mouth to speak.

"No," I'd interrupt. "Don't you dare say 'nothing,' Cordelia. Aren't you sick of that by now?" She'd chuckle a little and swirl her wine around her glass. Finally, she'd take a sip.

"We are not the first who with best meaning have incurred the worst," she'd say, looking into her drink.

I'd huff with impatience.

"Come on, Cordelia," I'd groan, rolling my eyes. "Speak what we feel, not what we ought to say."

There would be a long pause. Then Cordelia would say: "I cannot heave my heart into my mouth."

And there's no response to that. She's right. Some things are too heavy to lift to words. They sit in the pits of our stomachs until, with time, they digest—or they settle in the subtext. So I'd pick up the bottle, refill our glasses, and Cordelia and I would drink.

4.3   Othello:

Beast with Two Backs

Sex is one thing.

The *idea* of sex is something else.

"This is hard to show you," I told David as I slid my laptop, with its essay full of secrets, across the bed. "Also, I'm worried that my paragraph structure is confusing."

David began to read.

I sat next to him. This was uncomfortable. I didn't want to read over his shoulder, but I wasn't sure what else to do with my eyes. I looked at David. His Adam's apple moved. He had swallowed as he read.

I climbed off the bed and walked into the bathroom. I splashed water onto my face. Just as I had done years earlier, in Spain, before I bent over to inhale that first line of cocaine, I glanced up at the mirror above the sink.

Acts of self-destruction are supposed to follow a dramatic moment with a mirror, right?

I turned off the faucet.

Back in the bedroom, David had finished reading. I leaned against the doorframe.

"So," I said.

David climbed off the mattress and wrapped his arms around my waist. I stiffened.

"I love you," he said. "You're so brave." He paused for a second, then added: "And there's nothing wrong with your paragraph structure."

Weeks later, when that essay (with David's encouragement) appeared in the Modern Love column of the *New York Times,* it ended with those words.

The response was overwhelming. Hundreds of emails poured into my inbox from people around the world. I heard from people of all ages and backgrounds, with stories, questions, and fears just like mine. I got an email from a woman close to my age who wrote to me *from her refugee camp* to ask how she should tell her boy-friend, also a refugee, about her own spanking fetish. (Before her country fell into brutal civil war, she had been an English teacher, which is why she was able to read my *New York Times* article.) We struck up a friendship.

"I'm always happy to talk about spanking," I wrote to her one day. "But I feel embarrassed to focus on that when you face such bigger problems."

"I have many problems in my life, yes," she replied. "But it is the loneliness that is the worst. It is the feeling I am broken." Her words took my breath away.

"Great article. From a fellow . . . Brasenose alum," a man named Cyan wrote to me, only a few hours after the essay appeared online. (He had read about my educational history on my website.)

I called for David to come look at my computer screen. Years earlier, when I had spent that term at Oxford University, study-ing Shakespearean cartography, Brasenose had been my college, too.

"A Brasenose person wrote to me!" I exclaimed. "Small world, huh?"

David snorted.

"That's not his point, Jillian," he said.

I scrunched up my nose.

"Why would he lie about that?" I replied.

David laughed.

"I'm sure it's true that he went to Brasenose," he said. "But *that's not his point.*"

My eyes widened.

"Oh," I said, as the implication of Cyan's ellipsis dawned on me. "*Oh.* I'm so gullible."

David kissed the top of my head.

"Yeah," he agreed, walking off.

Cyan followed me on Twitter. I followed him back.

But the most common question I received, given the essay's unresolved ending, was: What happened next?

Like I said, the idea of sex is one thing.

Sex is something else.

"Get on your hands and knees," David suggested, only a few days after the article ran. "I'm in the mood to do this doggy style."

I giggled.

"Okay," I agreed. The point is, my butt was right in David's face. And he didn't even *touch* it. Not once.

"Do you feel paralyzed by pressure?" I asked after, my fingers on my forehead. "Are you overwhelmed?"

"I promise, I'm not overwhelmed," David said. "I just forgot. That's it."

I looked up and pointed at my computer. The screen showed my email inbox. In the previous hour, I had received twenty-eight new unread messages. Most of them were from people who wanted to talk about my essay.

"People around the whole world heard what I'm trying to tell you," I said, starting to cry. "How are you the only one who missed the message?"

"Oh, honey, I got the message," David said. "I just forgot."

He smiled.

I tried to brush away my tears. But I was *terrified*.

"We can take it slow," I insisted. "We'll go at whatever pace makes you comfortable. I don't want to rush you. But you have to talk to me."

"There's nothing to talk about," David replied. "I love you. I support you."

I shook my head.

He did spank me sometimes, of course. Much more often than he had before. But something was missing.

As our sexual life struggled to find its footing, our professional lives exploded. David was swamped with his clinical year of medical school. For my part, the gamble I'd made when I cut out my heart and sold it to the *New York Times* for five hundred bucks paid off. Suddenly, I was a journalist. Editors invited me to pitch them stories about sexuality; I responded with other ideas. I got to write about human rights in North Korea, tourism in Bosnia and Herzegovina, nuclear security in Iran, and dozens of other issues, for publications I'd idolized for years. Work often took me away from New York. Even when I was in town, David was usually at the hospital.

Months passed, and I woke up in the Philippines.

The theater company I had worked for when I lived in Singapore had flown me back to Asia to deliver a new series of Shakespeare lectures in conjunction with their newest production, and I took advantage of the transpacific flight to work on articles for the *Washington Post*, *Slate*, and the *Atlantic*. Journalism inflamed the same part of me that had been so focused on international politics back when I lived in Spain, and I was hungry to learn as much as I could.

One morning, I tweeted a question about the Spratly Islands, a disputed archipelago off the Philippine, Malaysian, and Vietnamese coastlines.

An instant message window popped up on my screen.

"Why are you learning about the Spratlys?"

I frowned at the user name. At first, I didn't recognize it. Then I realized it was Cyan—the fellow "Brasenose alum" who had praised my spanking article six months earlier.

"Oh, that's right," I typed back. "You work in foreign policy, don't you?" Cyan and I had never had a conversation in real time before, but I'd followed him on Twitter long enough to get a sense of his job. He sometimes tweeted a remark about one of my articles, but other than that he left me alone.

"I focus on North Africa and the Middle East, but I've done some Asia work," he replied. "I might be able to answer your questions."

"Why are you awake?" I asked. "Isn't it like three A.M. in the U.K.?"

"It is," he wrote. "But I live in D.C. now."

For months, I'd avoided friendships with people who had emailed me in response to my spanking article. But this was different, wasn't it? Cyan and I shared an alma mater. If he had been a few years younger, we would have been at Brasenose at the same time.

Besides, it's not like I could talk about disputed Asian archipelagos with just anyone.

"Cool," I typed. "Why are these tiny islands such a big deal?"

In *Othello,* the surface of things doesn't reflect the continental shelf that lies below.

DURING SHAKESPEARE'S LIFE, people said the liver, not the heart, was the seat of love. In *Twelfth Night,* for example, Orsino, ranting to Cesario that female love is superficial compared to male love, claims that women love from the palate, not the liver:

> *There is no woman's sides*
> *Can bide the beating of so strong a passion*
> *As love doth give my heart; no woman's heart*
> *So big, to hold so much; they lack retention.*
> *Alas, their love may be call'd appetite,*
> *No motion of the liver, but the palate,*
> *That suffer surfeit, cloyment, and revolt,*
> *But mine is all as hungry as the sea,*
> *And can digest as much. Make no compare*
> *Between that love a woman can bear me*
> *And that I owe Olivia.*

—*Twelfth Night*, 2.4

Livers appear throughout the canon. In *Love's Labor's Lost*, for example, Berowne says of some erotic poetry: "This is the liver-vein, which makes flesh a deity." In *Twelfth Night*, when one character senses that a mean-spirited romantic trick will work, he remarks: "This wins him, liver and all." In *The Merry Wives of Windsor*, Pistol describes Falstaff as "with liver burning hot," and in *Much Ado About Nothing*, one character says of Claudio that "if ever love had interest in his liver"—that is, if Claudio had truly loved his betrothed—he would not have suspected her of infidelity. In *Antony and Cleopatra*, when a soothsayer tells a woman that she "shall be more beloving than beloved," the woman retorts: "I had rather heat my liver with drinking." (The philosophy that love lives in the liver wasn't unique to Shakespeare's England: some traditional Arab cultures also believed that when a person falls in love, the beloved steals his or her liver.)

But Shakespeare didn't associate the liver only with love and erotic passion: he also connected it to courage (as in *Macbeth* and *Hamlet*), to jealousy (as in *The Winter's Tale*), and to anger (as in *Troilus and Cressida*). Strong emotions are born in the liver. They travel through our bodies in its bile.

In Shakespeare's words: "Reason and respect make livers pale and lustihood deject."

The point is, I think about livers.

"Can we play tonight, maybe?" I asked David, on one of the rare days when he and I were both home.

"Of course," he said. "Sure."

I ducked my head. I felt guilty, like a sex offender. I worried I was pressuring a good man into something repulsive against his will.

"I'm sorry," I said. "I just . . . need it."

David gave me a hug.

"You don't need to apologize, honey," he said. "It's fine."

That night, David came up to me.

"Do you want to watch a movie?" he asked.

I blinked.

"Oh," I said. "Oh."

"*Total Recall* is on Netflix," he added.

I shifted on my feet.

"Or we could watch *Secretary*," I offered. "It's not perfect, but it might spark some conversation."

David sighed.

"Can we save it for another night?" he asked, rubbing his eyes. "I'm so tired. It was a long week at the hospital."

I pulled my lips into my mouth, rubbing them against each other.

"Sure," I said. "Of course."

In *Othello*, things go unconsummated. From lusty beginning to tragic end, sex is just an idea.

OTHELLO BEGINS IN Venice. Roderigo, a wealthy gentleman, is complaining to Iago, an ensign, that Roderigo's crush, Desdemona, has just eloped with a Moor named Othello.

The racial specifics of the term *Moor* are open to debate. Technically, the Moors were the Islamic inhabitants of North Africa, Sicily, and the Iberian Peninsula, but during Shakespeare's life the term was also used to describe anyone of African descent, regardless of religion. Othello does say "I am black," but Elizabethans routinely referred to anyone with dark hair as "black," so it's also possible that Othello is North African or Middle Eastern. (My friends in Oman imagined Othello as a fellow Arab.) However, as Virginia Mason Vaughan points out, Roderigo calls Othello "thick lips," which was a common racial slur used by sixteenth-century explorers in sub-Saharan Africa and points to that region as Othello's place of origin. In any case, Othello is a person of color—and racial tension permeates every detail of his play.

Roderigo is desolate at news of Desdemona's elopement, but Iago reassures him that he has a plan to disrupt their marriage. Iago hates Othello—in part because Othello, an honored general, passed him over for a promotion in favor of Cassio, a mere "arithmetician" with far less battle experience, and in part because, according to rumor, Othello has slept with Iago's wife, Emilia. Iago wants revenge. He and Roderigo wake Brabantio, Desdemona's father, to tell him about the secret marriage. Iago paints a lurid portrait, saying, "Even now, now, very now, an old black ram is tupping your white ewe."

The mere idea of this sexual miscegenation is so strong that Brabantio flies into a rage. At the Venetian senate, he accuses Othello of using witchcraft to seduce his daughter. But Othello recounts how words, not witchcraft, won Desdemona's love. He summons her to confirm that account. Desdemona arrives and declares her love, loyalty, and allegiance to her new husband. As

Brabantio storms out, he plants this ominous seed in Othello's ear: "Look to her, Moor, if thou hast eyes to see. She has deceived her father, and may thee."

But before Othello and Desdemona can celebrate their new marriage, Othello is ordered to go to Cyprus, where he will command the Venetian forces against a hostile Turkish fleet. Desdemona begs to travel with her new husband, and they leave for Cyprus immediately. Roderigo, Cassio, Iago, and Emilia, Iago's wife, go, too.

As I said, geography is destiny. What happens in Cyprus would be unthinkable in Venice.

THE FIRST TIME Cyan and I met in person, it was on my territory. He had a conference in New York City, and invited me to join him for lunch. Given the circumstances under which we had met, I wore baggy jeans and a blue fleece. I wanted to look asexual.

I arrived at the pizzeria fifteen minutes early. "If I disappear today," I texted to Peng as I waited, "I was last seen with Cyan Agbaria at Bleecker Street Pizza on Seventh Avenue."

"If you disappear today," Peng replied, "I'll kill him myself."

I sat on a tall stool, swinging my feet. I already knew that a person named Cyan Agbaria, with a job title and face that matched Cyan's Twitter profile, did exist. I'd done enough Internet research to confirm that. But it didn't occur to me until I sat there that, in theory, a sexual predator could have lured me to this pizzeria using a stolen identity.

I glanced at faces in the crowded restaurant. I glanced at my butter knife.

The door opened, and I laughed with relief. Cyan's face matched the one I had seen online.

"So you're you," I told him.

"Who did you think I'd be?" he asked.

I shrugged.

"Someone dangerous," I joked.

"I'm not dangerous." Cyan laughed. An uncertain frown crossed his face. "At least, I don't think I'm dangerous," he added.

He wasn't. For the next six hours, Cyan and I talked about Oxford, international politics, and his job as an adjunct professor of Middle Eastern and Islamic Studies in D.C. Like a loose thread that unravels a sweater, the conversation didn't end. Lunch led to a walk, which led to coffee. Coffee led to another walk, which led to yet another coffee.

In the months to come, I would learn that Cyan doesn't even like coffee.

When he first invited me to meet, I had assumed that Cyan would want to talk about kink. Why else would he want to meet me? But the subject didn't come up. In fact, Cyan ignored the topic with such ease that I began to wonder whether he was even a fetishist at all. Maybe David and I had misinterpreted the ellipsis in his first email. Maybe, once again, I'd imagined connections that didn't exist.

When Cyan mentioned D.C.'s hierarchical political culture, it was my chance to probe the mystery.

"D.C. sounds kinky," I joked. "All those people in suits running around calling each other 'sir.'"

Cyan laughed. It was an odd laugh, both bitter and dry. Then he paused.

"A colleague once asked me why I'm the only person at the university who never calls the department chair 'sir,'" he finally admitted. "But I can't. It's just too—"

I bit back a smile.

"You don't need to explain," I interrupted. "I get it."

Cyan nodded.

"Yeah," he agreed. A pause lingered between us.

When we finally said good-bye, I was happy. I'm not immune

to hypocrisy, and for years I had worried that other spanking fetishists, were I ever to meet them, would be everything I didn't want us to be: weird, creepy, damaged, subhuman, aberrant, violent, unstable. I feared Cyan might confirm my worst fears about myself. But he did the opposite. Cyan was normal. Even better, he was smart. He was polite. He was successful. When the sunlight touched him, he didn't burst into flames.

"He wants to sleep with you," David declared.

I wrinkled my nose. "I don't think so," I replied. "He didn't flirt with me at all."

"Glad to hear it," David said. "But he still wants to sleep with you."

I laughed. "I don't have to be friends with him if you don't want me to," I offered.

David waved off the suggestion.

"Be friends," he said. "I trust you."

Othello and Desdemona sail to Cyprus. And Cyan became my friend.

As months passed, the cautiousness of our first conversation gave way to candor. For more than two decades, I had been walking on eggshells: first, because I was terrified of any disclosure that might reveal my shameful secret, and later because I was terrified that any misstep would reflect badly on kinky people as a group. I even felt that way around David. But with Cyan, I could stop tiptoeing on eggshells and finally give in to gravity.

I collapsed on the floor of Cyan's kitchen in D.C. with dramatic flourish.

"You have a dishwasher!" I gushed, as I lovingly pressed my hands against the appliance's metal face. "A dishwasher is the only thing missing from my life. I hate washing dishes. It's the worst thing in the world."

Cyan laughed.

"Some things are worse," he pointed out.

I shook my head.

"No," I said, deadpan. "Nothing in life is worse than washing dishes."

He smiled.

"Then I must be a sadist," he joked. "Because now all I want to do is make you wash dishes."

My work often took me to Washington; his work often brought him to New York. When it did, we hung out. Most of the time, our friendship felt normal. We argued about politics and talked about our jobs. David and Cyan even chatted over the phone a few times, which made the friendship feel aboveboard.

But it was the first time I'd been friends with another spanking fetishist, and I had to admit that the relationship had unusual details. Once, at lunch with Cyan, I wanted to brush my hair. I reached into my purse to grab my hairbrush—and froze.

Cyan was browsing the menu. My brush is square, wooden, and thick—in other words, just a hairbrush to anyone *other* than people like us.

I excused myself and brushed my hair in the bathroom.

Later, when I admitted to Cyan what I'd done, he laughed. I didn't have to explain. He understood. It was as if we shared a linguistic and cultural shorthand only people like us could understand.

That spring, Al Jazeera English brought me to their D.C. studio to discuss an article I'd written on one of their news shows. It was my first major television appearance, and it didn't go well. I blew it. Cyan met me outside the studio after the segment to give me a tour of the Washington Mall, but I couldn't focus. Instead, I scrolled through Twitter, looking for masochistic confirmation that I had been the nonsensical mess I feared.

Cyan snatched my phone out of my hand and deposited it in his pocket.

"Stop worrying about your interview," he said. "Is that clear?"

I sighed.

"Yes," I said.

"Yes *what*?" he joked, in a soft voice.

I rolled my eyes. But my liver had just moved.

"Very funny," I said. "You need a girlfriend, Cyan."

He sighed.

"I really do," he agreed.

Cyan and I didn't talk about kink every day, or even every time I saw him. But when we did, it was great. For more than a year, I had explained my fetish: to David, to my friends, to the media. Cyan required no explanations. With him, I could stop being a symbol of kink and just be myself. For once, I didn't have to answer questions—I could ask them. Cyan and I talked about our fetish's most challenging details: its intersections with misogyny and heteronormativity; its relationship to child abuse and spousal battery; its place within the broader BDSM community; its comparison to self-mutilation. We laughed about our mutual attempts to access fetish erotica from the Middle East. We argued about the different kinds of spankings—erotic, maintenance, "good girl," punishment, "funishment," stress relief, rhythmic, role play, just-for-fun, power exchange—and the irony that people like us use spankings for both pleasure and punishment. (Trust me, our community can debate that paradox until we're all blue in the face.)

"Don't say 'community,'" Cyan said.

"Don't say 'spanko,'" I replied.

"Deal," Cyan agreed.

We're all semanticists, apparently.

Cyan was a "switch"—someone who alternates between dominant and submissive roles, depending on the partner and context. He was single, but had a long list of play partners. (Every time we hung out, his phone buzzed with text messages from them.) I love leather implements, such as belts and straps; Cyan preferred wood toys, such as paddles and canes.

"How patriotic," I joked. "Brits love canes."

Cyan stuck his hands into his pockets.

"It has something to do with our school system, I suspect." He shrugged.

I nodded. Like every spanking fetishist in the world, I'd inhaled Roald Dahl's *Boy* enough times throughout my childhood to be intimately familiar with Britain's traditional approach to school discipline.

"Were you ever caned at school?" I asked.

Cyan gave me an amused grin. "No," he said. "It was banned from our government schools when I was about ten years old, so I was a bit too young."

"Oh, right," I said.

"But I've been caned as an adult," he added.

That caught my attention.

"Wow," I said. "When?"

"Not so fast, kid," he replied. "If I'm going to tell you that, you have to tell me something, too."

I leaned against the wall next to him.

"What do you want to know?" I asked.

He looked at me. His eyes flickered with thought.

"Have you ever switched?" he finally asked.

I shook my head.

"No," I said. "I don't have a dominant side."

Cyan chuckled.

"I doubt that very much," he replied. "I don't think someone without a dominant side would write the way you do."

I blushed. That was kind.

"That's just my work." I shrugged. "It's different."

"Is it?" Cyan asked.

I looked down and scuffed my foot in the soil.

"I answered your question," I said. "Now you have to tell me when you've been caned."

Cyan grimaced.

"When I was at Oxford, I went into London to see professional dommes a few times," he said.

"What was that like?" I asked. He shook his head.

"In my case, not great," Cyan said. "At that point, I didn't want physical gratification so much as I wanted to feel like someone understood me. And that's not something one can buy, is it?"

I scratched my nose to hide a smile.

"It's hard for me to imagine your submissive side, Cy," I said. "You're so dommy around me."

Cyan's lip twitched with amusement.

"This is Washington," he said. "Everyone here wants to dominate something."

I laughed. Blood flowed to my liver.

Don't forget: *Othello* isn't about sex. It's only about the *idea* of sex.

But everyone still ends up dead.

OTHELLO AND THE others arrive in Cyprus prepared for war. But the battle has already been won: a storm felled the Turkish fleet before it even landed on the island. That night, as everyone celebrates, Iago gets his rival, Cassio, drunk and sends his friend, Roderigo, to provoke a fight with him. The ensuing brawl disturbs Othello, who flies into a rage and strips Cassio of his promotion. Cassio, humiliated and distraught, begs Iago for help. Iago assures Cassio that his best bet is to ask Desdemona for help.

Desdemona is sympathetic to Cassio, and agrees to plead with Othello on his behalf. Meanwhile, Iago subtly suggests to Othello that Desdemona and Cassio are having an affair, so that each time Desdemona pleads on Cassio's behalf, Othello's suspicions deepen. But Othello is a general, an experienced battle tactician. Mere suspicions aren't enough. Othello demands "ocular proof" of infidelity. So Iago persuades his wife, Emilia, who is Desdemona's attendant, to steal a handkerchief that Othello gifted to Desdemona during their courtship. Iago drops the handkerchief in Cassio's room. When Othello sees Cassio with it, he becomes convinced of Desdemona's alleged infidelity and strangles her in their bed.

Emilia realizes what her husband has done and reveals Iago's deception. Like many Shakespearean tragedies, *Othello* is a bloodbath: at the end, Iago murders Emilia, Othello commits suicide, and Iago is taken away to be tortured.

The power of suggestion is a potent drug. On Iago's lips, words are weapons. Armed with nothing other than language, he engineers a massacre. Iago's verbal power is so terrifying that, according to Norrie Epstein, during one Old West production of *Othello*, an audience member pulled out a gun and shot the actor playing Iago to death.

I like to quote Shakespeare. But in this case, the rapper Eminem said it best: "Words are a motherfucker."

"You identify as a masochist, not just a bottom?" Cyan clarified, the last time I saw him before things changed. "Does that mean you actually love pain?" I was sitting on a ledge in downtown D.C., tapping the heels of my feet against the stone.

I ran my hands along the front of my jeans. I had puzzled over that question for years.

"I wouldn't say I love it, exactly," I admitted. "I'm *curious* about pain: how different implements feel, the different marks they leave, how pain changes in different hands. How it never, never feels quite like I remember. How bruises evolve, like sunsets. I'm curious about that."

Cyan nodded.

"Yeah," he said. "I understand."

"But sometimes I think curiosity and love are the same thing," I added. "So maybe I do love pain after all."

Our eyes met, and we burst into awkward laughter.

"Does that sound twisted?" I asked, bringing a hand to my lips to partially cover my face.

"Not to me," Cyan said. "But our kink has a twisted edge. I don't think any of us is truly comfortable with it."

I bristled.

"I'm comfortable with it," I snapped. "Why else do you think I wrote that article?"

Cyan eyed me.

"I think you wrote it because you're lonely," he said. "But it didn't work. I think now you feel more alone than ever."

I didn't realize it until he spoke, but that was true. It was so true I felt incised by him.

"That's not true," I said.

Cyan gave me a sidelong glance.

"Okay," he said.

I didn't know what to say.

"When will I see you again?" Cyan pressed.

"I'm coming to D.C. a week from next Thursday," I admitted. "I'll be in town a whole week."

Cyan hopped up to sit on the ledge beside me.

"So can I see you then?" he asked.

I squinted past a memorial into the distance.

"You want to see me again so soon?" I asked.

"Jillian," he replied, "when you're in town, I want to see you every day."

For all *Othello*'s talk about sex, no one actually has it. I am convinced that Desdemona and Othello never consummate their marriage, and that Desdemona dies a virgin. (I am not the only person to think so: T. G. A. Nelson and Charles Haines argued the same in their 1983 article "Othello's Unconsummated Marriage.") Shakespeare littered his text with hints of this secret. At the beginning of the play, for example, Brabantio summons Othello to the Venetian court, after their secret elopement but before Othello has a chance to sleep with his new bride. "True, I have married her. The very head and front of my offending hath this extent, no more," Othello explains—in other words, his offense at this point is limited to the wedding ceremony, and nothing else. Their aborted wedding night also explains why Othello is so eager to bring Desdemona to Cyprus with him, and why she is so eager to go. Othello underlines this point when Desdemona joins him at the front, telling her: "Come, my dear love, the purchase made, the fruits are to ensue; that profit's yet to come 'tween me and you." But, once again, they are interrupted—this time, by Cassio's drunken brawl with Roderigo, which explains why Othello is furious enough to strip Cassio of his rank. Even Iago knows that Othello hasn't had a chance to sleep with Desdemona, since he tells Cassio: "He hath not yet made wanton the night with her." And near the end of the play, when Desdemona asks Emilia to put the sheets from her wedding night on her bed, why would she make that request unless the sheets were unstained with blood, and therefore a symbol that, she hopes, could pacify Othello by reminding him of her purity?

Othello's marriage, like his battle plan for Cyprus, remains unconsummated.

The week after seeing Cyan, when I got back to New York, I was swamped with work. I had an important meeting lined up to pitch a story to *The New Yorker,* and I was nervous. To make things worse, I was running behind schedule.

My cell phone beeped. It was a text message from Cyan. He had agreed to give some professional advice to a friend of mine who was working on a Ph.D. in Cyan's field, and Cyan wanted to apologize for having been slow to respond to my friend's email.

Frustrated and in a hurry, I replied automatically.

"Don't apologize," I typed, as I pushed my way through a crowd on Broadway. "You know how I want you to talk to me."

It was an unthinking and irresponsible flash of truth.

I shoved the phone into my purse and rushed into the meeting. I didn't see Cyan's response until a few hours later.

"Oh, Jillian," he had written. "It makes me so happy when you're honest."

It was my mistake. I opened that door; Cyan just walked through it. The person who is responsible, and culpable, for everything that happened next is me.

Othello and Desdemona built their marriage on a thousand stories, a world of sighs, the witchcraft of a million words. But it fell apart in a single breath.

It's hard to build things. It's much easier to tear them down.

David walked into our apartment and dropped his stethoscope and keys on the nightstand. By this point, he had decided to go into emergency medicine and spent most of his time in the ER.

"We had another patient with end-stage liver disease today," he said. "I wonder if that's how my father will die."

I paused. I wasn't sure what to say.

"Is that something you worry about?" I asked.

David shrugged.

"I worry more that he'll get high, jump in his car, and take a family of five out with him when he goes," he said. "Liver failure might be a mercy."

I nodded.

"What exactly do livers do?" I asked.

David scrunched up his face with thought.

"Well," he said, "it's no accident they're called *live*-ers. We can't live without them. They process the toxins in our bodies, for one."

I slid my hands around his waist.

"Did I ever tell you that in Shakespeare's day, they described livers the way we describe hearts today?" I asked. "They said love grows in the liver."

David grinned.

"I like that idea," he said. "Love processes our toxins, right?"

I pressed my forehead into his chest and said nothing.

"We're going through a rough patch right now, David," I admitted.

David rubbed his hands on my back.

"I know," he said.

I pulled back.

"I wish—I wish we could talk, you know?" I said.

David sighed and walked into the bedroom.

"I'm so exhausted, Jillian," he said. "You don't understand what my job is like."

I followed him into the other room.

"I'm exhausted, too," I said.

"We do talk," he replied. "What do you want to talk about? You want to talk about *spanking*?"

A shadow crossed my face.

"Don't say it like that," I said.

David sat on the bed and closed his eyes.

"Talk to Cyan about it," he said. "Isn't that why he's still around?"

Tears pricked the backs of my eyes.

"But when I talk to him, I'm *not* talking to you," I said. "Doesn't that bother you?"

David's eyes opened.

"Of course it bothers me," he said. "Fuck it, maybe you should just sleep with him. Get it out of your system."

I ran my fingers through my hair with frustration.

"The fact that you think I want to *sleep with him* tells me everything," I growled. "You don't even know what he gives me that you don't."

"What does he give you?" David replied.

"I'm not even sure myself," I admitted. "Friendship, maybe."

David shook his head.

"That guy is not your friend," he snarled. "He's just another one of those *fucked-up spanking freaks* who wants to get in your pants."

I didn't say anything. I didn't need to. My face said enough.

David blanched.

"I'm sorry," he said right away. "I didn't mean that. You know I didn't mean that."

I nodded. I knew that he *believed* he didn't mean it. But maybe, just that once, his words had come from a more honest place.

"It probably is fucked up," I agreed. "The truth is, I think I'm fucked up, too."

I meant it. I had become my own Janus: the two-faced god that Iago swears by in *Othello*. In public, I was confident about my sexuality and the sociopolitical and pathological questions it raised. But privately, I hesitated every time a psychiatrist sent me an unsolicited email in response to my *New York Times* article to offer "reparative therapy" for my "illness." ("You think you're happy," the head of a psychiatry program at a major university wrote to me when he read my article, "but you're not.") A handful of paragraphs hadn't healed my lifelong ache.

I said one thing but often feared another. How could I expect David to be any different?

He stood up and wrapped his hands around my upper arms.

"I don't think you're fucked up, Jillian," he said. "I don't know why I said that. I'm just so tired."

I wanted to cry, but couldn't.

"I really do love you," I said, shaking my head.

David wrapped me in his arms.

"Just hang in there, okay?" he said. "We'll figure this out."

Would we? Worry gnawed at my insides. I loved David. I had chosen David. But I was excited to spend a week in the same city as Cyan.

Too excited.

I boarded the bus at Penn Station. The woman in the seat next to me was already on board. When I saw her face, I swore out loud.

"Fuck," I said.

"Well, good morning to you, too," Emilia drawled.

I plopped down next to her. My sigh sounded like a groan.

"It's a bad sign that you're here," I muttered, shaking my head. In her most memorable scene, Emilia discusses infidelity with Desdemona—and delivers an impassioned defense of it.

Emilia chuckled.

"You didn't expect to see Desdemona here, did you?" she asked. "She's an angel, God bless 'er. But you're no angel, and you have nothing to learn from one."

I sighed.

"I cheated on John," I said. "I know I have it in me." I felt sick to my stomach.

Emilia patted my leg.

"Well, honey, you know my opinion on this," she said.

I nodded.

"'It is their husbands' faults if wives do fall,'" I recited, quoting Emilia's words to Desdemona from *Othello*. "But I don't agree with that. None of this is David's fault. He's the best man I've ever known. I can't fault him for being too good for me. I can't fault him for being less *fucked up* than I am." Maybe David, like Dylan before him, was just too good—too whole, too unbroken—for me.

Emilia crossed her arms.

"Then what's really going on, sweetheart?" she asked.

I began to cry.

"I'm so lonely," I admitted. "David says he loves me, and I know he *thinks* he does. But how can he love me if he doesn't understand me? He has no idea who I am."

Emilia shrugged.

"Can anyone really know another person?" she asked.

I pressed my fingertips into my eyes to stop the tears and inhaled a long, shuddering breath.

"Maybe Cyan knows me," I muttered.

At that, Emilia laughed outright. Her laugh was sharp and mocking, like the screech of a bird.

"Oh, come," she scoffed. "That's the silliest thing I've ever heard."

I nodded.

"I know," I admitted.

Emilia smoothed my hair.

"So what are you going to do, honey?" she asked.

My phone beeped. I reached into my purse to grab it.

When I sat up, Emilia was gone.

Cyan had sent me a text message.

"Are you hungry?" he asked.

"Starving," I replied.

"Good," he wrote. "When you get into town, we'll have lunch."

"Don't talk to me about food right now," I typed. "Pink elephants and all that."

He replied with a question mark.

"If I say, 'don't think of pink elephants,' you'll imagine pink elephants, right?" I explained. "Talking about lunch will just make me hungrier. It's the power of suggestion."

"Ah," Cyan replied. "I understand."

His next question appeared on my screen in pieces. Each line echoed like drops from a faucet in a sink.

"So what would happen—"

Drip.

"If I said—"

Drip.

"Don't think of yourself—"

Drip.

"Over my knee—"

Drip.

"For a sound spanking—"

Drip.

"As your ass turns pink—"

Drip.

"And then red—"

Drip.

"And then pale purple—"

Drip.

"From the weight of my hand?"

I stopped breathing.

In *Othello*, sex goes unconsummated.

But my *Othello* chapter is almost over.

"You're an asshole," I typed.

I did not press send.

"Are you picturing it?" Cyan wrote. "Or are you still thinking of pink elephants?"

Drip.

4.4 Cymbeline:
What We May Be

"What are you doing?" Helena shouted, shaking my shoulders.

I looked at her.

What was I doing? I was in a taxi, on my way to Cyan's apartment, smashed between a bunch of opinionated figments who wouldn't leave me the hell alone.

What was I doing? I was going to ask Cyan to spank me, just once, just to let myself *be myself* one last time. David would never know.

What was I doing? I was going to tell Cyan that our banter had become too explicit and that it had to stop. We could still be friends.

What was I doing? I was going to negotiate some kind of polyamorous dynamic, where David could have vanilla sex with his species and I could have sexless beatings with my own.

What was I doing? I was going to kick *both* men to the curb and get on an airplane again. There's a whole world of ways to avoid myself.

An email I had received in response to my first article haunted me.

"I admire your desire to make it work with this vanilla guy," a woman had written. "I tried that, too. But people like us are different. Your relationship is doomed. He needs someone who speaks his language. And you need someone who speaks ours. If you love this man, you'll let him go."

Maybe she was right.

Really—what the fuck was I doing?

"It doesn't matter what you do," Emilia scoffed, twisting around to face me from the taxi's front passenger seat. "Men are all but stomachs, and we are but food: they eat us hungrily, and when they are full, they belch us. One way or another, you'll get belched."

Caliban nodded beside me.

"You're a devil, a born devil, on whose nature nurture can never stick," he agreed, putting an arm around my shoulders. "You can't change."

Helena shook her head.

"This is a mistake," she insisted. Friar Lawrence nodded in agreement.

I bristled.

"But Cal is right," I pointed out, nestling my head into the space between his neck and his shoulder. "I can't change this part of me. God knows I've tried."

King Lear laughed.

"Thou shalt not die," he said, with scornful disdain. "Die for adultery? No, the wren goes to't, and the small gilded fly does lecher in my sight. Let copulation *thrive*."

I glanced up. King Lear winked.

My skin crawled.

"You can't give up!" Helena insisted, her hands on my shoulders. "The course of true love never did—"

Berowne cut her off.

"Let affection overpower oaths," he interrupted, elbowing

Helena out of the way. "Admit it—you want to know the thing you are forbid to know."

Frustration boiled in my chest.

"Yeah, so says the guy who ends his play *alone*," I snarled.

Berowne blanched.

"I do not end up alone!" he insisted. "In *Love's Labor's Won*, the sequel to—"

"*Love's Labor's Won* doesn't count!" I cried. "No one has read it!"

"It does too count!" Berowne shrieked.

"Oh yeah?" I roared, gesticulating around the taxi. "Then where is *Cardenio*, huh? If lost plays count, why isn't Cardenio in here right now?"

Lady Macbeth stretched out in the backseat.

"To be fair, *Cardenio* is probably about the Cardenio character from *Don Quixote*, who falls into erotic madness," she mused. "So I could argue that—"

My eyes widened. I turned on her.

"Are you about to suggest that *I'm* the insane one, *Purell*?" I growled. Iago snickered.

Lady Macbeth shrugged.

"Takes one to know one," she said.

I lunged at her across the taxi. I wanted to claw out her eyes.

Friar Lawrence and Hermione each grabbed one of my arms.

"Shut up, bitch," I shouted at Lady Macbeth, fighting to free myself from the Friar's grip. "You just want to watch the world burn."

"Deep down, isn't that what you want, too?" Goneril purred.

I froze.

"No," I said, shaking my head, terrified, as Friar Lawrence and Hermione released me. "I don't want that."

"Ignore them all," Kate whispered. "These opinions mean nothing. What do *you* want?"

I blinked at her. What did I want?

"For the love of God, just do *something*," Hamlet groaned. "I can't tolerate another round of indecision paralysis."

Iago reached across the taxi and ran his fingers through my hair. The tips of his nails dragged against the skin on my scalp. Electricity ran down my spine.

He leaned over to whisper in my ear.

"After the cats and blind puppies have drowned," Iago murmured in a cashmere voice, "it's your turn to step into the water."

I recoiled. In his mirror eyes were all my sins remembered.

I pressed the palms of my hands against my face.

"Shut up!" I screamed. "Leave me alone! There isn't enough room in this taxi for all of you!"

Silence fell.

"Maybe just one of us, then?" a voice finally said.

I dropped my fingers from my eyes. Only Helena was still with me. The others were gone.

She put her hand atop my own.

"If you won't listen to me," Helena said, glancing toward the taxi driver, "at least listen to him." Then she was gone.

The taxi pulled to a stop in front of Cyan's apartment.

I stepped out of the backseat and walked up to the driver's window.

"How much?" I asked, reaching for my wallet. The driver looked up.

"This ride's on me," Fidele said.

I sighed.

Cymbeline's romantic core is not dissimilar to *Othello*'s: a man (Posthumus), egged on by a manipulative friend (Iachimo), suspects his wife (Imogen) of infidelity. But although they share this seed, *Othello* and *Cymbeline* grow into very different plays. To test his suspicions, Posthumus challenges Iachimo to seduce Imogen and bring back proof of her unfaithfulness. So Iachimo sneaks into Imogen's room while she sleeps and steals the bracelet that Posthumous gave her at their wedding. Just as Desdemona's stolen handkerchief confirms Othello's suspicions, Imogen's stolen bracelet is, for Posthumus, "ocular proof" of his wife's infidelity. Posthumus orders his servant Pisanio to murder Imogen. But Pisanio, anguished, can't bring himself to kill her. Instead, he warns Imogen that she is in danger, and Imogen goes into hiding in the caves of Milford Haven, disguised as a young man named Fidele.

Fidele means "faithful."

"Welcome to Milford Haven," Imogen joked from the driver's seat of the taxi, pulling off the hat that hid her long hair.

I fought back tears.

"This is not my 'blessed Milford,'" I said, glancing at Cyan's apartment building. "There is no haven here."

Imogen pursed her lips with disapproval.

"So you're going to cheat," she said.

I looked down.

"I've done it before," I admitted. "I'll never be like you."

"That's not necessarily true," she challenged me. "What do I get right? What does Helena get right? What do we do right that so many other characters screw up?"

I shook my head.

"I don't know," I said.

"Think," she insisted. "There is a very specific answer."

Cymbeline is listed in the First Folio as *The Tragedie of Cymbeline*, but it doesn't meet the traditional standards of a tragedy. In fact, *Cymbeline*'s most gruesome death is conveyed with dark humor: Imogen wakes up next to a headless corpse and describes it in the form of a lover's tender *blason*. But *Cymbeline* isn't quite a comedy, either. It turns the traditional comedic form upside down: rather than end with a wedding, it begins with one. *Cymbeline* scrambles genre.

"Comedy and tragedy aren't your only options," Imogen

reminded me. "What other kinds of plays are there? What is *Cymbeline*?"

I sighed.

"It's a romance," I admitted. The romances are a category of Shakespeare's later plays, which includes *Cymbeline*. The romances tend to be complex comedies with a few common traits: tragic elements mix with comedic ones; young lovers exist, but are not the central point of the work; magic and fantasy blend with reality.

Imogen nodded.

"That's right," she said. "If your life isn't a comedy or a tragedy, let it be a romance—a sublime and hazardous journey into the unknown. You want romance because you want adventure. We already know how comedies and tragedies will end. Only romance is unforeseeable."

> *O curse of marriage!*
> *That we can call these delicate creatures ours,*
> *And not their appetites!*
>
> —*Othello*, 3.3

I inhaled and glanced to Cyan's door.

POSTHUMUS HAS A DREAM.

It's a weird one.

At this point in *Cymbeline*, he believes that Imogen, upon his orders, is dead. He is racked with guilt and regrets his homicidal mistake, even though he still believes Imogen was unfaithful. (He bemoans having killed a wife "much better" than himself for "wrying but a little.") Britain has gone to war with Rome, and Posthumus, hoping to be killed in battle, disguises himself as a Roman solider and ends up in a British jail, awaiting execution. He goes to sleep in his cell.

"O Imogen," he says, as he falls asleep. "I'll speak to thee in silence."

Posthumus is an orphan. It's worse than that, actually—not only did he lose his parents, he lost his entire family. His father died before he was born. His mother died in childbirth. His two older brothers died in wars. Posthumus never got to know any of them. The grief of these losses haunted Posthumus throughout his life: "He did incline to sadness, and oft-times not knowing why," Imogen says.

But just when it seems like *Cymbeline* will dissolve into tragedy, the deus ex machina appears.

In sleep, Posthumus dreams of his lost family. They gather around him and summon the "thunder-master"—Jupiter, the Roman god of thunder. Posthumus's dead father, Sicilius Leonatus, scolds Jupiter for having let Posthumus fall into imprisonment, saying: "Thou orphans' father art, thou shouldst have been, and shielded him from this earth-vexing smart."

Jupiter descends in thunder and lightning.

"No more, you petty spirits of region low, offend our hearing: hush!" he commands. Happiness and satisfaction await Posthumus, Jupiter tells them.

"Whom best I love, I cross," he explains. "To make my gift, the more delay'd, delighted."

Good things, in other words, come to those who wait.

What is intimate is what is *inmost*, whatever that may be. The deepest trauma in Posthumus's psyche—the one that had to be resolved before he could be a whole person—was the loss of his family. It was always about that pain. Posthumus didn't lose his mind because he thought Imogen slept with someone else: he lost it because he thought she had, like everyone else always had, left him.

In a life where no one was ever there for him, Posthumus just wanted to believe that Imogen would be there.

It wasn't a sex thing.

My friend Abby is, like me, a spanking fetishist. Our stories are similar: we looked up the same words in the dictionary, read the same books, and blushed when the same movie scenes appeared onscreen. (The big difference is that Abby was never spanked as a child and was therefore spared having her sexuality nonconsensually inflicted on her at an early age.) And Abby, like me, does enjoy sex. But it occupies a far less critical space at the core of our identities than our fetish does.

That's why although Abby identifies as heterosexual, she had a deeply fulfilling relationship with a dominant woman named Samantha. Abby and Samantha loved each other—and, yes, Samantha disciplined Abby every time she broke one of their mutually agreed-upon rules—but they never had sex. It wasn't a sexual relationship, but, for Abby, it was every bit as intimate as one, if not more so. When that relationship ended, Abby was *more* devastated than she had been after the breakup of any previous sexual relationship. Sex is intimate. But it's not the only thing that is. Abby and I have both tried to masturbate to the thought of sex but found the experience as gummy and anticlimactic as masturbating to the thought of toothpaste. We are not asexual, but neither are we "sexual" in the normative sense: we exist in an undefined third space.

My fetish makes gender irrelevant. It makes conventional physical attractiveness irrelevant. It makes even *sex* irrelevant.

Does it make love irrelevant, too?

Cyan disappeared into the next room. When he returned, he was holding a belt.

"This is the one I told you about," he said. (Earlier that week, Cyan had texted me about a new belt he bought to use with one of his recent play partners. "I know a good trick with belts," I had replied. "But I'll tell you about it later.")

"So what's the trick?" he asked.

"Here, I'll show you," I said, reaching out.

Cyan handed me the belt. I looked at it, turning it over in my hand. The outer side was smooth, and the inner side was faintly rough. The leather was thick.

"You fold it like this, right?" I said, folding the belt so its smooth half was outside.

"Yes," he said. "Of course."

I reversed the fold, so that the leather bent against the direction of its normal curve.

"This is better," I said, passing it back to him. "Trust me."

"Really?" he asked, frowning at it. "Huh." He flicked his right wrist back and whipped the belt against his left palm. The crack echoed through the room.

I shook my head.

"Don't do that," I said.

"Why?" he asked.

"Because I like that sound," I said, sliding onto a bar stool.

"I know you do," Cyan said.

"I know you know," I replied.

Cyan grinned.

"Want a drink?" he asked.

"Yes," I replied. "Please."

"Red or white?" he asked.

"Whiskey," I said.

"I bought this white at a winery in Virginia last year," Cyan replied, ignoring me. He opened his refrigerator and removed a tall green bottle. He pulled a corkscrew from a drawer.

"Wait, don't open a special bottle," I interjected. "I'm not—"

Cyan looked over his shoulder at me.

"It's too late," he said. "The cork is pierced."

"Now I feel bad," I protested as he poured. "I'm not staying long."

"Don't worry about it," he said. He poured one glass, handed it to me, and put away the bottle. He wasn't having any. I rarely saw him drink.

I sipped my wine.

I swallowed.

I hesitated.

"I never asked what drew you to North Africa and the Middle East," I said.

Cyan raised an eyebrow.

"You want to talk about work?" he asked.

I shook my head.

"No," I said, looking down. "But I just realized I never asked you that."

Cyan leaned against the cabinets in his kitchen. He cleared his throat.

"Why are you curious?" he asked.

"It doesn't matter," I said.

Cyan was frowning at the floor.

"In '97, there was a massacre in Relizane," he said. "It's a long story."

I looked at him.

"Where is Relizane?" I asked, mentally flipping through a list of global conflicts from the late nineties. "Algeria?"

He nodded.

"Were you there?" I pressed.

Cyan's lips formed the thin line between a grimace and a smile.

"I'll tell you about it someday, kid," he said. "But not today."

I nodded.

"Sure," I said, blinking fast. "Someday."

After Posthumus sees his family inside the jail cell, he wakes. He assumes it was merely a dream—until, to his astonishment, he finds a tablet from Jupiter still beside him.

It says:

When as a lion's whelp shall, to himself unknown, without seeking find, and be embraced by a piece of tender air; and when from a stately cedar shall be lopped branches, which, being dead many years, shall after revive, be jointed to the old stock and freshly grow; then shall Posthumus end his miseries, Britain be fortunate and flourish in peace and plenty.

"'Tis still a dream," Posthumus says, amazed. "Or else such stuff as madmen tongue and brain not; either both or nothing; or senseless speaking or a speaking such as sense cannot untie."

The jailer arrives and tells Posthumus that it is time for his execution.

"I am merrier to die than thou art to live," Posthumus replies. He is ready for death.

But Shakespeare hits rewind.

In *Cymbeline*, every old wound heals. No one repeats the choices that echoed into grief the first time around. King Cymbeline doesn't repeat King Lear's mistake and throw away his daughter. Posthumus doesn't repeat Othello's mistake and murder the wife he suspects of infidelity, or Leontes's mistake and throw her in prison. The lovers don't repeat Romeo's or Antony's mistake and commit suicide when each thinks the other is dead. The King doesn't repeat Hamlet's mistake and kill a man he does not recognize.

Cymbeline walks the precipice of tragedy. But it does not fall.

"I need to ask a favor, Cy," I said. "It's going to be difficult for me."

He frowned.

"Okay," he said.

I spoke into my wineglass.

"I hope you have a really good summer," I said, carefully. "But . . . I hope I won't hear about it."

A pause. I swallowed.

"And I'll need your help to make sure I *don't* hear about it," I finished. "Because if I hear from you, I'm scared I'll respond."

Cyan frowned.

"What does that mean?" he asked.

I wrapped my arms around my stomach. I couldn't meet his gaze.

"We can't be friends, Cy," I said. "We're not really friends now."

There was a long pause.

"Why are you saying this today?" he asked.

I shifted on my stool.

"All morning, I wanted—" I broke off. This was embarrassing. I looked down.

"I just wanted to come over here and clean up your apartment."

Cyan looked surprised.

"Wait, why does that matter?" he said. "So you're a nice person."

I looked at him.

"Come on, Cy," I said, in a low voice. "That's not what it means."

He crossed his arms over his chest.

"We're *friends*, Jillian," he insisted.

"My 'friends' don't put me in this headspace, Cyan," I replied. The truth was, no one had put me in that headspace since John.

Cyan sighed and rubbed the bridge of his nose with his knuckles. He walked across the kitchen, reopened his refrigerator, and picked up the bottle of wine.

"So what does this mean, exactly?" he said, pouring himself a glass. "We're never going to talk again?"

I shook my head.

"I don't know," I muttered. "Maybe."

He leaned against the cabinet. I looked at the floor.

Cyan shook his head.

"We're just friends," he said again. "I've never touched you."

I rubbed my eyes.

"It's not really physical, this thing we do," I said. "It's wordplay. That's the part that matters."

Cyan took a sip of his wine and frowned.

"Well, of course I'll respect your wishes," he said. "You won't hear from me again."

I nodded and blinked. Seconds passed.

"You're not losing anything today, Cy," I finally said, in a bitter voice. "You have these conversations with so many women."

Cyan looked up. His face was tight.

"What 'conversations' do you assume I have, Jillian?" he asked.

I pressed my eyes into my fingertips and tried to laugh. It sounded forced.

"Conversations about the Spratly Islands, of course." I sighed.

Cyan nodded. He was looking at the floor.

I was not prepared for this. When I had tried to foresee this conversation, I'd imagined that Cyan would respond with indifference or, at worst, anger. But this was sadness. I hadn't considered the possibility that Cyan would look sad.

I stood up.

"Did you have any other questions?" I asked. Maybe a brusque, businesslike tone of voice would cauterize the wound.

Cyan looked at me. He seemed tired.

"It looks like you're leaving," he said. "So I guess I don't."

I clutched my umbrella, bracing myself against emotions that threatened to make me stay. Cyan walked me to the front door and put his hand on the knob to open it.

"It's a shame," he muttered.

I looked at the floor.

"Some words are more sexual than sex," I mumbled. "This isn't fair to David."

The best sex advice I'd ever heard, delivered by a virgin on the far side of the world, echoed in my mind: Find a good man and figure it out. You're not dead yet.

I stepped outside. Cyan closed the door behind me.

Khalila was right: Love is miraculous. But Soraya was right, too. Love is only half a miracle. The other half is choice.

It's just not always a painless choice.

Blinded by tears, I stumbled into the street and poured myself into a taxi.

AT THE END of *Cymbeline*, Posthumus learns that Imogen is still alive.

"Hang there like fruit, my soul, 'til the tree die," he says, embracing her. In his dream, Posthumus finally takes control of the greatest trauma in his life—the loss of his family—and becomes the whole person Imogen deserved.

My point is, a tree's fruit falls. But, with water, it grows again.

The taxi pulled up to the apartment I had rented. I paid and stepped outside.

In front of the building there was a tree, its long, thin branches speckled with buds of early spring. I scrubbed away my tears with the back of my hand and reached up to rip a branch from the trunk. As I jogged up the steps to my door, I stripped the buds off the branch. They fell behind me like bread crumbs.

I let the door slam shut. Helena was sitting on my bed.

I pointed at her. My chest rose and fell with breath and steadied me.

"This is your fault," I said. "You're the one who started this. But I'm the one who ends it."

Helena slid off the bed, eyeing the switch in my hand. She raised an eyebrow.

"What do you think you're doing?" she asked. "You don't dominate anything. You never have."

I crossed the room and grabbed a fistful of hair at the base of Helena's neck. She gasped out a laugh of pain and disbelief. I twisted her head to the side to speak in her ear.

"You are set in ink, but I am not," I said in a low voice. "I write my own story. I choose what I dominate, and I choose what dominates me. Understood?"

Helena looked at me.

"I understand," she said.

"Good," I replied, releasing her hair. She rubbed the red spot where the hair had strained against her skin.

I leaned the switch against the bed.

"I refuse to live half empty," I told her. "Turn around."

Slowly, she obeyed me.

I stepped up behind her and ran my fingers along the hem of Helena's dress, letting the fabric dance against my fingertips. My hands slid under her skirt and up the backs of her thighs to her underwear. I pulled them down to her knees.

I picked up the switch again. Our eyes met.

I pointed at the bed.

"Bend over," I said.

Helena put her hands on the bed and stretched down, slowly. From behind her, I slid the fabric of her skirt up to her waist.

I ran my hand against the unmarked skin on her butt. It was perfect. Pristine. Untouched.

Blank pages beg for language.

I stepped back and flicked my wrist. The switch made a loud crack at impact. Helena winced and arched her shoulders as the wood made contact.

"Why am I spanking you?" I murmured.

I reached out to brush my fingertips against the white mark that was turning red.

Helena looked back over her shoulder at me. There was a satisfied gleam in her eye.

"Because this is a metaphor," she said.

I hit her three more times, harder. Helena sucked in a breath.

"Does that feel *metaphorical* to you?" I asked, leaning forward to catch her gaze.

"It's a metaphor for your desire to master Shakespeare," Helena replied, breathing hard.

I seared a fifth red welt onto her skin, parallel to the first four. Helena grimaced and shook her right hand in front of her chest, as if the motion would release the pain. It occurred to me that I could paint a bar code on her body if my aim were accurate.

"It's a metaphor for your desire to take control of your sexuality," she said.

This time, I aimed the switch at the sensitive skin at the tops of her thighs. Helena cried out as it hit, again and again, fighting to catch her breath. On her skin I wrote paragraphs, pages, volumes of red words that turned purple in my sight. I watched her face. I watched her chest. I watched every bead of sweat that ran down the crevice of her ass. Her pain was mine; her body was mine; my body was hers. In attention and agony, we were one flesh.

"Or maybe," Helena murmured, her voice low, when I finally stopped beating her, "you want to punish yourself for what happened with Cyan."

I paused.

Helena's butt was zebralike in banded symmetry. With my left hand, I reached out and spread her cheeks apart to reveal the space between. I spit into the fingertips of my right hand and wiped the liquid across the black bull's-eye at the apex of her gorge, then placed the tip of my switch against the wet spot.

"When we feel," I said, leaning forward to press my weight against the wood, "we don't have to think." The point of the stick disappeared into Helena, like a lock into a keyhole. Her body expanded to swallow it whole.

She inhaled. I exhaled.

"How does it feel?" I asked.

"It hurts," Helena murmured. I nodded.

"Do you have any more theories to share?" I asked. I pressed the stick an inch deeper.

Helena shook her head. Her hips trembled.

"Good," I replied.

I pulled the switch out and dropped it to the floor.

Helena reached behind herself and put her hand on top of my own.

With both of our hands still pinned to the back of her body, Helena stood up and turned around to face me. Our hands slid across her skin as she moved. It was a dance without music.

"I didn't say you could stand up," I told her.

"I'm being disobedient," Helena replied. Her eyes were gentle, tender, forgiving, full of trust. She put her hands on my waist and pulled my dress up, off my body, and leaned forward to kiss me. Together, our mouths tasted sweet, but also tart. I thought of Demetrius. I understood why he describes Helena's lips as cherries—a fruit whose sugar is cut with the tang of acid.

Helena dropped to her knees in front of me. She pulled me down to her level, her torso close to my own. She picked up my hand, pressed my palm against her chest, and inhaled. The rhythm of her heartbeat fluttered against my hand.

"Can you feel it?" she asked me. "Do you recognize that rhythm?"

I swallowed.

"I do," I murmured. "I feel it."

Helena leaned forward to whisper in my ear. I tipped my face down and slid my hands around her waist.

"I know what you want," she said. "You're looking for three little words inside a haystack of language. You're looking for the words that will teach you how to love."

I pulled back to look at her.

"Yes," I said. "Tell me."

Helena smiled. She leaned close to my ear.

"Speak to him," she said.

I exhaled with audible frustration.

"From *Twelfth Night*, I know," I said, dragging my fingers through my hair. "And in *Hamlet*, he wrote 'speak to her.' Speak to him, speak to her. Shakespeare wants us to speak. Everyone keeps telling me that. But I'm speaking! I've spoken! He doesn't hear—"

Helena grasped my chin and leaned forward. The tip of her nose was inches from my own.

"When did I give up on Demetrius?" she pressed.

My breath stopped in my throat.

Helena *never* gives up on Demetrius.

Every nerve ending in my body tingled. I reached out and put my hands on Helena's face, running them against the smooth perfection of skin that had never been damaged by a day off the page. She pulled me toward her, and we kissed. Our kiss was deep and furious, as if effort and intensity would break the skin barrier between us.

I pulled back and scanned her torso, letting my gaze linger on the pockmark at its core. I reached out to touch it. My fingers dipped into the dent.

"Why do you have a belly button, Helena?" I murmured. "Most Shakespeare characters don't have mothers. You don't have a mother."

Helena forced a smile.

"I cut it into myself," she said. "I wanted to reach my liver."

My chest squeezed tight, like a fist.

I bent down and pressed my lips against the wound, circling the tip of my tongue around the scar she had sliced into her core.

"Wrong hole," Helena said. I glanced up to meet her eyes.

She giggled.

I wrapped my hands around Helena's hips and flipped her over, onto her knees. She laughed with surprise at the abrupt gesture. I smacked her bruised butt, hard, with my palm.

"Get on your stomach," I ordered.

Helena put her face in her hands.

"Jesus Christ, Jillian," she groaned, laughing uncomfortably.

I tilted to the side to catch her gaze.

"What?" I asked, my eyes wide and innocent. "Did I say something weird?" Helena cringed and pressed the back of her hand to her forehead.

"It's just a bit soon to joke about that, isn't it?" she asked.

I shook my head.

"No," I replied, patting the palm of my hand gently against her ass. "It is much too late." I pushed forward against her hips, and Helena rolled down onto her belly, like a wave.

I bent over to rest my forehead on her bottom. Helena winced as my weight pressed against her welts. The space between her cheeks was warm and soft, like a pillow.

"You're the one I want to speak to," I told her, pushing my face into that dark crevasse between her hips. "You're the one I want to know." I reached up to grab the sharp handles of her hipbones, ran my tongue along the line at the bottom of her ass and in a circle around the spot I had punctured earlier. Helena moaned with pleasure and pressed her pelvis against the floor. My hands traveled down the curves of her body to slip inside her from the front.

"You already know me," she murmured.

I shook my head.

"I don't," I admitted. "But I'm trying."

Helena exhaled and stretched her body along the ground. I ducked my head down to see what my fingers were doing between her legs. I had never really *looked* at a vulva. Culture told me to expect a flower, but there was nothing horticultural about it. Instead, what filled my eyes was pink and vulnerable, like the raw flesh of an open wound. It mirrored the marks I had left on her ass in perfect red-and-pink symmetry.

"Do you like what you see?" Helena asked, propping her chest up on her arms.

"There's a path that leads inside you," I replied. "I like that."

She rolled onto her back to face me and reached up to touch my face.

"Would all other women could speak this with as free a soul as I do," she murmured.

My mouth followed my hands. I found a slip of delicate tissue, as fragile as an oyster, with my teeth. I bit down on it—gently at first, and then harder, until a barrier gave way and cherry salt, as warm as semen, slithered onto my tongue.

As she groaned, Helena's hands strained against the floor. Her back arched above the ground, revealing, for a second, the purple fingerprints I had left on her skin. Helena's gasps were colored with pleasure and with pain; with every physical detail that silences the cerebral for the sexual. In climax, we found Shakespeare. He lives in the moment when doubt, self-consciousness, and fear disappear, even if only for a second; the moment when our bodies alight with feeling, and we do not ask or even wonder what it means; the moment when the physical world takes over and we speak to each other in a voice more wondrous than language.

Then I sat up and looked around the room. Helena was gone. On the ground next to me was a book, thick with pages as delicate as tissue. I didn't hesitate. In one fluid tear, I ripped a page free and wiped away the oil between my legs.

ACT FIVE

Is Shakespeare a masochist?
Of course. He is the king of masochists; his writing thrills with that
secret.

—*The Black Prince,* BY IRIS MURDOCH

5.1 As You Like It:
What You Will

The word *lonely* didn't always exist.

Shakespeare invented it.

Before him, the word *lone* existed. But Shakespeare was the one who took that solitary state and turned it into a feeling. In *Coriolanus,* the title character describes himself as "like to a lonely dragon, that his fen makes fear'd and talk'd of more than seen." That's the first time *lonely* appeared in print. It makes a perfect sound. The *o* at its middle gasps for help. The *y* at its tail trickles out just as the world itself ends: not with a bang, but with a whimper.

Lonely.

I came home.

"Why are you crying?" David asked.

He wasn't angry. He was concerned.

I shook my head, looking at the floor of our apartment.

"I asked Cy not to contact me anymore," I said. "He won't."

I put my face in my hands.

David wrapped his arms around me. My face dampened his shirt.

"I love you," he said.

And that was true. I didn't deserve it. I didn't even understand it. But that afternoon, as I cried in my fiancé's arms over the loss of another man, David held me, and did not let go.

"I won't ever be really sadistic, you know," he said, softly.

I paused.

"Good," I finally replied. "Because a real sadist would refuse to hurt a masochist."

Shakespeare invented the word *lonely*.

But he also invented its cure.

As You Like It is my favorite play.

It begins, as so many of Shakespeare's stories do, in a bad place. This time, it's a dukedom in France. Duke Frederick usurped his older brother, Duke Senior, and exiled him into the forest of Arden. Duke Senior's daughter, Rosalind, was only allowed to stay at court because of her close friendship with her cousin Celia, who is Duke Frederick's daughter.

Things are bad elsewhere in town, too. Orlando, the son of a nobleman, has fallen on hard times and decides to challenge Charles, the Duke's prized wrestler, to a match. But Orlando's brother Oliver, who hates Orlando, persuades Charles to "accidentally" kill Orlando during the course of the wrestling.

The wrestling match takes place before the entire court, including Rosalind and Celia. Rosalind is almost immediately taken with Orlando. "O excellent young man!" she cries with delight when Orlando, despite his smaller stature, overpowers Charles. After the match, Duke Frederick congratulates Orlando—but the mood sours when Frederick realizes that Orlando is the son of Sir Rowland de Bois, who had allied himself with the deposed former Duke, Rosalind's father. Rosalind and Celia are both horrified by how Duke Frederick treats Orlando. Rosalind gives Orlando her necklace to console him. Orlando is so mesmerized by Rosalind that he cannot even find the words to thank her for the gift. "Can I not say, 'I thank you'?" he berates himself, as Rosalind leaves.

At the sound of Orlando's voice, Rosalind gets excited. "He calls us back!" she cries, and then calls out to him: "My pride fell with my fortunes, I'll ask him what he would! Did you call, sir?!" She runs away from Celia to return to him.

Orlando still cannot find the words to speak.

Rosalind never has that problem.

"Sir, you have wrestled well," she flirts, "and overthrown more than your enemies."

When Orlando returns home, his servant warns him that Oliver plans to kill him that night. Meanwhile, Duke Frederick has changed his mind about allowing Rosalind to remain at court. Orlando and his servant flee the dukedom just as Rosalind and Celia, joined by a court jester named Touchstone, also leave in search of Rosalind's banished father—Rosalind disguised, for safety, as a young man called Ganymede.

Orlando and Rosalind both go to the same place: the Forest of Arden.

The Forest of Arden is where things get good.

"IT'S NOT THAT I want David to 'slap my ass,'" I told Peng, rolling my eyes.

For non-fetishists, spanking seems easy and obvious. But it's not. The details of our fetish are so specific that it's even difficult for people from other branches of the BDSM tree to fully absorb them. We can tell the difference. ("I need a real *spanko* spanking," a friend, who met her boyfriend through the general BDSM community rather than our specific subculture, complained to me once.) If it's difficult to teach other kinky people what we need, how could I explain it to David?

"He'll never know me if he can't understand this part of me," I said.

Peng nodded.

"And it felt like Cyan could," she offered.

I sighed.

"It was just easier," I said, frowning. "This thing is part of him, too."

Peng shrugged.

"So it's like you're engaged to someone from a different religion," she pointed out.

I winced with embarrassment.

"Spanking isn't my religion," I said.

Peng squinted at me.

"No offense, Jillian, but it kind of seems like it is," she said. "How do religions attract converts?"

We were waiting for lunch at a Mexican restaurant in East Harlem. As I mulled over the question, Peng absentmindedly arranged her fork and knife to rest parallel to the edge of the table. I smiled.

Peng and David could be the same person. In temperament, demeanor, and outlook, they're identical. (Which might explain why they're among the rare breed of people with the superhuman patience it takes to tolerate me.) Their similarity is perhaps best expressed by their mutual affection for parallel lines. Whenever I clean the apartment, I focus on dust, grime, and other bits of dirt. When David "cleans" the apartment, as far as I can tell, he just puts things in parallel lines.

"I guess religions have conversion classes?" I said.

Peng nodded.

"So why not think of it as a class?" she suggested.

I laughed.

"You want me to design a syllabus?" I deadpanned. "The Art and Practice of Beating Me?"

Peng shrugged.

"Why not?" she said. She was serious.

I should have thought of it myself. That's more or less what Rosalind does.

Rosalind and Celia settle into the Forest of Arden. (They are safe there, but Rosalind nevertheless chooses to remain disguised as Ganymede—her disguise offers her more than protection: it's a liberation.) Orlando also finds safety and comfort in the forest, but he still pines for Rosalind and carves simple love poems to her on the forest's trees.

Orlando's poems aren't amazing. Touchstone, the court jester who joined Rosalind and Celia in their flight, mocks them:

TOUCHSTONE
If a hart do lack a hind,
Let him seek out Rosalind.
If the cat will after kind,
So be sure will Rosalind.
Wint'red garments must be lined,
So must slender Rosalind.
They that reap must sheaf and bind;
Then to cart with Rosalind.
Sweetest nut hath sourest rind,
Such a nut is Rosalind.
He that sweetest rose will find,
Must find love's prick and Rosalind.

The last syllable of Rosalind's name, you'll notice, does not actually rhyme with *hind, kind, lined, bind, rind,* or *find*—Touchstone is exaggerating Orlando's clumsiness. And he's not the only one: the scholar Bertrand Evans called Orlando "only a sturdy booby." But Rosalind doesn't want Touchstone (or me, or Bertrand Evans) to tease Orlando.

"Peace, you dull fool!" she snaps at Touchstone. "I found them on a tree."

"Truly," Touchstone points out, "the tree yields bad fruit."

Rosalind hopes the verses could have been written by Orlando, but doesn't dare to think it's possible—after all, she believes he is still back at court. So when Celia tells her that she ran into Orlando in the woods, Rosalind is at first shocked into near silence. ("Orlando?" she asks. "Orlando," Celia confirms.) But Rosalind, unlike her beloved, rarely lacks for words. She recovers and goes on:

ROSALIND
What did he when thou saw'st him? What said
he? How look'd he? Wherein went he? What makes
him here? Did he ask for me? Where remains he?
How parted he with thee? And when shalt thou see
him again? Answer me in one word.

Rosalind is stuck in her Ganymede disguise, but she decides to make the best of it. "Ganymede" finds Orlando in the forest and confirms that Orlando is indeed the author of that arboreal poetry. When Orlando complains how awful it is to be mired in unsatisfied love, Ganymede offers to cure Orlando of his love sickness by pretending to be Rosalind and enacting every terrible stereotype about lovers.

"I would not be cured, youth," Orlando responds.

"I would cure you," Ganymede replies, "if you would but call me Rosalind and come every day to my cote and woo me."

In other words, Orlando and Rosalind, disguised as Ganymede, will act out the fantasy of the relationship they desire.

Bingo.

"That's what I need to do?" I asked. "Turn kink into a class?"

Peng nodded.

"Take that tangle," she said, pointing at my head, "and put it into parallel lines."

Years of experience have taught me that it is best to follow Peng's advice immediately, and in the most literal way possible.

The next day, when David and I were in the shower, I drew a horizontal line in the steam on the shower wall. It was parallel to a crack in the tile.

"I like this already," David said.

I laughed.

"Imagine this line is a pain scale," I said, pointing at the shower wall. "This end is no pain, and that end is extreme pain."

I drew a short tick mark through the line, about three-fourths of the way to the "extreme pain" end.

"Imagine this line is my pain threshold," I explained. I drew an x just past that point. "That's where I need to go," I said. "Just past my limit."

"That's the sweet spot, huh?" David said.

I smiled.

"Yeah," I said. "But I can only get there if I'm in the right headspace. That's why I need your help."

In 1896, George Bernard Shaw described what sets Rosalind apart from other characters. "She makes love to the man," he wrote, "instead of waiting for the man to make love to her."

It would be, just as Imogen had told me, a sublime and hazardous journey into the unknown. We had a lot of work to do.

I wiped the back of my hand across my mouth.

"Thanks, Jilly," David breathed happily. "Your turn!"

He picked me up off my knees and dropped me on the bed.

I shook my head.

"Nope," I teased. "I don't want sex. You know what I want."

David rolled his eyes.

"We can do both," he pointed out.

I shook my head again.

"Nope, nope, nope," I insisted. "Spanking isn't a side dish to sex for me. I want you to really understand that it satisfies me fully. And today, it's all I want."

I rolled onto my stomach. David started spanking me.

"This is *really* all you need?" David asked. "It's enough?"

"Mmm-hmm," I murmured into the pillow.

"But you come so easily," he mused.

I turned my head to the side to make eye contact with him.

"And what do you think I'm thinking about during every orgasm?"

David laughed.

I didn't. I was dead serious.

David raised his eyebrows.

"Every time?" he asked.

"Every. Single. Time." I turned my face back into the pillow.

"Huh," I heard David mutter behind me.

He kept spanking me. I dropped into the blissful oblivion of my fetish, and didn't realize how much time had passed—forty-five minutes, David later guessed—until, out of the corner of my eye, I noticed him pause for a second to shake out his hand.

I pushed myself up onto my elbows.

"Does your hand hurt?" I asked, surprised. It had never occurred to me before that spankings would hurt his hand, but of course they can. (In the fetish community, we even have an expression for it. If a bottom says, "I assed his [or her] hand," it means he or she took such a long hand spanking that it left bruises or blood blisters on the top's palm.)

David's from the Midwest. He tried to tough it out.

"It doesn't hurt," he said. "I'm fine." He kept hitting me.

I suppressed a smile.

"There are other things you can use," I pointed out. (I'd assumed that was obvious—after all, I literally handed him a belt on, like, our fifth date. But if I've learned anything, it's that when it comes to human sexuality, *nothing* goes without saying.)

"Like what?" David asked.

So that was Lesson Number One: implements.

"This is plastic," I said, days later, lifting a paddle brush in my right hand. "And this is wood," I added, nodding to the brush in my left hand. "Wood is more painful than plastic. It's also more painful than leather."

David nodded.

I picked up a wooden spoon.

"This is a spoon," I continued. "As far as I'm concerned, cooking is its secondary utility."

Fetishists call household implements that can be repurposed for kink "pervertibles." There are lots of pervertibles: hairbrushes, bath brushes, rulers, belts, spatulas, wooden spoons, and more. I get distracted at Bed Bath & Beyond. (Books can be pervertibles, too. I'm under no illusions about what my friends will do with hardcover copies of this one.)

That solved the problem of David's manual discomfort. The good news for his hand was "bad" news for my butt.

"Ow!" I laughed into a pillow, weeks later. (We spread these "seminars" out over a period of months.) David had just hit me hard—very hard—with a wooden hairbrush.

"What number was that?" he asked.

"A six?" I suggested. We were measuring the intensity of different strokes with scientific meticulousness: it could only have been David's idea.

"Okay," David noted, with professionalism. "So this one hurts more than the belt."

I nodded.

"Yes," I confirmed.

"You have a crazy pain tolerance, Jilly," he observed. "How do I push you past a six?"

I giggled over a flutter of nerves.

"Hit me that hard, but don't stop," I admitted. "Just lay into me."

David nodded.

"Got it," he said. Soon after, we achieved a nine.

"What the hell is a ten?" David marveled.

I laughed.

"No rush," I said. "We'll figure it out."

Another week, I swallowed three shots of candor—also known as whiskey—and, red with shame, finally introduced the word *scold*.

"You want me to scold you?" David clarified.

"Yes," I mumbled, squinting at the ceiling. "It's not like I'm externalizing internal guilt. I don't think I *deserve* to be scolded. It just—it helps me drop into the right headspace."

David shrugged.

"Okay," he said.

"It's so weird," I moaned.

"Is it more weird than putting the produce section of the Asian foods aisle up your—"

"Hey," I interrupted, pointing at him. "Don't dis ginger."

We were drunk. Things got funny.

"You buy three-dollar beverages, have *two* sips, and then *never—finish—them,*" David ranted, spanking me. "It makes me *crazy.*"

David rarely unloads. I was oddly charmed to discover that this was the secret resentment he'd been bottling up inside.

"That's what you're upset about?" I laughed, squirming. "Iced tea?"

"What is the point of ordering a drink if you don't finish it?" David continued. "Three dollars here, three dollars there—"

I was still laughing.

"The tea I bought yesterday was too sweet," I pointed out. "You're a doctor—did you really want me to drink unhealthy sugar water just because I paid for it?"

David paused. I had made a good point.

He fell back on a classic.

"I'm the one who is talking now, not you," he said, ignoring my rebuttal. "This thing you do with drinks is *killing me*. You are torturing me with tea."

He was serious. It was hilarious.

(My friend Kelley, who is very committed to BDSM ethics, would be furious if I didn't mention that alcohol complicates consent. For safety's sake, BDSM practitioners must be especially conscious of those lines. David and I both understand that. But our bodies are our own, as is our relationship. David and I have enough experience with each other to feel comfortable playing drunk, and we know when we're too inebriated to consent. So cut us some slack, okay?)

"Did it feel good to get that off your chest?" I asked afterward.

David grinned.

"You know," he said, "it really did."

I laughed.

But David wasn't the only one who had a thing or two to learn. Eventually, the student became the teacher.

"It's not like you've made a great effort with vanilla things, either," David snapped one day.

Oh, shit. He was right.

I had things to learn, too. Which is why, weeks later, I was in our kitchen, wearing stilettos and a frilly apron over black lace lingerie. (To put this in context, my preferred pair of "erotic" underwear says "ONE TOUGH COOKIE" alongside cartoons of the eponymous snack.) There was a lasagna in the oven and a glass of scotch in my hand. I'd found a soundtrack for the evening by searching for "porn music" on YouTube. It was all very normative.

I felt—

Well, bored, to be honest. David wasn't home yet. I had been standing there, restarting my porn music, for more than half an hour.

I picked up my phone.

"No one ever says how boring sexy surprises can be," I texted

Peng. "I have this big reveal planned, but he's not home yet. So I'm just waiting."

"That's why you bring a book to sexy surprises," Peng replied. "Always bring a book."

David's key scraped the lock.

Months passed like this.

For more than six years, that damn folder—"David, If You Find This, Please Don't Look Inside"—had been sitting on my hard drive. Even after I wrote about it in my first *New York Times* article, it stayed closed. I always knew that, even if David found it, he would respect my wishes and leave its contents unread.

But every class has a final lesson.

"You also have a clown fetish, don't you?" David said, settling in front of my laptop. "I knew it."

I laughed. "Don't tease me, babe," I said. "This is hard for me."

David sighed. "You're about to show me some super cool, edgy, sadomasochistic, like, *French* erotica," he said. "And it'll make my stupid porn seem lame."

I shook my head.

"No, honey," I replied. "That's really, *really* not what's about to happen."

"It's like I'm marrying an onion," David said, squinting into the distance. "So many layers. And every one makes my eyes water."

I snapped my laptop shut.

"That's it," I said. "I'm not sharing my heart, or my soul, or my thoughts, or anything with you, *ever again*."

David was laughing.

"That was a joke," he said. "You're not an onion."

"Well, now I feel like an onion," I pouted.

"You're not an onion," David repeated. "I take it back."

"Say I'm an artichoke," I demanded. "My layers taste good, and they don't make you cry."

David pressed his lips together to suppress a laugh.

"You're an artichoke," he agreed.

"And my heart is, like, the best part," I finished.

David raised his eyebrows.

"Oh, wow," he said. "This metaphor really carries."

I grinned.

"Yeah!" I cheered, proudly.

"And artichokes take a lot of work, too," David added.

I stomped out of the room.

Twenty minutes later, after David got me to admit that, yes, like an artichoke, I do require a lot of work—but, he added, artichokes are worth the effort—we went back to my computer.

"Okay," I told David. "As you know, my fetish deals with power dynamics. Things like discipline and hierarchy turn me on."

David nodded.

"Okay," he said.

"So, like, the military is one example of that kind of power structure," I said. "Religious groups are an example of that, too."

David nodded again.

"Okay," he repeated.

This was so embarrassing.

"My point is, if something were to mix military hierarchy with religious discipline," I continued slowly, "I'd find a lot of *potential* in that, right?"

David nodded.

"Okay," he said.

I scrunched up my face.

"Can you think of anything that combines those two aesthetics?" I asked. "Military and religion?"

David shrugged.

"No, I can't," he said. "But I bet you're about to tell me."

"You'll figure it out," I said, cringing, "if *the force is with you*." I covered my face with my hands and flopped over onto the couch, as if I had just died.

David was cracking up.

"Oh, my God," he said, laughing. "You're into sadomasochistic *Star Wars* porn."

I dropped my hands from my face.

"It's not porn, exactly," I insisted. "They're stories. I read *stories*."

David squinted.

"That might be worse, love o' mine," he said. "That means you're into sadomasochistic *Star Wars* fan fiction."

I made a face.

"I didn't say I was into the perfect writing quality, *David*," I snarled.

"Okay, show me," he replied.

A few minutes later, David was inside my secret folder. (The stories were on my hard drive instead of online because, after the website where I had found them disappeared for a while, I panicked. If the website were to disappear again, it would take 90 percent of my private sex life with it. So I copied every single story into Word documents—and thank goodness I did, because a few months later, the website did disappear for good.)

I'll just say it: It's a bunch of stories about Qui-Gon Jinn spanking Obi-Wan Kenobi. I'll never again be able to watch a Liam Neeson or Ewan McGregor movie without blushing.

"Wow," David said, as he scrolled through my collection.

"Yup," I said. I curled my legs up on the couch.

"But you don't like the *Star Wars* movies," he said.

"Trust me, I'd like them if they were like this," I replied.

"These aren't even characters from the good *Star Wars*," David teased. "Is Jar Jar Binks in here?"

I snatched my computer away.

"Don't be mean," I said. "You've never shown me your porn."

"It's embarrassing," David replied.

I raised my eyebrows and pointed at the computer.

"Most of those stories are from a website called 'Padawan Punishment,'" I said. "Is your porn more embarrassing than that?"

"I don't think *anything* is more embarrassing than that, dear," he replied, patting my shoulder with mock sympathy.

"Ha, ha," I said. "Now you have to show me yours."

Thirty minutes later, after we plowed through a bottle of wine to lubricate the situation, David and I sat next to each other on the couch, staring at a video on his laptop screen. A woman was giving a man a blow job.

"This is a couple having oral sex?" I asked.

"Yeah," David replied. "It's one of my favorites."

We continued to watch.

"Does anything else happen?" I asked.

"Well," David added, "in a minute, another man comes in. And she gives him a blow job, too."

I looked at David. I could not imagine a less embarrassing kind of pornography.

I put my hand on his.

"I love you, vanilla bean," I said.

He squeezed my hand.

"I love you, too, my young apprentice," he replied.

I laughed. At some point, we have to let all the anxiety, insecurity, and self-loathing go and laugh about it. Our sexual secrets can only humiliate us if we let them. Sex, even weird sex, *even* sexless sadomasochistic *Star Wars* fan fiction, isn't embarrassing. It's funny. It's great.

David took a deep breath.

"The thing is," he said, "the next guy in this video is actually that woman's husband."

I smiled and shook my head.

"I get it, I get it," I joked. "Your porn is super respectable, don't rub it in."

David frowned.

"No, you don't understand," he said. "That means the man she's with right now *isn't* her husband."

I squeezed David's hand.

"It's a fantasy, honey," I reassured him.

He squinted at the screen.

"But I like this type of scenario," he said, in a tone of voice I recognized. "I *really* like it."

I blinked.

"David," I asked. "What are you . . . ?"

He scrunched his lips together.

"I'm not sure," David said, his eyes fixed on his screen. "But the truth is, I find the thought of you over someone *else's* knee incredibly . . ."

We turned to look at each other.

" . . . hot."

AT THE PEAK of *As You Like It*'s sexual urgency, Orlando speaks for all of us.

"I can live no longer by thinking," he says.

But he won't have to. *As You Like It* is a comedy.

And you know what they say about how comedies end.

Beneath Ganymede, there is a girl. Even when Orlando couldn't see her, Rosalind was always there. It just took some time to coax her out.

It's possible to know—*really know*—other humans. I have to believe that.

From David's (sexually normative) perspective, his biggest triumph was when he spanked me so well, with such a perfect buildup of pain, that I had an orgasm while I was over his knee.

"But I didn't even touch you!" David said, astonished.

I sat up and eyed the wooden spoon in his hand.

"Well, *that* touched me," I pointed out.

"Oh, my God," David said. "My mind is blown."

I laughed. Although I'd never climaxed during a spanking before, I had known it was possible for a while. I'd even come close with David a few times, but I never told him. I didn't want him to feel pressured, or to think that spankings are supposed to lead to climax, when that's not true at all. (It's not even something I'd want to happen every time.)

"Do you feel like a stud?" I asked, grinning.

David nodded.

"Hell, yes," he said. "I just made my fiancé come *using only my mind*."

I squinted.

"Sure, honey," I agreed, in a dry voice. "Your mind—plus millions of conversations, months of practice, and a wooden spoon."

David laughed and kissed the top of my head.

"Exactly," he joked. "Easy."

But from my perspective, that orgasm wasn't the best part. The best part took place months later, in a war zone. That's an improbable setting for a spanking scene in this narrative, I realize, so I'll explain.

For years, David and I had hoped that our careers in global health and journalism, respectively, could eventually come together. To our delight, we weren't wrong. When we plan ahead, David and I can work in the same places at the same time. In this country, David volunteered at a hospital while I worked on a magazine story about pirate prisons.

Let me give some context. The situation in this country, which has been in a civil war for decades, is not a game, and my journalism job brings me into the lives of real people. I refuse to write something that could harm them. So, for lack of safer options, suffice it to say that—in a city I will not describe, through means I cannot disclose, with the help of people I will never name—I snuck into a prison to interview someone I was not supposed to meet.

A few hours later, David and I were alone in a safe house, on our way back to the relative safety of a neighboring country. David had already finished his service at the hospital, so this interruption didn't derail his work. But I also hadn't warned him about my unauthorized—and, in my defense, unforeseeable—prison visit in advance.

David wasn't thrilled.

"That's right, I forgot," he roared, only half joking, as he paced around the room. "You have a death wish! You want to die!"

We had been living in the hospital where David worked. We'd had enough privacy for sex, but it had been a while since we'd had enough privacy for an activity that requires loud slapping sounds.

"Gosh, if only there were some way to punish me for this reckless display of journalism," I teased in a singsong voice.

David shook his head.

"Hell no," he said. "If I reward this insanity with a spanking, every time I look away you'll try to get yourself killed."

I climbed on the bed and bounced up and down on my knees.

"Please?" I begged, clutching my hairbrush in front of me, like a bouquet. "It's not a reward, it's a terrible, *terrible* punishment."

David crossed his arms in front of his chest and glared at me. I changed tactics.

"Okay," I negotiated. "If you give me a spanking right now, I promise to never sneak into a prison again."

David laughed and gave in.

"Fine," he said, sitting on the bed and pulling me over his knee. "But I'm going to hold you to this promise."

He started spanking me with his hand. I snuggled my face into the pillow.

"Repeat after me," David said. "I will not sneak into prisons."

"I will not sneak into prisons," I repeated. "Unless it's for a really good story."

David picked up the hairbrush and pounded it on my butt.

"That wasn't our agreement," he growled.

"Wait, wait," I yelped into the pillow, trying to crawl away from the hairbrush. "That hurts! I'm not ready!"

David held me in place and kept hitting my butt.

"You told me to ignore you if you said that," he reminded me.

I shook my head.

"No, but this time I mean it," I begged. "Maybe I'm not a fetishist anymore. It's a miracle! I'm cured!"

David laughed.

"You told me to ignore that, too," he said.

"Damn it!" I said, giggling into the pillow. "I told you too much!"

Things continued along these lines for another twenty minutes. By then, I'd fallen into the sweet spot where my endorphins overpowered the pain. The glow was so all-consuming that I almost didn't notice when David began to alternate the intensity of slaps.

Slap *slap!* Slap *slap!* Slap *slap!* Slap *slap!* Slap *slap!*

I giggled and pushed my torso up on my elbows.

"Are you playing the drums?" I joked.

"Nope," David replied.

Slap *slap!* Slap *slap!* Slap *slap!* Slap *slap!* Slap *slap!*

I frowned. There was something familiar about the tune.

"Is that a song?" I asked.

David laughed.

"Good grief, girl," he said. "I'd think you of all people would know."

Slap *slap!* Slap *slap!* Slap *slap!* Slap *slap!* Slap *slap!*

I looked over my shoulder.

"Oh, wow," I said. "You're not—?"

David bobbed his head, with a smug grin.

"Yup," he said.

David, my boy with the baseball cap, was spanking me to the rhythm of iambic pentameter.

"Love is merely a madness," Rosalind tells Orlando, "and, I

tell you, deserves as well a dark house and a whip as madmen do. And the reason why they are not so punished and cured is that the lunacy is so ordinary that the whippers are in love, too."

Screenwriters like to give lovers a "meet-cute." It's that moment when two people meet for the first time, often in an adorable and memorable way, and see something familiar and beloved in each other. They know they've found something special.

But who says lovers only get one meet-cute? Why can't a lifetime include many of them, as each partner meets the more intimate selves inside the other's Russian doll? Shakespeare seemed to think it was possible. He gave many of his lovers more than one meet-cute. Rosalind and Orlando have at least three: there's the first meet-cute, when Rosalind sees Orlando win the wrestling match and purrs "O excellent young man!" with a lusty growl. There's a second meet-cute in the forest, when Ganymede finds Orlando and banters with him. And there's yet another meet-cute at the end, when Ganymede abandons "his" disguise to reveal the woman inside.

I believe in love at first sight. But I also believe in evolution. Love at first sight is real love, but it's an infant love. As love matures, we meet again and again, and discover new parts of our partners for the first time. I'd like to think that Rosalind and Orlando will cycle back to meet each other for the rest of their lives.

Livers regenerate. They're the only organ that can.

I pushed my hips back, off David's lap, and sat next to him on the bed. I put my hands on his shoulders. Nine years after I read his story from an Internet café in Seville, seven years after he first kissed me on a balcony at Stanford, and two years after I handed him my heart in a thousand words, I fell in love with the man I'd always loved.

"Hi," I said.

David smiled.

"Hi, honey," he replied.

Two months later, in the bedroom of our three-hundred-square-foot apartment in New York City, David and I got married. After the ceremony, David smashed the lightbulb I had given him seven years earlier. We framed the shards.

Shakespeare's comedies, as they say, often end with a wedding. After that, there are epilogues. We usually don't get to see the married couples' sex lives. So I will, as I've always done, follow Shakespeare's example. I will inhale his words, and let them cycle through my body, until they exhale as my own.

That's just a fancy way to say I'll steal Rosalind's last speech from *As You Like It*.

ROSALIND
It is not the fashion to see the lady the epilogue;
but it is no more unhandsome than to see the lord
the prologue. If it be true that good wine needs
no bush, 'tis true that a good play needs no
epilogue. Yet to good wine they do use good bushes;
and good plays prove the better by the help of good
epilogues. What a case am I in then, that am
neither a good epilogue, nor cannot insinuate with
you in the behalf of a good play! I am not
furnish'd like a beggar, therefore to beg will not
become me. My way is to conjure you, and I'll begin
with the women. I charge you, O women, for the love
you bear to men, to like as much of this play as
please you; and I charge you, O men, for the love
you bear to women (as I perceive by your simpering,
none of you hates them) that between you and the
women the play may please. If I were a woman, I
would kiss as many of you as had beards that pleas'd
me, complexions that lik'd me, and breaths that I
defied not; and I am sure, as many as have good

beards, or good faces, or sweet breaths, will for my
kind offer, when I make curtsy, bid me farewell.

With that, I'll draw a veil around my husband and his wife. This time, a few details of our marriage will stay between us.

Rest assured: it hurts me more than it hurts you.

I LOVE SHAKESPEARE the same way I love spankings.

Neither is easy at first. The poetry, like the pain, hurts. It's jarring and uncomfortable. It takes a few minutes to adjust.

But then, in both cases, endorphins kick in.

Blood circulates.

Heat rises.

Things start to feel better: first tolerable, then comfortable, and then (if it's done right) downright blissful. The unfamiliar Elizabethan English begins to feel simple and magical. The pain starts to feel like pleasure. In an instant, Shakespeare and spankings both feel so natural to me.

And they're both that much more satisfying because they hurt at first.

I ran across an empty subway platform and slipped through the car doors just before they closed. The train coughed and pulled away from the station to take me home.

I slid into a seat.

It was nighttime. It felt like there was no one else on the C Train that evening. There are moments when, against all odds, even New York feels lonely.

But I wasn't alone.

I felt His eyes on me before I saw Him. The hairs on the back of my neck lifted, like sunflowers that look toward the dawn. I turned around.

Just as I'd expected, there He was: the Man with a Million Faces.

My chest squeezed around my heart.

"Hi," I said.

"Promise me this subway tunnel isn't some metaphorical birth canal," He replied.

I burst into laughter.

"Oh, God," I groaned, shaking my head. "It's not."

He plopped down into the seat next to me.

"So you're going to write a book about me and spanking, huh?"

I blushed.

"I guess so," I admitted. "Do you mind?"

He winked.

"Just give me some material to *shake my spear* to and I'll be happy."

I giggled.

"That's all I get?" I joked. "A masturbation pun?"

He shrugged.

"What did you expect?" He said. "I devoted a whole sonnet to 'having traffic with thy self alone.'"

The train paused in the darkness of the tunnel. I swallowed the lump in my throat. The train trembled, and so did I.

I looked down and shook my head.

"I'm scared that I will never really know you," I told Him.

He nodded.

"I hear that from a lot of people," He said. "I hear it from students, I hear it from actors. Ken Branagh said it to me last week."

"Really?" I asked.

He nodded.

"I'll tell you the same thing I tell everyone: If you look in my words to find me, you're searching for the wrong thing. Don't forget: the purpose of playing was, and is, to hold the mirror up to nature. You may not know me, but I know you. All of you."

My eyes filled with tears.

"Damn it," I said, scrubbing my face with the back of my hand. "You've made me cry."

He leaned back in His seat. "That's my way," He said, with a grin. "I give you an awesome masturbation joke, then I change your life. I'm the best."

I laughed through my tears.

"Oh, kiddo," He said, reaching out to brush my cheek. "You'll be okay."

I caught His hand.

"Will we?" I asked, urgently. "I'm not sure. Will we ever stop being so lonely? Is there a cure for this plague you named?"

He smiled.

"Do what I did: tell stories about the hearts we have, and the rhythm they all share," he said. "Forget morality; forget politics, convention, and reception; forget psychology, theology, and pathology; and *speak*. Speak to be understood. Speak as liberal as the north. Speak in many sorts of music."

He squeezed my fingers.

"And when you can't find your own words, borrow mine. I left them here for you."

I sighed and pressed my hands against my face.

When people talk about sexuality, they often talk about "empowerment." I'm not sure why. I have never felt empowered by my fetish. To this day, I still don't. If my sexuality empowers me, it's only in the same way as my heartbeat: it is always there, and always has been there—and when it goes away, so will I.

Sometimes we see a cloud that's dragonish, a vapor sometime like a bear or lion, a towered citadel, a pendant rock, a forked mountain, or blue promontory with trees upon't that nod unto the world—and mock our eyes with air. At some point, I would need to stop idling in fantasy and get off the train. I was tired. My eyes ached from looking for things I will not find.

I was the only person in the car. I knew that.

I opened my eyes, blinking against the harsh fluorescence of the train.

But He was still there. He hadn't left.

He never leaves.

I smiled.

"I love you," I told Him. "You're the love of my life."

He touched my hand. Our fingers intertwined.

"For your sake, honey, don't let that be true," He said. "Give your love to the ones who will love you back, okay?"

I nodded.

"I know," I told Him. "I do want that."

He waved away my doubt, as if it were an irksome fly.

"'Tis in ourselves that we are thus or thus," He said. "Our bodies are gardens to which our wills are gardeners."

I pressed my lips together and looked down.

"Are you saying," I asked, fighting to suppress my smile, "that love is fertilized with *will*?"

He winked.

"I am."

I laughed, shaking my head. It's a lovely thought. It buoys me.

Our train pulled into a station, and the doors slid open.

"Is this our stop?" He asked.

I glanced out the window at the platform: Chambers Street. We weren't home yet.

I curled my knees up to my chest and rested my head on His shoulder.

"No," I said. "But we're getting close."

Works Referenced

All quotes from Shakespeare are taken from *The Riverside Shakespeare*. 2nd ed. Edited by G. Blakemore Evans and J. J. M. Tobin. Houghton Mifflin, 1996.

A Midsummer Night's Dream: Stand and Unfold

Ania Loomba. *Shakespeare, Race, and Colonialism*. Oxford University Press, 2002.

Access Denied: The Practice and Policy of Global Internet Filtering. Edited by Ronald Deibert, John Palfrey, and Rafal Rohozinski. The MIT Press, 2008.

Women's Rights in the Middle East and North Africa: Progress Amid Resistance. Edited by Sanja Kelly and Julia Breslin. Freedom House, 2010.

Norman N. Holland. "Hamlet: My Greatest Creation." *Journal of the American Academy of Psychoanalysis* 3 (1975).

Plato. *Symposium*. Translated by Robin Waterfield. Oxford University Press, 1994.

2.1 The Tempest: Were I Human

W. H. Auden. "The Sea and the Mirror." *Collected Longer Poems*. Random House, 1968.

Virginia Mason Vaughan and Alden T. Vaughan. *Shakespeare's Caliban: A Cultural History*. Cambridge University Press, 1993.

Mary Gaitskill. *Bad Behavior: Stories*. Simon & Schuster, 1988.

" . . . that question is a pinch more stinging than bees" is a reference to *The Tempest*, 1.2.

"You smell like a fish, Cal. . . . A strange fish" is a reference to *The Tempest*, 2.1.

"There are brave new worlds to find" is a reference to *The Tempest*, 5.1.

2.2 The Winter's Tale: An Aspect More Favorable

Andrew Gurr. "The Bear, the Statue, and Hysteria in *The Winter's Tale*." *Shakespeare Quarterly* 34 (1983).

Anderson, Mark. *Shakespeare By Another Name: The Life of Edward de Vere, Earl of Oxford, the Man Who Was Shakespeare*. Gotham, 2006.

Scott Crider. "Weeping in the Upper World: The Orphic Frame in 5.3 of *The Winter's Tale* and the Archive of Poetry." *Studies in the Literary Imagination* 32 (1999).

2.3 Romeo and Juliet: These Violent Delights

Geoffrey Chaucer. *The Canterbury Tales*. Translated by David Wright. Oxford World's Classics, 2008.

" . . . as one dead in the bottom of a tomb" is a reference to *Romeo and Juliet*, 3.5.

2.4 The Taming of the Shrew: Rough with Love

John Davies. "In Francum." *The Poems of Sir John Davies*. Edited by Robert Krueger. Clarendon Press, 1975.

James M. Bromley. "Social Relations and Masochistic Sexual Practice in *The Nice Valour*." *Modern Philology* 107.4 (2010).

Thomas Middleton. *The Collected Works.* Edited by Gary Taylor and John Lavagnino. Oxford University Press, 2010.

John R. Yamamoto-Wilson. *Pain, Pleasure and Perversity: Discourses of Suffering in Seventeenth-Century England.* Burlington: Ashgate Publishing Company, 2013.

David Savran. *Taking It Like a Man: White Masculinity, Masochism, and Contemporary American Culture.* Princeton University Press, 1998.

Stephen Orgel. "Nobody's Perfect: Or Why Did the English Stage Take Boys for Women?" In *Displacing Homophobia: Gay Male Perspectives in Literature and Culture.* Edited by Ronald R. Butters, John M. Clum, and Michael Moon. Duke University Press, 1989.

Dana E. Aspinall. "The Play and the Critics." In *The Taming of the Shrew: Critical Essays.* Edited by Dana E. Aspinall. Garland, 2001.

3.1 *Hamlet: Nothing, My Lord*

Emily Dickinson. *The Complete Poems of Emily Dickinson.* Edited by Thomas H. Johnson. Back Bay Books/Little, Brown, 1960.

G. Wilson Knight. *The Wheel of Fire: Interpretations of Shakespearean Tragedy.* Routledge Classics, 2001.

Thucydides. *History of the Peloponnesian War.* Edited by M. I. Finley. Translated by Rex Warner. Penguin Classics, 1972.

Elaine Showalter. "Representing Ophelia: Women, Madness, and the Responsibilities of Feminist Criticism." In *Shakespeare and the Question of Theory.* Edited by Patricia Parker and Geoffrey Hartman. Methuen, 1985.

Pauline Réage. *The Story of O.* Grove Press, 1965.

Aristotle. *Nicomachean Ethics.* 2nd ed. Translated by Terence Irwin. Hackett Publishing Company, 1999.

" . . . two months later—no, not even that much, not two" is a reference to *Hamlet,* 1.2.

3.2 *Twelfth Night: What Should I Do*

Stanley Wells. *Shakespeare, Sex, and Love.* Oxford University Press, 2010.

William Shakespeare. *'Utayl (Othello).* Translated by Khalil Mutran. Cairo: Dar al-ma'arif, 1976.

Neil Barbour. *The Arabic Theatre in Egypt.* University of London Press, 1935.

Ferial J. Ghazoul. "The Arabization of *Othello.*" *Comparative Literature,* vol. 50, no. 1 (1998).

Peter Chelkowski. *Islam in Modern Drama and Theatre.* New York University Press, 1984.

M. M. Badawi. "Shakespeare and the Arabs." *Cairo Studies in English* (1966).

3.3 *Love's Labor's Lost: Wonder of the World*

Juliet Dusinberre. *Shakespeare and the Nature of Women.* 3rd ed. Palgrave Macmillan, 2003.

Gordon Williams. *A Dictionary of Sexual Language and Imagery in Shakespearean and Stuart Literature.* Bloomsbury Academic, 2001.

3.4 *Antony and Cleopatra: Here Is My Space*

Antony and Cleopatra: New Critical Essays. Edited by Sara M. Deats. Taylor and Francis, 2004.

Sophocles. *Oedipus Rex.* Translated by Sir George Young. Dover Publications, 1991.

4.1 *Macbeth: Double, Double*

" . . . hoisted it into the air like Yorick's skull" is a reference to *Hamlet,* 5.1.

"Stars, hide your fires: let not my boyfriend see my black and deep desires" is a reference to *Macbeth*, 1.4.

Peter Stallybrass and Margreta de Grazia. "The Materiality of the Shakespearean Text." *Shakespeare Quarterly* 44 (1993).

Bruce R. Smith. *Homosexual Desire in Shakespeare's England: A Cultural Poetics*. University of Chicago Press, 1995.

John Donne. *The Essential Donne*. Edited by Amy Clampitt. Ecco Press, 1996.

Marjorie Garber. *Shakespeare After All: The Later Plays* (Macbeth, Lecture 6). Harvard University Extension School Video Lecture Series. http://freevideolectures.com/Course/2746/ENGL-E-129-Shakespeare-After-All-The-Later-Plays/6#.

"'Privacy' palters with us in a double sense" is a reference to *Macbeth*, 5.8.

Harold Bloom. *Shakespeare: The Invention of the Human*. Riverhead Books, 1998.

"But the only alternative is to unsex myself" is a reference to *Macbeth*, 1.5.

4.2 *King Lear:* Speak

Jane Smiley. *A Thousand Acres*. Reprint ed. Anchor, 2003.

4.3 *Othello:* Beast with Two Backs

Virginia Mason Vaughan. *Othello: A Contextual History*. Cambridge University Press, 1996.

Norrie Epstein. *The Friendly Shakespeare: A Thoroughly Painless Guide to the Best of the Bard*. Penguin Books, 1992.

T. G. A. Nelson and Charles Haines. "Othello's Unconsummated Marriage." *Essays in Criticism* 33 (1983).

4.4 Cymbeline: *What We May Be*

"After the cats and blind puppies have drowned . . ." is a reference to *Othello*, 1.3.

"In his mirror eyes were all my sins remembered" is a reference to *Hamlet*, 3.1.

5.1 As You Like It: *What You Will*

Iris Murdoch. *The Black Prince*. Penguin Classics, 2003.

Bertrand Evans. *Shakespeare's Comedies*. Oxford University Press, 1960.

"I devoted a whole sonnet to 'having traffic with thy self alone'" is a reference to Sonnet 4.

"Speak in many sorts of music" is a reference to *Twelfth Night*, 1.2.

"Speak to be understood" is a reference to *Love's Labor's Lost*, 5.2.

"Speak as liberal the north" is reference to *Othello*, 5.2.

"Sometimes we see a cloud that's dragonish . . . and mock our eyes with air" is a reference to *Antony and Cleopatra*, 4.14.

Acknowledgments

This book would not exist without three amazing people: my brilliant editor, Cassie Jones, and my wonderful agents, David Kuhn and Becky Sweren. Cassie, thank you for taking a chance on me. I feel so blessed to have had the privilege of working with you. I hope this book will make you proud. I'm also grateful to Kara Zauberman, Kenny Hoffman, Sharyn Rosenblum, Emily Homonoff, Tavia Kowalchuk, Serena Wang, Greg Villepique, Fritz Metsch, Sunil Manchikanti, Michael Accordino, Andrew DiCecco, Beth Silfin, and the entire team at William Morrow.

Vauhini Vara helped me take a few steps closer to the writer I aspire to be. Thank you, Vauhini. This would have been a very different book without your wise, thoughtful feedback.

Thank you to the many friends who soothed my crippling insecurity and insatiable appetite for feedback over the last two years: Rachel Yong, Paz Pardo, Melissa Anelli, Aida Mbowa, Elisha Maldonado, Elyse Klein, Mike Wood, Guy Molnar, Kevin Farrell, Erin Ryan, Kelly McKenzie, Xiao Ying-tai, Cathy Reisenwitz, Terry Kosdrosky, and Molly Katz. I especially want to thank Rahul Kanakia: a good man, generous friend, and fantastic author.

My career—and my life—would not be what it is today without the kindness of strangers. I will always be grateful to Amy O'Leary, Susan Dominus, Rebecca Mead, Suzy Spencer, and Toni Bentley, who had no reason to share their words of wisdom with me but did so anyway. I'm also grateful to Daniel Jones, who gave me my first break in the literary world when he chose my essay to run in the *New York Times*.

Robert Draper gave this book its title, but his influence on me (and my work) runs deeper than he knows. Thank you, Robert. It is not every person who, at the peak of an amazing career, reaches out to help people at the beginning of their own. Cathryn Jakobson Ramin has also been my friend, teacher, and mentor since before I had a single national article to my name. Thank you, Cathryn.

Patricia Parker and David Ivers are the reasons I fell in love with Shakespeare. Thank you, thank you, thank you. You both inspire me every day, and I am humbled to call you my friends. I hope you enjoyed my book.

My mother introduced me to two of the greatest joys in my life: Shakespeare and travel. Everything I am, and everything I've done, started with her. Thank you, Mom. I understand why you don't like this book. I hope someday you'll understand why I had to write it.

There is a long list of people who touched my life, and gave this story its heart, whom I cannot name here. You know who you are. Thank you for allowing me to share our stories. Thank you for the gardening lessons. Thank you for the adventures. Thank you for being my friends.

I love you, Peng, Erin, Ian, and Mark.

I love you, David.

Index